WAYFINDING

PictograficSystems

Nonverbal. Universal.

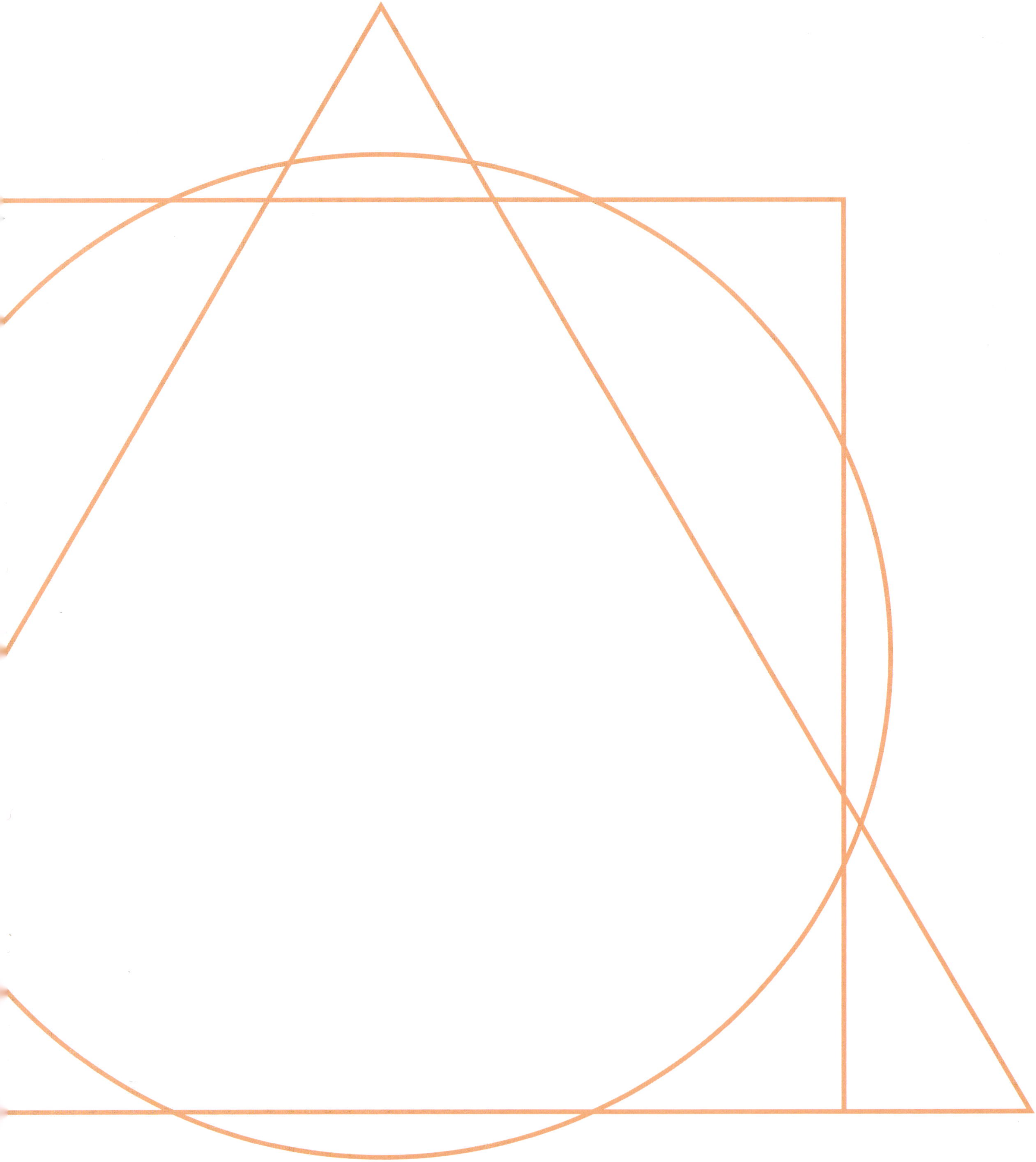

WAYFINDING

PictograficSystems
Nonverbal. Universal.

Paul Arthur and Branimir Zlamalik

FOCUS
STRATEGIC
COMMUNICATIONS
INCORPORATED

WAYFINDING
PictograficSystems
Nonverbal. Universal.

First published in 2005 by:
Focus Strategic Communications Incorporated
535 Tipperton
Oakville, Ontario, Canada L6L 5E1
www.focussc.com

Book, jacket and text design: Branimir Zlamalik, gb.com unlimited
Pictographs: Paul Arthur, Branimir Zlamalik
Layout: gb.com unlimited

Series 7 – Hazards in Parks and Recreational Areas – reproduced by permission of Parks Canada

ISBN 0-9731822-1-0

Library and Archives Canada Cataloguing in Publication

Arthur, Paul, 1924-2002.
PictograficSystems : nonverbal, universal / Paul Arthur and Branimir Zlamalik.

(Wayfinding)
Includes index.
ISBN 0-9731822-1-0

1. Picture-writing. 2. Signs and symbols. 3. Signs and symbols — Design. I. Zlamalik, Branimir, 1949– II. Title. III. Series.

P93.5.A78 2005 302.2′223 C2004-907414-8

10 9 8 7 6 5 4 3 2 1

To the late Paul Arthur
who showed us the way

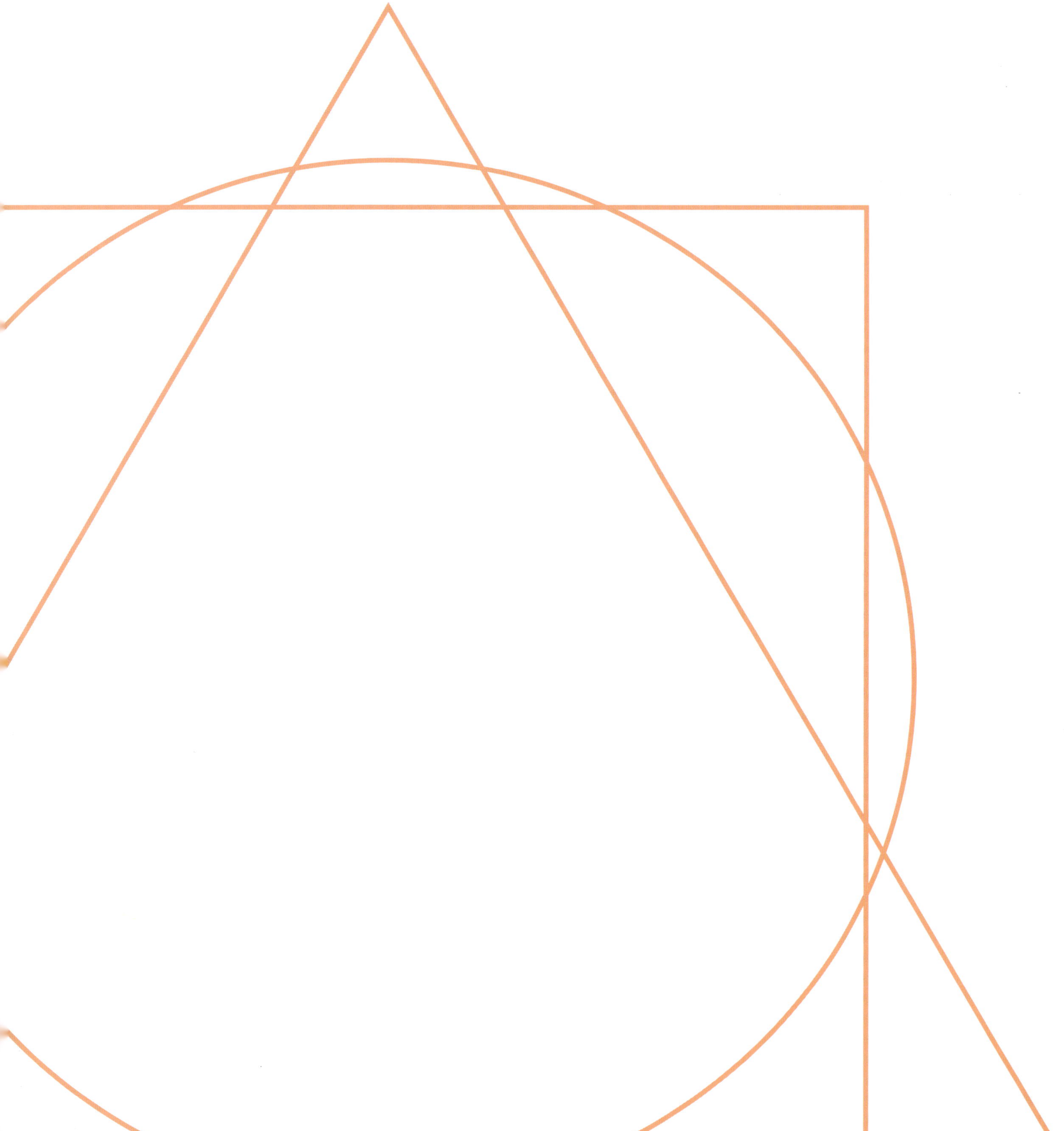

CONTENTS

This book of pictographs and their image content descriptors, or ICDs, is built on earlier (and still ongoing) research into the feasibility of the concept that we shall achieve the long-cherished dream of true internationalism in symbol signs only if we have a single, verbal, description for each of them. In the current absence of an organized collection of such descriptions, designers and others involved in the creation of pictographic images have no basis on which to develop their work. As a result, the topic "Restaurant" is rendered in no fewer than ten different ways (as pictured here). Doubtless, this figure could easily be doubled, if not tripled, if one looked hard enough.

I became convinced that a book on pictographs, organized by topic, would be a most useful document. It would also help to fulfill the goal of "universality of concept." On the other hand, universality of design is neither desirable nor needed, for reasons that are explained below. There is, however, a very real need for universality in terms of the essential content.

This book is organized as follows:

- **CATEGORIES:** major collections with subsets of topics (or referents)
- **TOPICS:** individual topics for which ICDs can be conveniently developed. In other words, there are no topics for which an ICD cannot be drafted. This is because the only purpose of an ICD in the first place is as a set of instructions to a designer who can "design" only what the ICD describes. No ICD, no possibility of design. This more or less limits us to things that are "tangible," although it does not exclude some of the intangibles such as costs or services. For example, the former could be represented by a dollar sign ($), while the latter could be a person in a peaked cap, evocative of the Maytag repairman.

Eventually, we will likely be able to develop a thousand topics in about two hundred categories of pictographic images representing common actions, services, objects or facilities of importance to us in our everyday lives. Because no common descriptions exist, we are constantly exposed to different pictographic images or symbols representing the same thing. If, however, we could agree on a common set of descriptors for each of these topics, the efficient use of pictographs in environmental communication would be enormously enhanced throughout the entire world. Differences in "the graphics" would be immaterial. In much the same way that we can recognize an almost unlimited number of approaches to the design of the letters of our alphabet (as long as every "A" has the general characteristics of "A-ness" and "Bs" of "B-ness"), we shall have no difficulty in recognizing different depictions or renderings of symbols (as long as each of them subscribes to the same understandable and commonly adopted verbal description). If we have commonly adopted what we think, collectively, constitutes such abstractions as "A's" and "B's," why could we not do the same thing with pictorial images?

It is irrelevant, for example, whether the head of the "Man" symbol is round or ovoid, whether his shoulders are rounded or square, whether he has long legs or short and so on. These differences in rendition need not affect universal recognition of the pictographic image for what it is – which is, after all, what really matters.

Paul Arthur

In *PictograficSystems: Nonverbal. Universal.*, topics are grouped for convenience into a series of categories according to their general use. Each is identified here first in its simplest form, as, for example, in "Parking." This, however, will give rise to a series of topics:

- You may park here

OR

- No parking

The same for the topic of "Smoking":

- This is a smoking lounge, you may smoke here

OR

- No smoking

We have used the ISO/CSA/ANSI method of categorizing these uses, as follows:

CLASSIFICATION	CATEGORY	NO.
◆ REGULATION	PROHIBITION	1.1
	OBLIGATION	1.2
◆ WARNING	CAUTION!	2.1
	DANGER!	2.2
◆ INFORMATION	EMERGENCY	3.1
	GENERAL INFO (including the concept of permission)	3.2

ISO – International Standards Organization
CSA – Canadian Standards Association
ANSI – American National Standards Institute

* **ISO/ANSI** substitute a blue disc and ISO does not recognize the red triangle

Note that some pictographic images are repeated because they may have slightly different meanings, depending on which series they are in.

Wash your hands (obligation)

***4034, 1.2** (Series 4 – Health Care Facilities)*
***6045, 1.2** (Series 6 – Safety in the Workplace)*

Hand-washing station, washroom (information)

***5044, 3.2** (Series 5 – Transportation, Travelers & Those in Transit)*

FORM	EXAMPLE
45° diagonal red slash (normally, top left to bottom right) **(NO SMOKING)**	
* disc **(KEEP DRY)**	
(SLIPPERY FLOOR)	
* **(EXPLOSION HAZARD)**	
(FIRST AID)	
(TOILETS)	

For the purposes of clarity of explanation only, examples of symbols incorporating pictographic images are provided, keyed by number to the ICDs. These examples are from the **PictograficSystems©** set.

PICTOGRAPHIC IMAGE

all on its own,
in positive form

all on its own,
in negative form

Smoke and cigarette together form an image, pictograph or pictographic image. All by itself like this, in positive or negative form, it is not a "symbol" because it has no meaning beyond a graphic reference to smoking. Whether it refers to "No smoking" or "Smoking area" is not made plain. In other words, the image is lacking the necessary graphic context that would make it a "symbol."

SYMBOL (SIGN)

No smoking

You may smoke here

Now the pictographic image has been provided with a graphic context that makes its purpose perfectly plain. This is called a "symbol" or a symbol sign, by virtue of the fact that the image has been placed inside a shape and has colors that give it the graphic context that was missing before as a simple "image."

SYMBOL (SIGN) WITH TEXT

Sometimes the symbol needs further amplification or explanation. In such cases, words are added in the manner illustrated. This is why it is called a "symbol sign with text."

TEXT (SIGN)

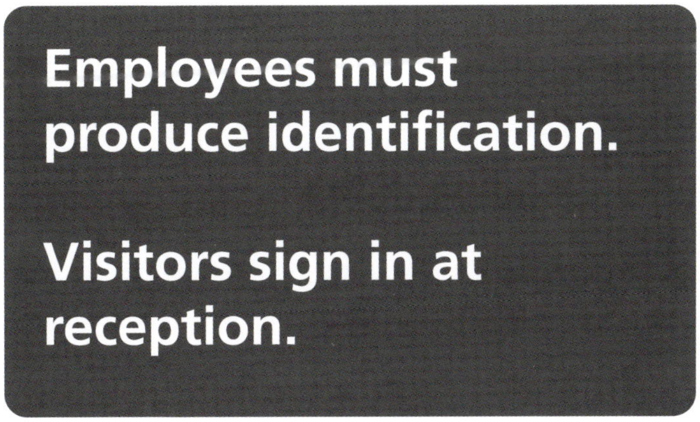

This is the logical conclusion to come to when a symbol sign is demonstrated to be impossible by virtue of there being no verbal description or ICD that can be created for it – in other words, when there are no words to describe what the suitable pictographic image would look like. In all such cases, resort to text and forget about graphic symbolism. Text signs follow the ISO color code in their field colors.

This is an aspect of the system that has been adopted worldwide, and that makes it possible for pictographic images to be translated into true symbols by providing them with a specific graphic context. Having established the system, it is equally important that the ways in which the component parts are described should be constant.

1.0
CLASSIFICATION 1.0: REGULATORY CATEGORIES 1.1 AND 1.2

1.1 Prohibition

1.2 Mandatory

The Canadian national standard (Z321) calls for a black, not a blue, disc for 1.2.

2.0
CLASSIFICATION 2.0: WARNING CATEGORIES 2.1 AND 2.2

2.1 Caution!

2.2 Danger!

ISO (7001) does not include the red triangle for 2.2; the US standard (Z535) replaces the red triangle with an orange one.

3.0
CLASSIFICATION 3.0: INFORMATION CATEGORIES 3.1 AND 3.2

3.1 Safety and emergency

3.2 General information

The blue square (3.2) also identifies the concept of permission, as in "You may smoke here."

This is the system that has been adopted worldwide, with minor variances, as indicated, and that enables pictographic images to be translated into true symbols by providing them with a graphic context. "Graphic context" means the ability to make multiple use of the same pictographic image for quite different purposes – depending on the actual context: No pedestrians, Watch out for pedestrians, or This is a pedestrian crosswalk and so on.

SHAPE CODES

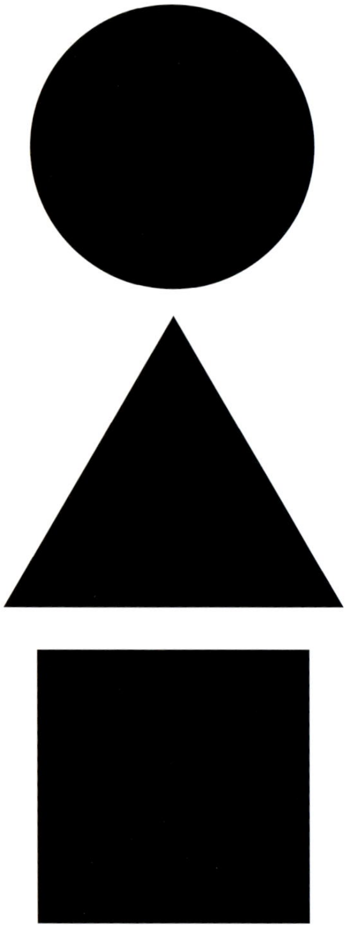

Shape codes is one of the ways that pictographic images, by the addition of graphic context, are transformed into symbols. Shapes are used for this, with circles (or discs) representing regulation, triangles for warning and squares for general information. This system is now used worldwide, and it is the basis – along with color coding – for many international standards. It is important, therefore, not to subvert the system by misusing it, as California has done.

Colors are the other way to provide graphic context.

MISUSE

Sometimes, there is misuse of a system that serves very well on the world stage to provide graphic context to pictographic images. The State of California, in an act that is the direct antithesis of inclusive design, has appropriated these two distinctive and universal shapes for the specific task of tactile identification of restrooms. (Only the triangle and the circle are tactile. The signs are accompanied by the words, Women and Men, also in tactile letters. Note the interesting visual illusion: the male looks, but isn't, taller than the female.)

COLOR CODING

Color coding is the second method for providing graphic context for pictographic images. Red identifies prohibition and danger; yellow is for caution; green is for emergency and fire protection equipment; and blue is for general information, including the concept of permission (as in "You may smoke here").

SOLIDS VS OUTLINES

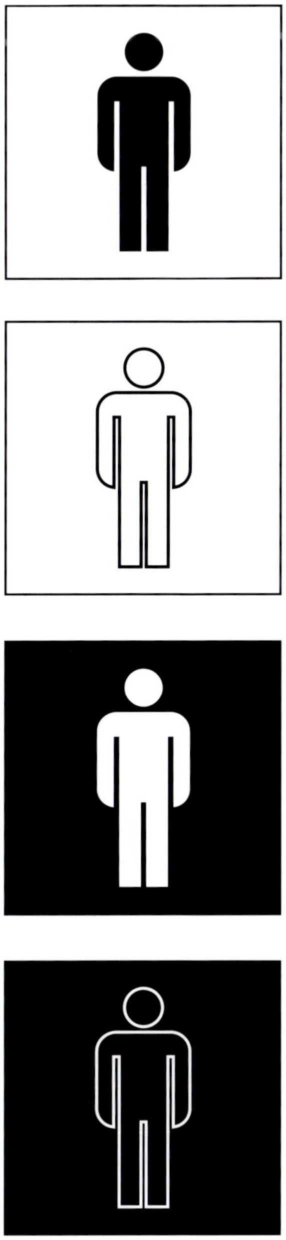

No matter what the color of the background is, solids make better pictographs than do outlines. On dark surfaces, these would actually be superior. The issue here, however, is that of solids vs outlines – with solid figures or elements always being more effective. There is something inherently complex about outlines, which is not the case when the very same image is made solid.

EXCESS INFORMATION

There is plenty of information in the example on the left without including a lot of elements that, while they also add up to the concept of "telephoneness," are purely gratuitous. If it's not essential, don't include it. (This is particularly important if an image is very small, such as a web page button.)

ELEMENT SIZE

The "gaps" between elements are important because they, too, are elements in the overall design. If they are inadequate, there is the real danger that the image will read only as a blob. Note the distinct difference between these two images: the image on the left can be read from further away than can the one on the right. Even up close, the left image is clearer than the right one.

UNIFORMITY

SIMPLICITY

The above two illustrations say it all; the one on the left is how, under normal circumstances, we would expect someone to use type. All the letters naturally belong to the same family, whereas the letters in the image on the right don't, and the result is simply bizarre. Uniformity of design in the creation of pictographic images is as essential a part of effective communication as anything else. The members of a family of pictographs should bear a recognizable similarity to each other in the same way that letters do.

There are two issues here. One has to do with the way a design, such as the one on the left, is graphically more complex and a lot less clear than the one on the right. The other issue has to do with the way in which we absorb and use information. Telling motorists to turn left, then canceling this instruction, is more complicated by far than just telling them that they must turn right in the first place. The figure on the right does that, simply and unequivocally. But guess which of the two is not being used?

ESSENCE

Only the essential components of the action or object are needed in an effective pictograph, and all extraneous information should be eliminated, no matter what. Thus, two walking legs and feet may be less "elegant" as an image, but they are a much better expression of the concept of "pedestrian" than is a whole body. (Nevertheless, both of them are present in PictograficSystems©.)

FAMILIARITY

If there is a choice, always opt for concepts and images that people are familiar with, over abstractions that don't mean anything – until, of course, they are learned. The original biohazard symbol, on the left, was actually chosen because it meant nothing. By contrast is one that does mean something. Evidence demonstrates that the right image is likely easier to remember and to identify because of long-held, and analogous, associations with poison. It is not as if this symbol were intended to be recognized by lab technicians only; the general public is also frequently exposed to it, in clinics and health care facilities (for example, on spent needle containers in labs where bloodwork is done).

COMPACTNESS

All other considerations being equal, the more compact the image, the larger (and clearer) it will read when inserted into a square. This is why the front view of a bus may be a better, and more adaptable, image than the side view.

CLARITY

Quite apart from the evidence of one's eyes, there is also research evidence to prove that the symbol on the left is more effective than the one on the right. Unfortunately, however, every standard throughout the world insists on the idea that the diagonal slash must obscure the pictographic image – thereby often rendering it difficult, or sometimes even impossible, to identify. The issue here, of course, is visual clarity. There is another related issue: avoiding ambiguity in the message.

AMBIGUITY

One of these illustrations is reasonably "clear" as to its meaning, while the other is not. Yet both are used to represent the same concept of a passenger elevator. The example on the left (from IATA) is ingenious in the idea of a floor with two holes in it for things to go up and down in. But it is too far away from what we are used to, which is a box that goes up and down in a shaft – even though this, in earlier images (without the lines representing the shaft), tended to look like a highly mobile toilet.

WORDS VS PICTURES

How much longer will North Americans go on displaying Latin words to identify the way out of a building, when most of the rest of the world uses a symbol sign for this purpose? There is another issue here: red vs green as safety colors, and particularly those associated with fire protection and emergency equipment. Does the color red really convey the concepts of "go" (or of "stop" and "danger")? Most of the world depicts such emergency-related concepts on green squares.

IATA – International Air Transport Association

CONSPICUITY

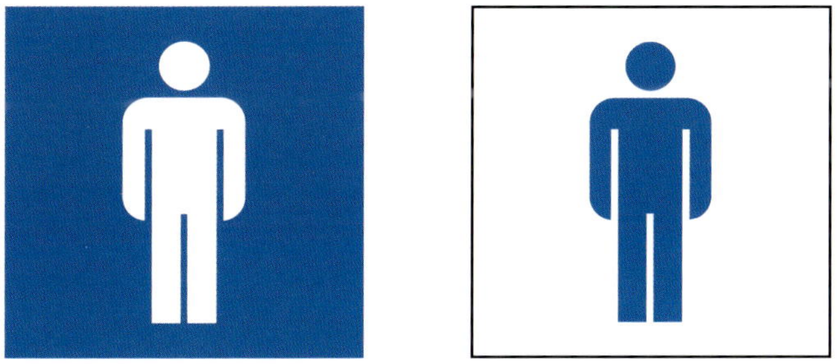

The "target value" of a sign is almost as important as the elements in the sign itself. If the sign is not easily noticed, or blends too easily into the wall on which it is displayed, it will not be noticed. This is true for all of us, but for the visually impaired, the example on the left is far better than the one on the right. In terms of "universal" or inclusive design, why not opt for the version that includes – or serves – the greatest number of people in our society? The only rationale for the example on the right has to do with matters that concern the personal taste of the interior designer.

SPECIFICITY

There is a difference between degrees of warning that have to do with whether the hazard involved is merely potential and cautionary – or imminent and dangerous. The yellow triangle (beside the door to an already locked electrical room in a building, for example) indicates the former, while the red one (at a transformer station) identifies the latter. There is a sufficiently long tradition of red being linked with danger and yellow with caution that many people will automatically recognize the difference. On the other hand, some things are worth taking the time, and the trouble, to learn.

0
1
2
3
4
5
6
7
8
Index

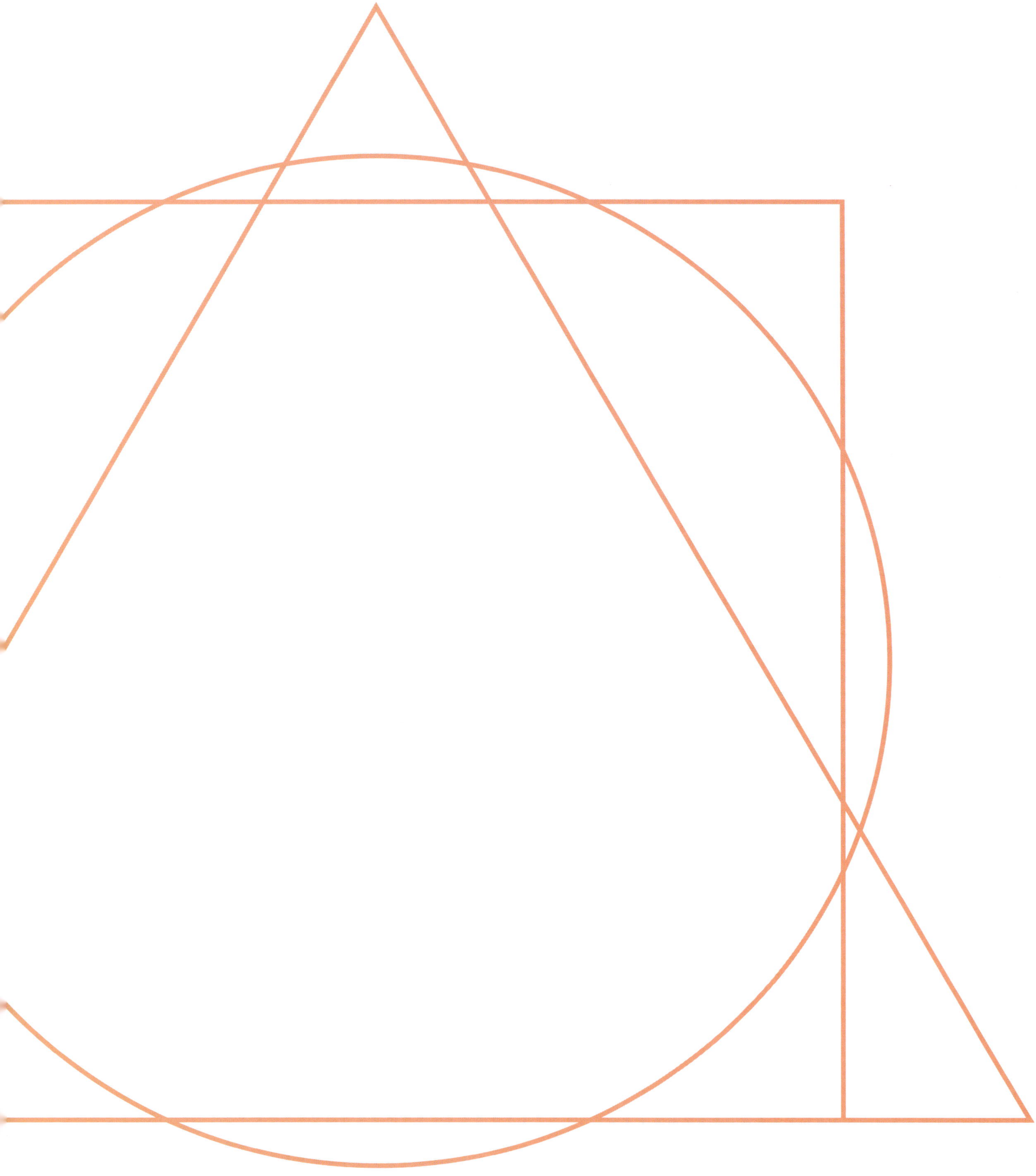

Series 0 – Pictographs common to all functions

0001

OCTAGONAL SHAPE, STOP

1.2 Stop

Note that the STOP sign brakes all the rules.

0002

P

1.1 No parking

3.2 Parking allowed

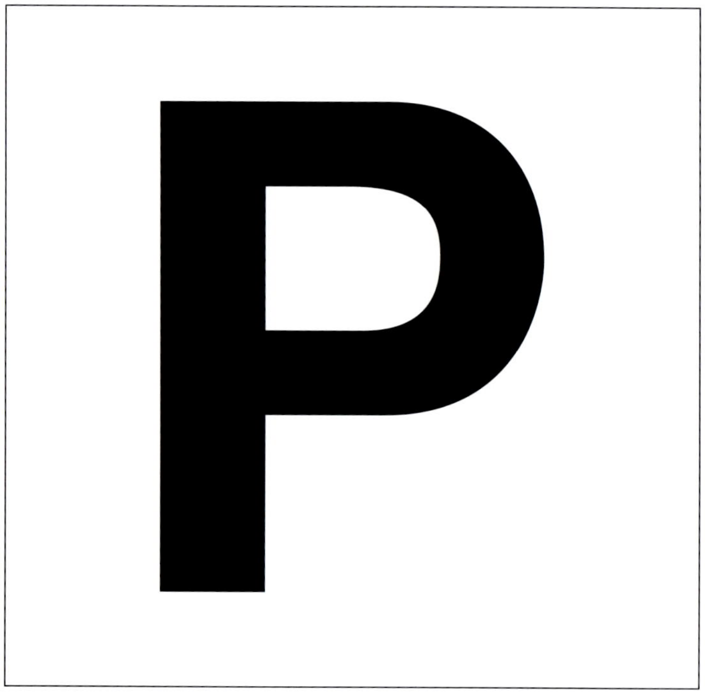

0003

WALKING LEGS

1.1 Stay put, do not cross
2.1 Caution! Pedestrians
3.2 Walk, cross

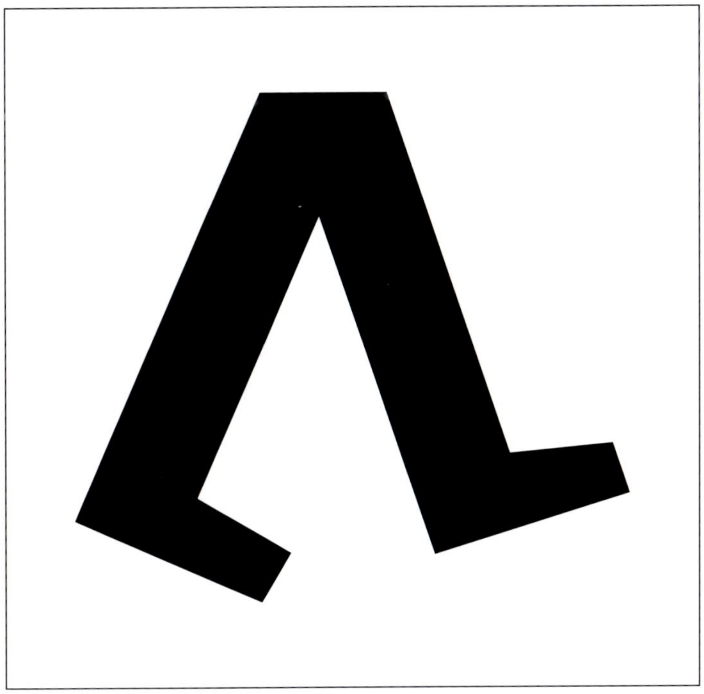

1.1

1.2

2.1

2.2

3.1

3.2

0004

HUMAN FIGURE, WALKING

1.1 Stay put, do not cross
2.1 Caution! Pedestrians
3.2 Walk, cross

1.1

1.2

2.1

2.2

3.1

3.2

0005

HUMAN FIGURE, WALKING, PARALLEL LINES

1.1 Stay put, do not cross

2.1 Caution! Crosswalk

3.2 Crosswalk

1.1

1.2

2.1

2.2

3.1

3.2

0006

HUMAN FIGURE, WHEELCHAIR

3.2 Symbol of access

1.1

1.2

2.1

2.2

3.1

3.2

RAMP (15° WEDGE SHAPE)

3.2 Ramp

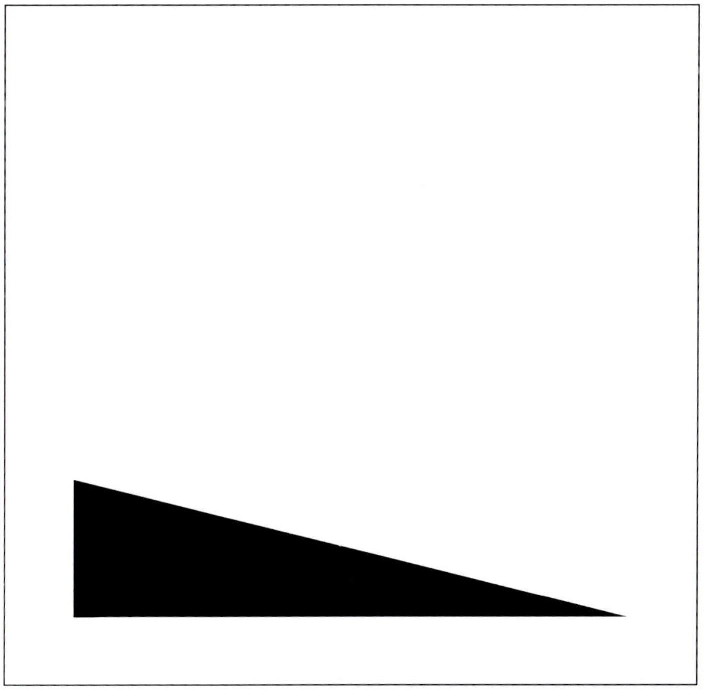

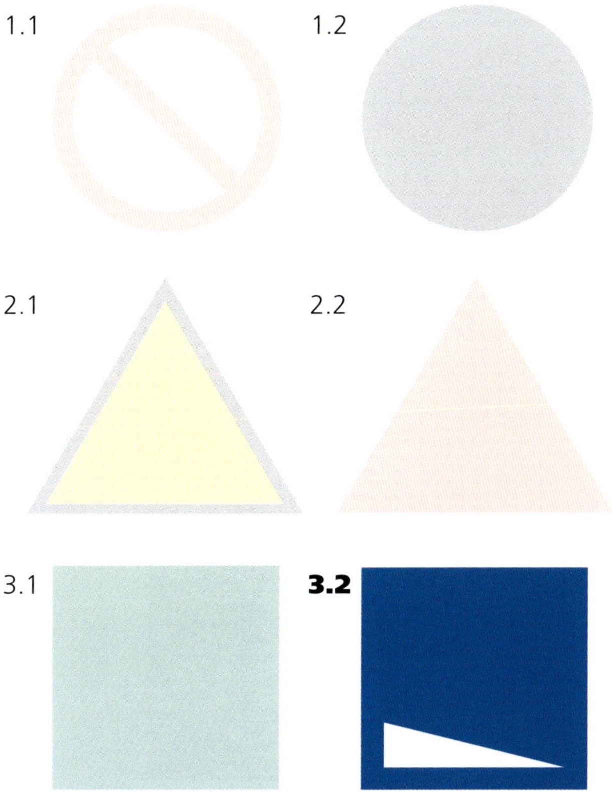

DIRECTIONAL ARROW

1.25 width stem (for all eight directions). See Series 8.

1.2 Obligatory direction

3.2 Identification of direction, this way

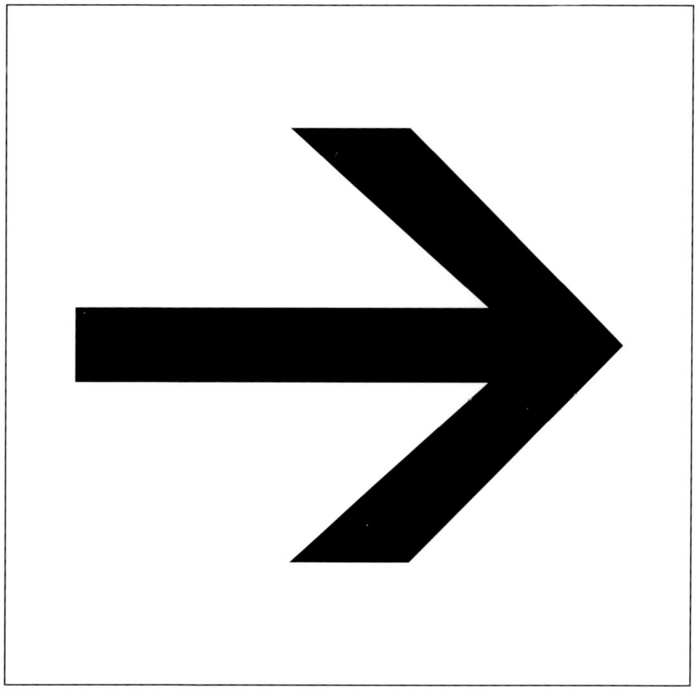

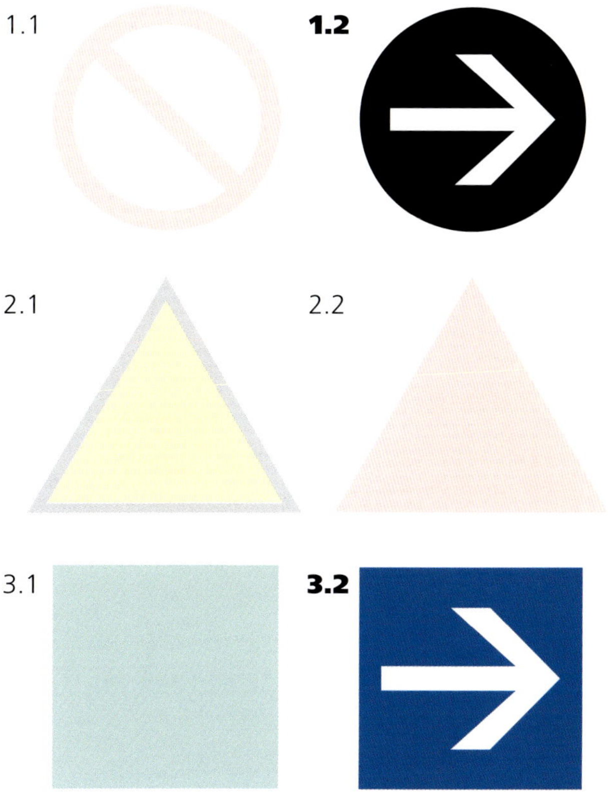

0009

DIRECTIONAL ARROW

1.5 width stem (for all eight directions). See Series 8.

1.2 Obligatory direction

3.2 Identification of direction, this way

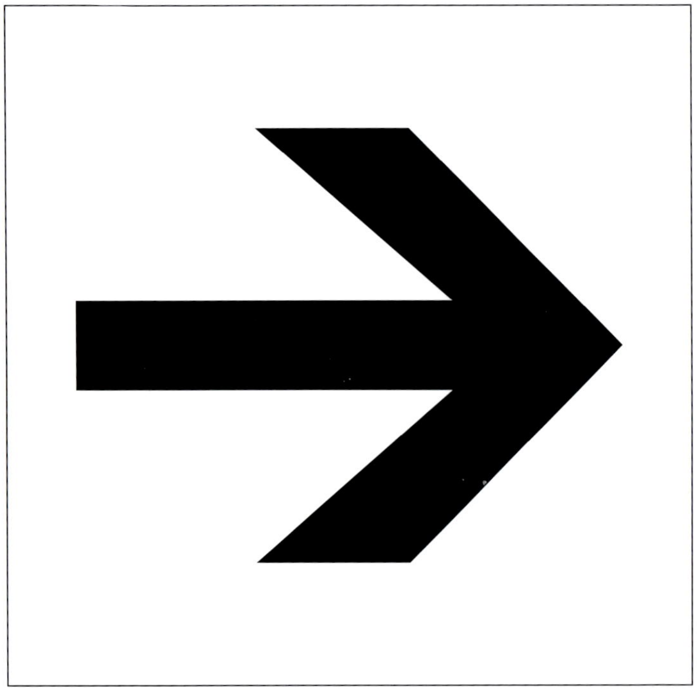

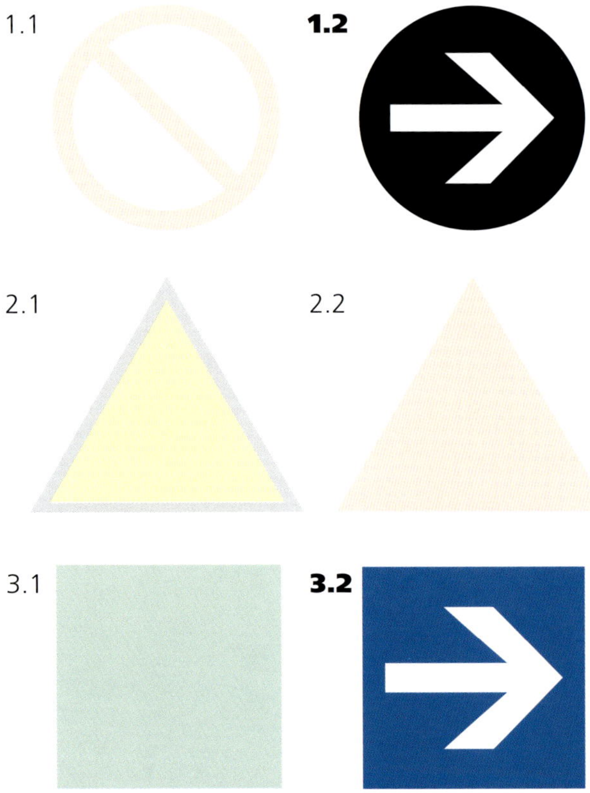

0010

DIRECTIONAL ARROW

Wedge-shaped arrow (for all eight directions). See Series 8.

1.2 Obligatory direction

3.2 Identification of direction, this way

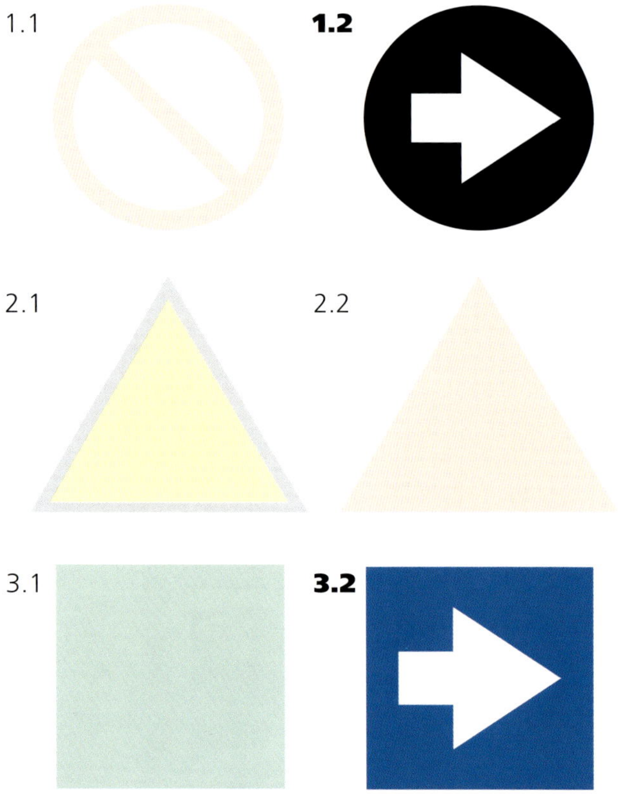

0011

ARROW, ENTERING THREE-SIDED BOX

1.1 No way in

3.2 Way in, entrance

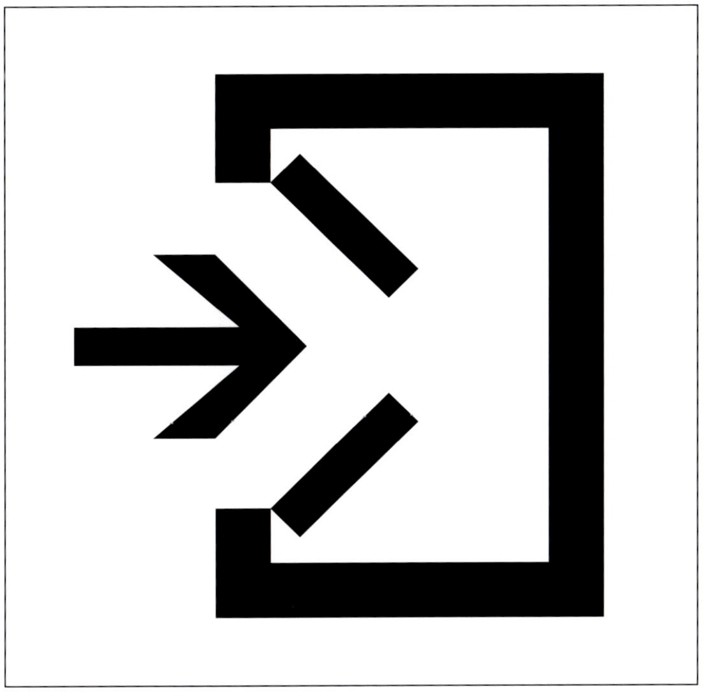

1.1

1.2

2.1

2.2

3.1

3.2

0012

ARROW, EXITING THREE-SIDED BOX

1.1 No way out

3.2 Way out, exit

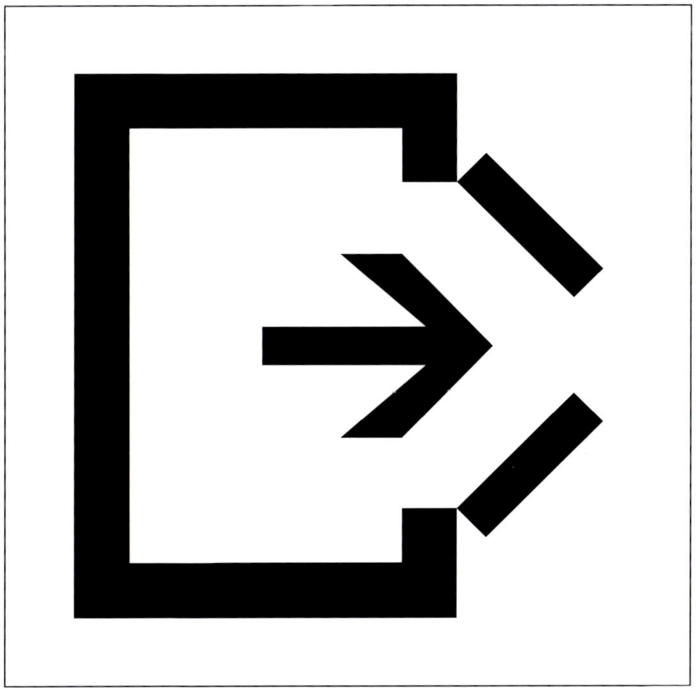

1.1

1.2

2.1

2.2

3.1

3.2

0013

DOUBLE HEADED ARROW, OPEN BOX

3.2 Shipping and receiving

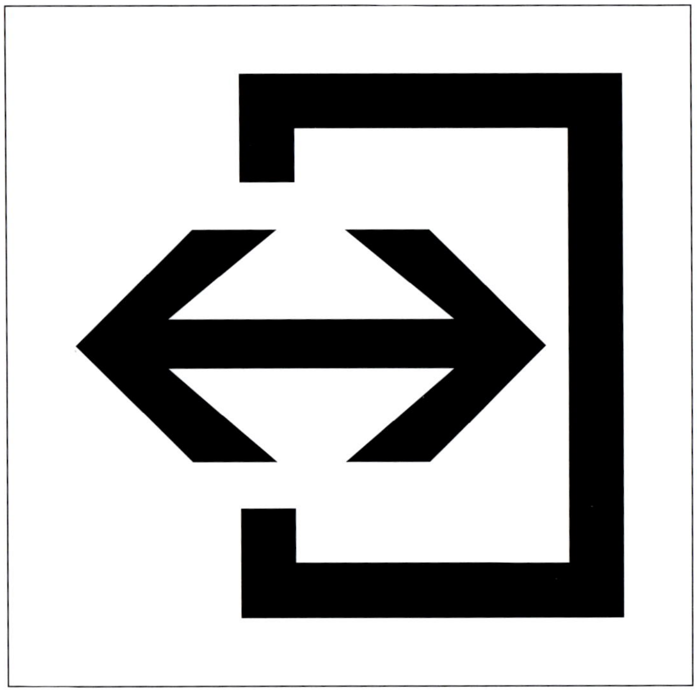

0014

DISC, VERTICAL BAR ACROSS

1.2 Enter

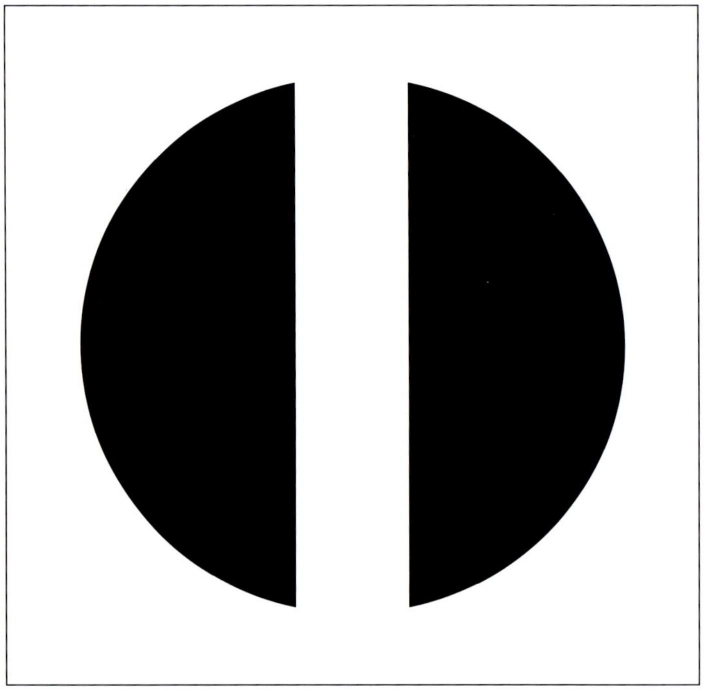

0015

DISC, HORIZONTAL BAR ACROSS

1.1 Do not enter

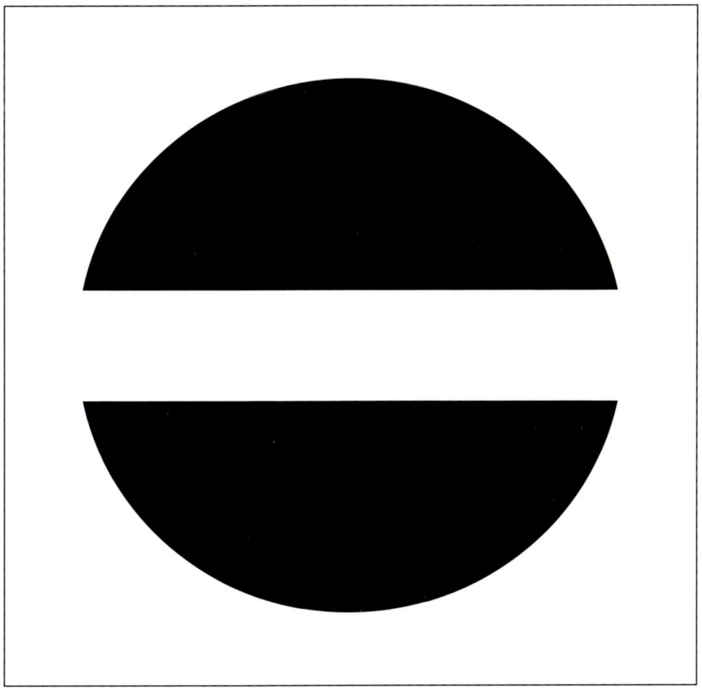

0016

QUESTION MARK

3.2 Information

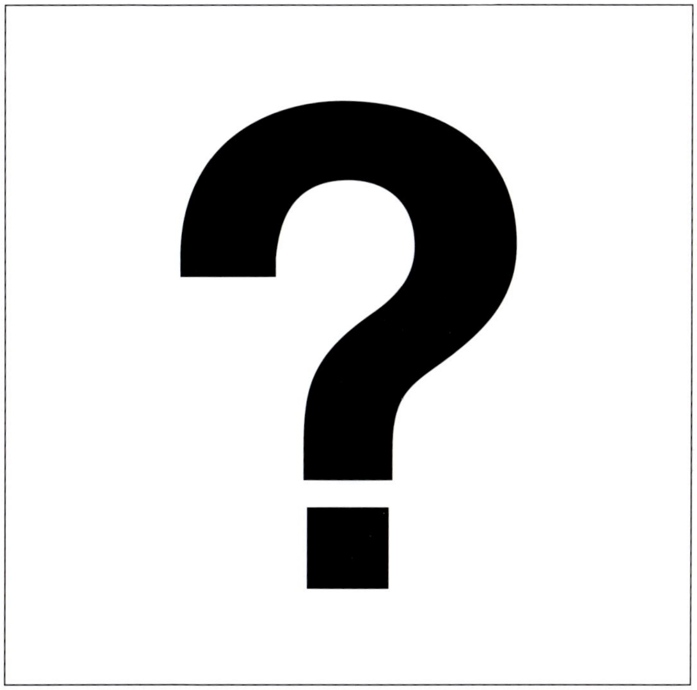

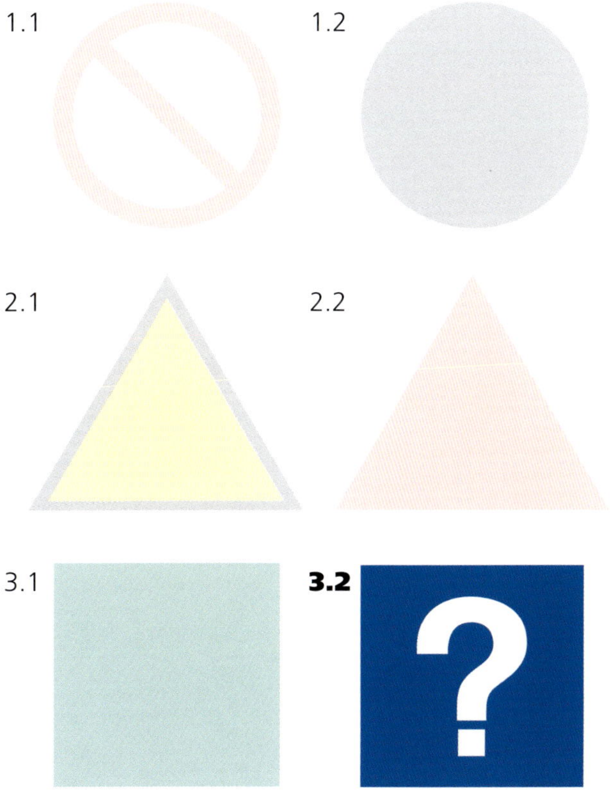

0
1
2
3
4
5
6
7
8
Index

0017

FIVE-POINTED STAR

3.2 Ground floor

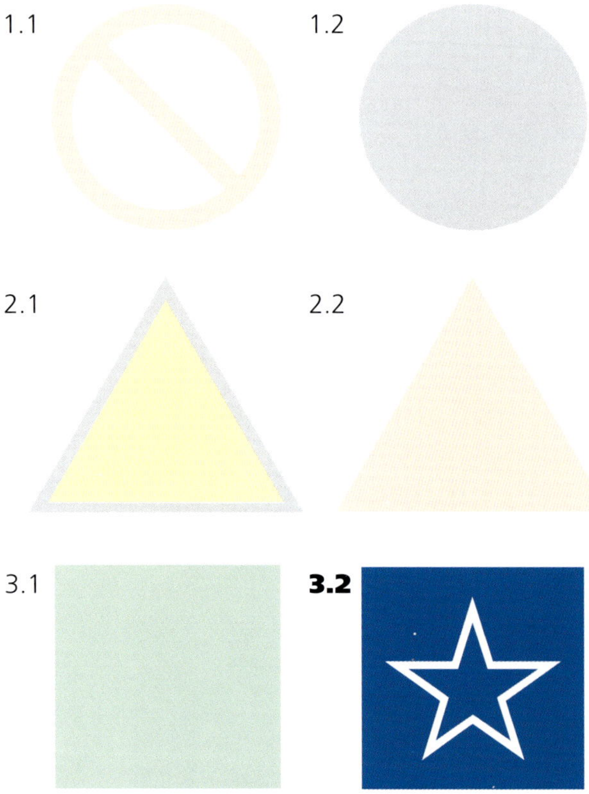

0018

HUMAN FIGURES, MOUNTING & DESCENDING STAIRS

3.2 Stairway

0019

HUMAN FIGURE, MOUNTING STAIRS

3.2 Stairway up

0020

HUMAN FIGURE, DESCENDING STAIRS

3.2 Stairway down

0021

HUMAN FIGURE, ESCALATOR

3.2 Up and down escalators

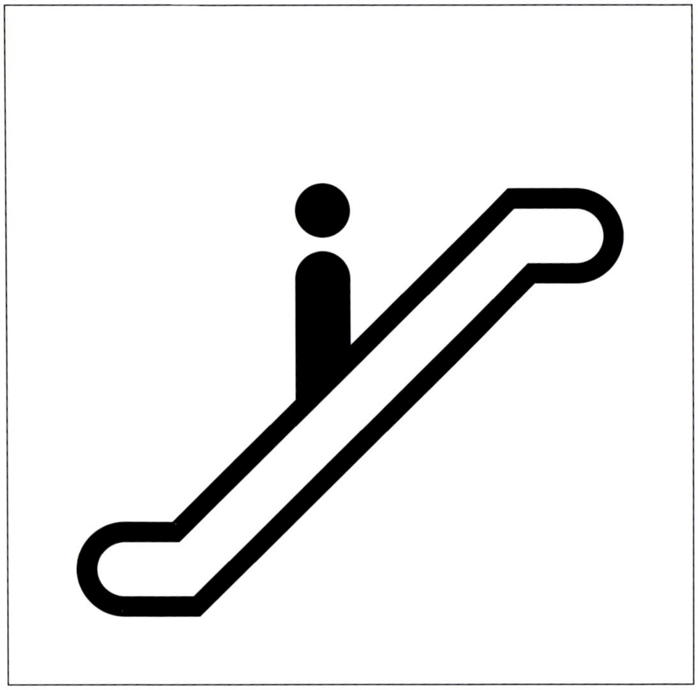

0022

HUMAN FIGURE, ESCALATOR, ARROW UP

3.2 Escalator up

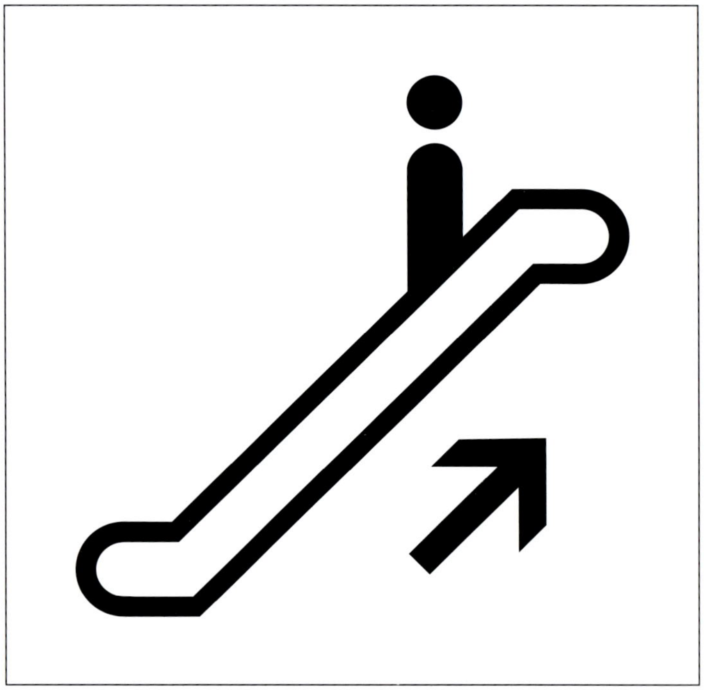

0023

HUMAN FIGURE, ESCALATOR, ARROW DOWN

3.2 Escalator down

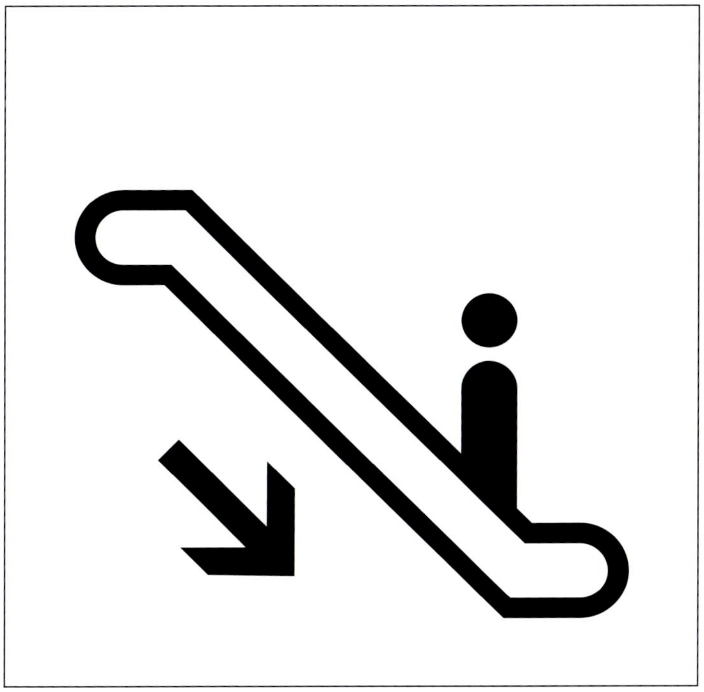

1.1

1.2

2.1

2.2

3.1

3.2

0024

ELEVATOR, HUMAN FIGURE, TOUCHING BUTTONS

1.1 Do not use elevator

3.2 Passenger elevator

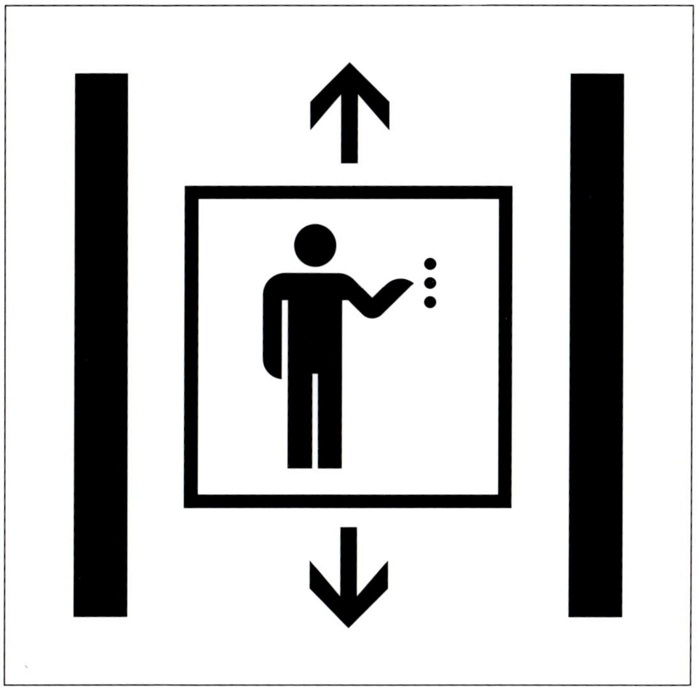

1.1

1.2

2.1

2.2

3.1

3.2

0025

ELEVATOR, HUMAN FIGURES

1.1 Do not use elevator

3.2 Passenger elevator

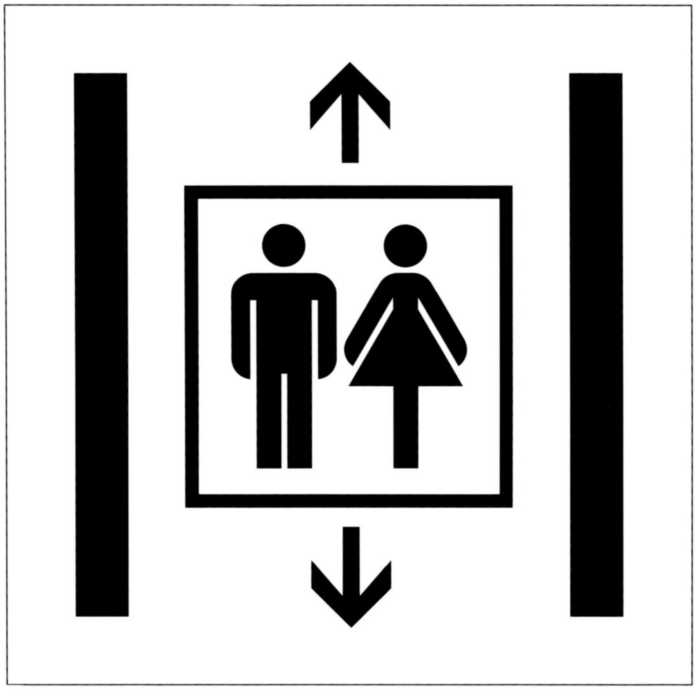

1.1

1.2

2.1

2.2

3.1

3.2

0026

ELEVATOR, SYMBOL OF ACCESS

3.2 Elevator with access

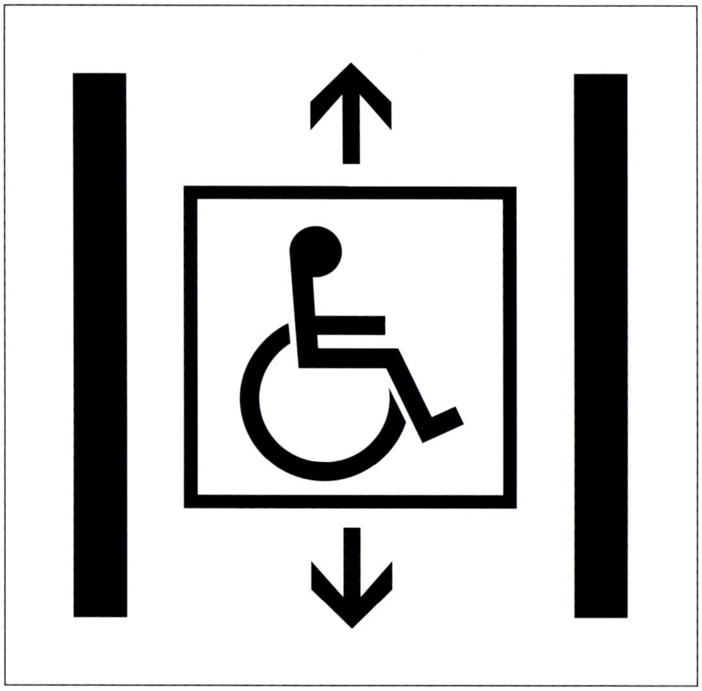

1.1

1.2

2.1

2.2

3.1

3.2

0027

ELEVATOR, HUMAN FIGURE, CRATE

3.2 Freight elevator

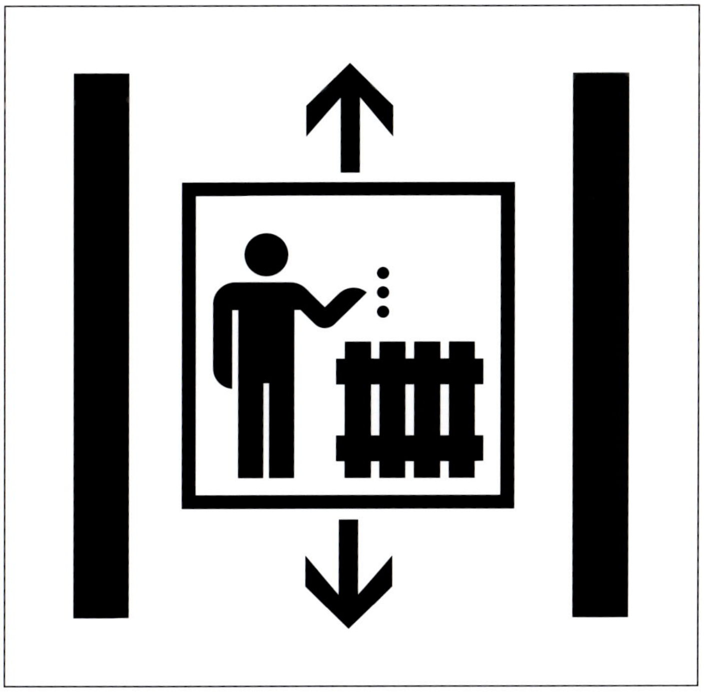

1.1

1.2

2.1

2.2

3.1

3.2

0028

ELEVATOR, CRATE, ON DOLLY

3.2 Freight elevator

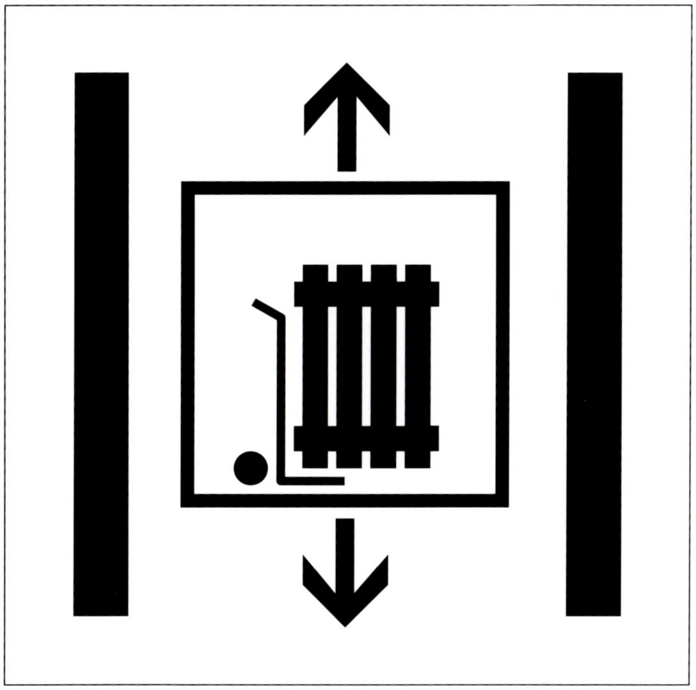

1.1

1.2

2.1

2.2

3.1

3.2

0029

ELEVATOR, P

3.2 Parking elevator

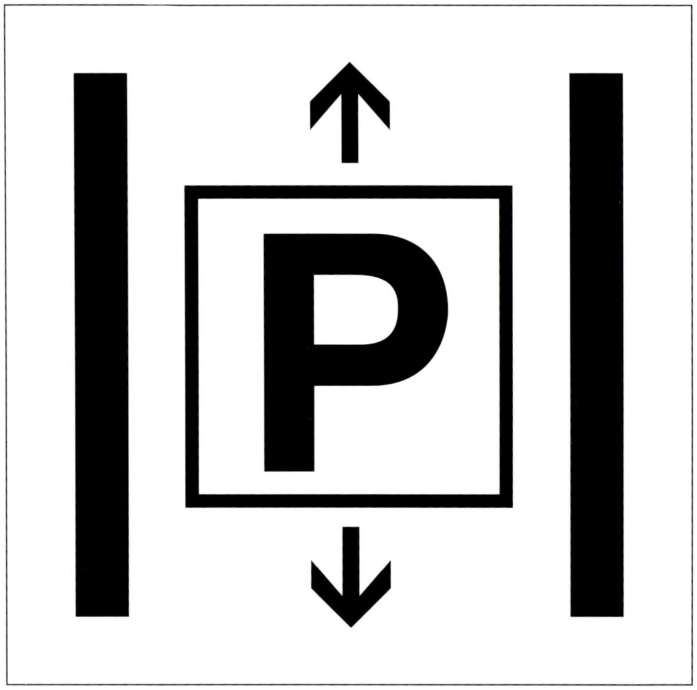

1.1

1.2

2.1

2.2

3.1

3.2

0030

HUMAN FIGURE, LOUNGE CHAIR

3.2 Lounge

1.1

1.2

2.1

2.2

3.1

3.2

0031

CIGARETTE, SMOKE RISING

1.1 No smoking

3.2 Smoking lounge

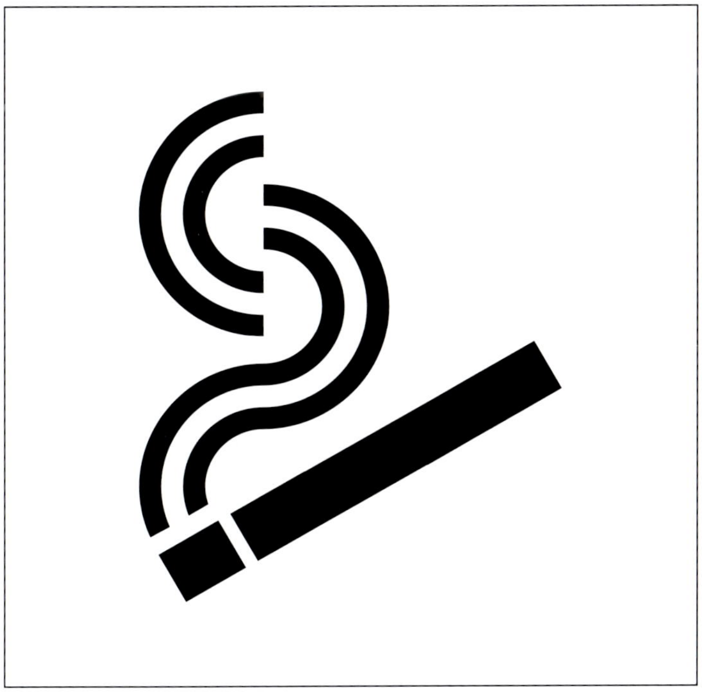

1.1

1.2

2.1

2.2

3.1

3.2

0032

CELLULAR PHONE

1.1 No cellular phones allowed

3.2 Cellular phones (store)

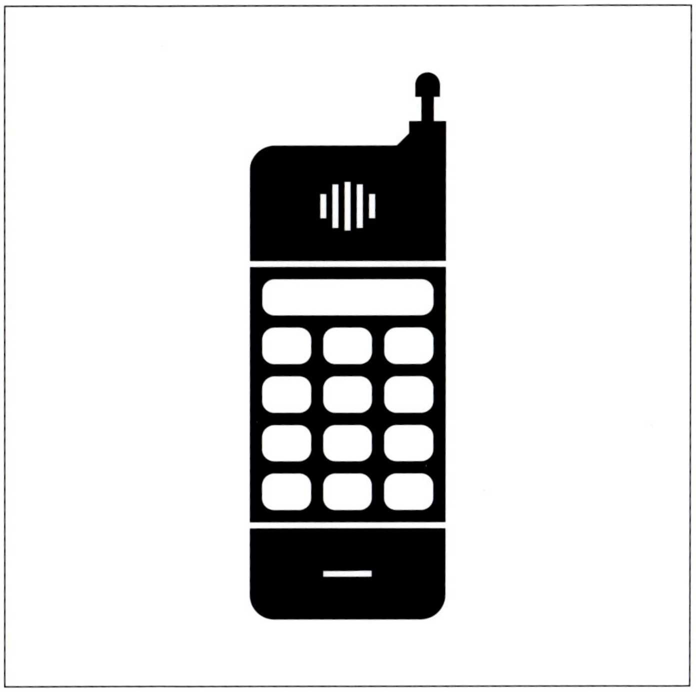

1.1

1.2

2.1

2.2

3.1

3.2

0033

HUMAN FIGURE, TRASH, (OPTIONAL RECEPTACLE)

1.1 Do not litter

1.2 Trash

1.1

1.2

2.1

2.2

3.1

3.2

0034

HUMAN FIGURE, OFF BALANCE, HORIZONTAL BAR

2.1 Caution! Slippery floor

1.1

1.2

2.1

2.2

3.1

3.2

0035

CUP, SAUCER

3.2 Coffee shop

1.1 1.2

2.1 2.2

3.1 **3.2**

0036

PAPER CUP, STRAWS

1.1 No drinks allowed

3.2 Snack bar, food court

1.1

1.2

2.1 2.2

3.1 **3.2**

0
1
2
3
4
5
6
7
8
Index

0037

ICE CREAM CONE, PAPER CUP, STRAWS

1.1 No food or drinks allowed

3.2 Snack bar, food court

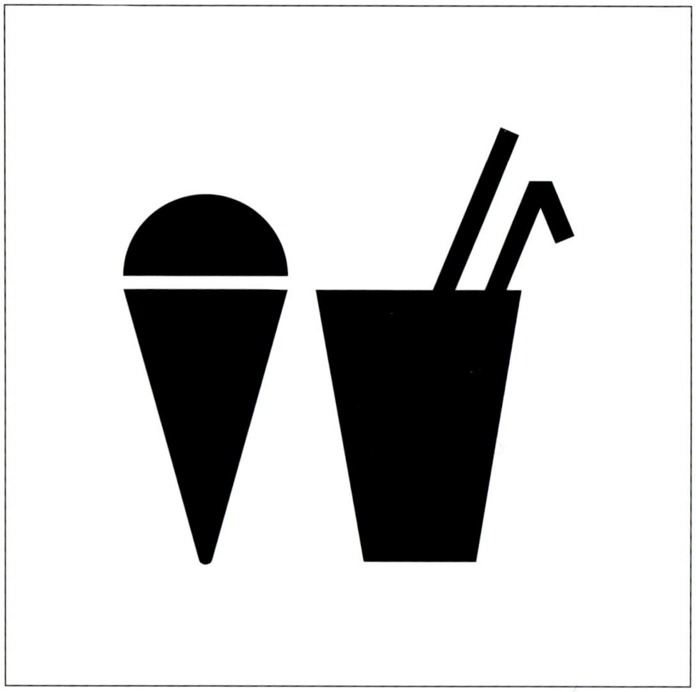

1.1

1.2

2.1

2.2

3.1

3.2

0038

HAMBURGER, PAPER CUP, STRAWS

1.1 No food or drinks allowed

3.2 Snack bar, food court

1.1

1.2

2.1

2.2

3.1

3.2

0039

FORK, KNIFE

3.2 Cafeteria, restaurant

0040

HUMAN HEAD, SPRAYING DROPS

3.2 Drinking fountain

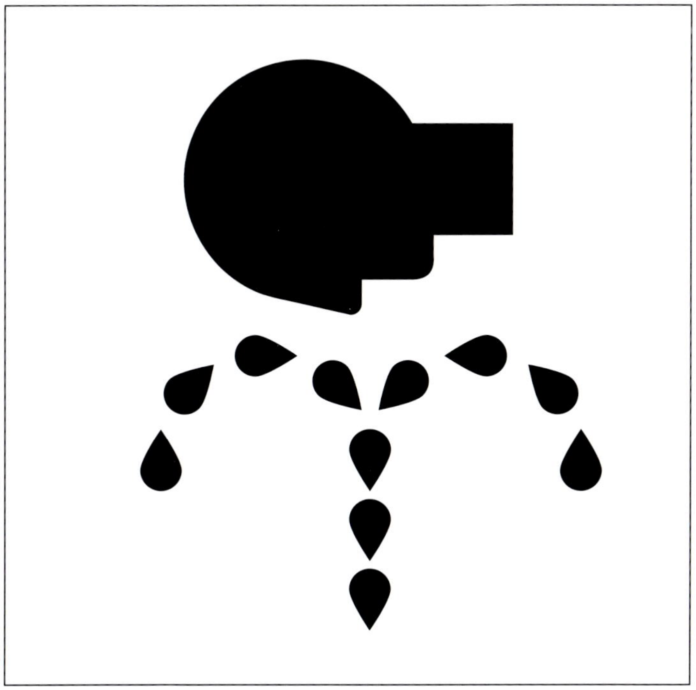

0041

SLOT, COIN IN HAND

3.2 Vending machine

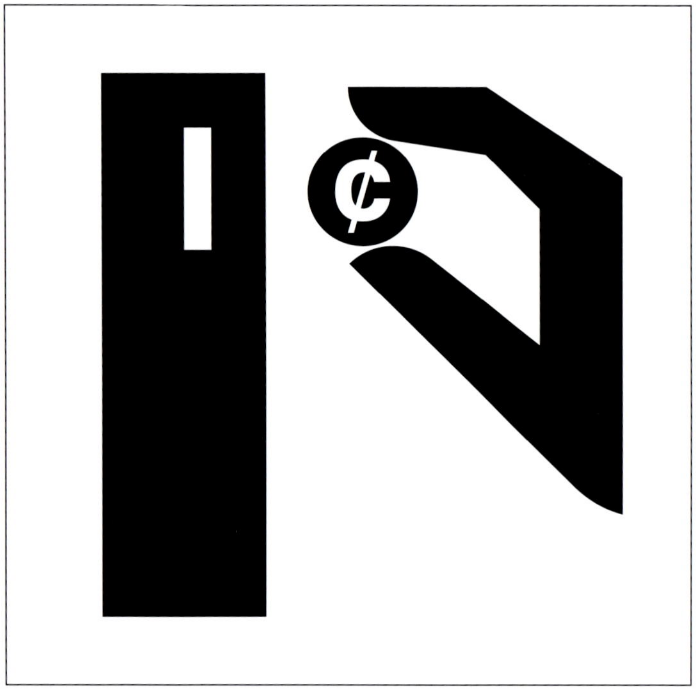

0042

SCREEN, KEYPAD, SLOT, CURRENCY SIGN

3.2 ABM (Automated Banking Machine)

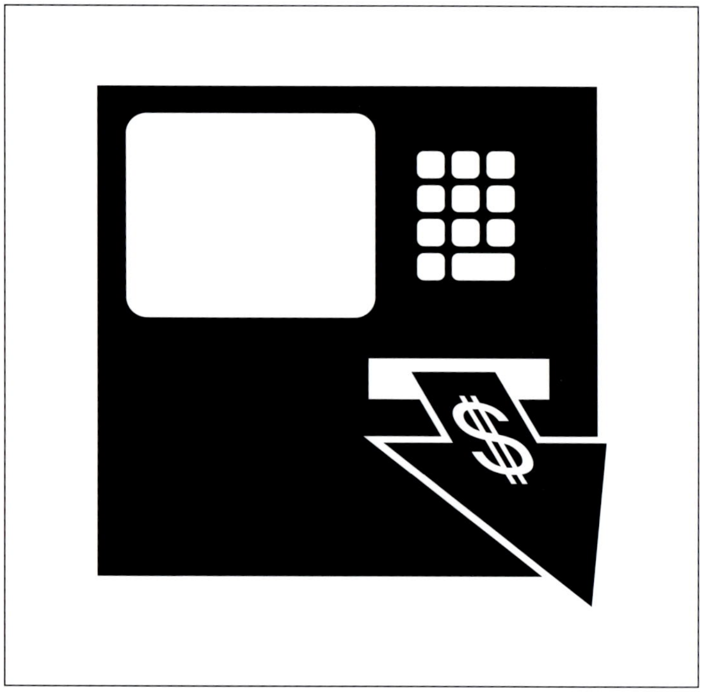

1.1

1.2

2.1

2.2

3.1

3.2

3.2

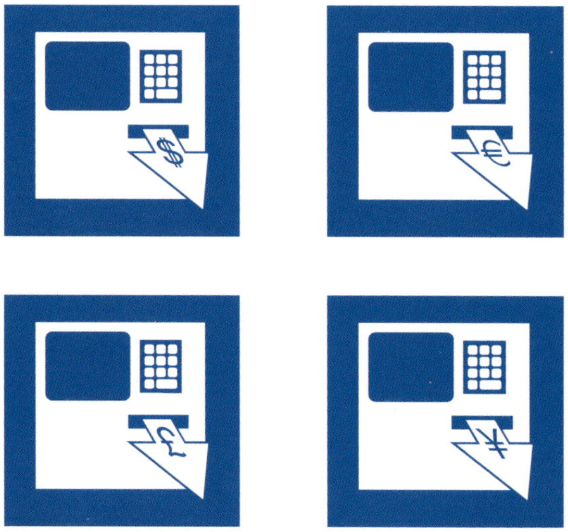

0043

CURRENCY SYMBOL

3.2 Cash, cashier

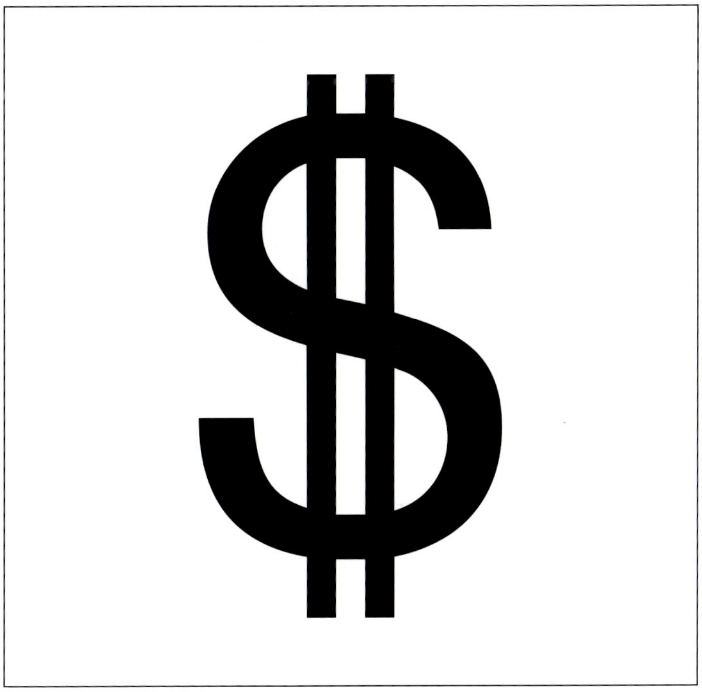

3.2

0044

PAPER MONEY, COINS

3.2 Foreign exchange

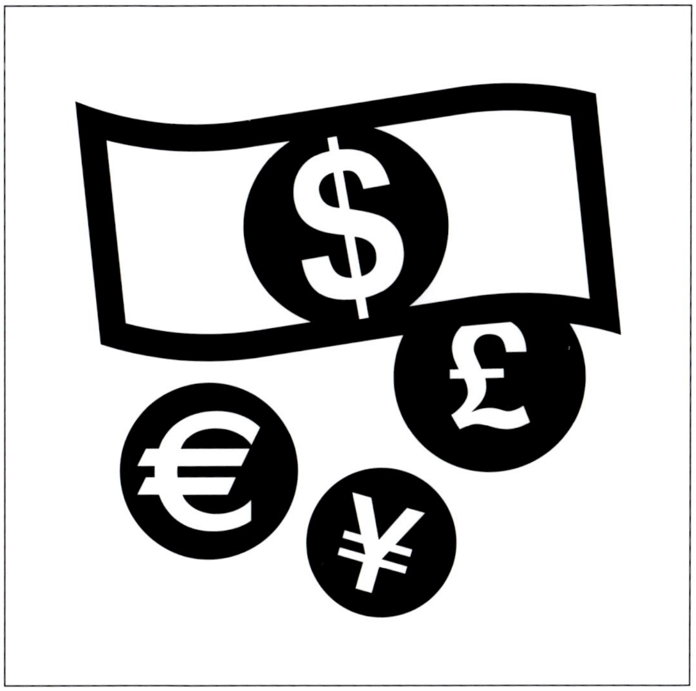

1.1

1.2

2.1

2.2

3.1

3.2

0045

HUMAN FIGURE, MAN, LEGS APART, TOILET

3.2 Toilet for men

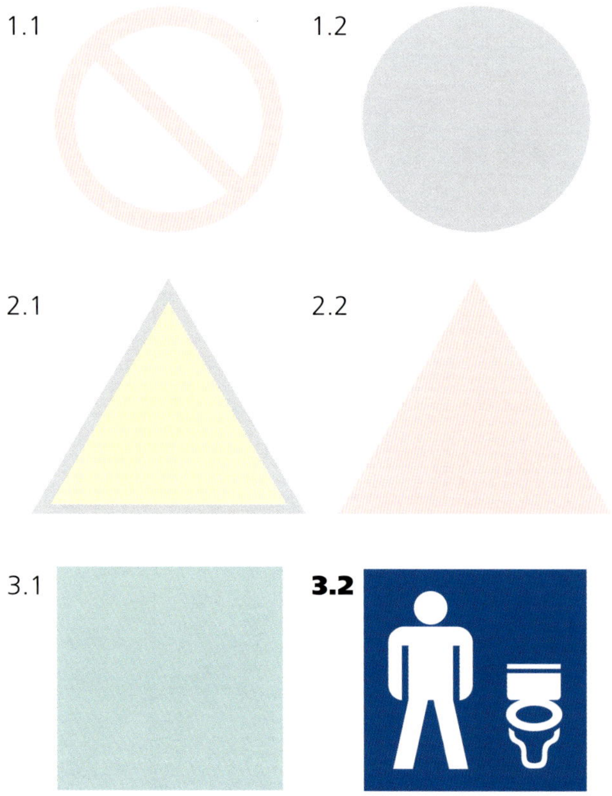

0046

MAN, LEGS APART, TOILET, SYMBOL OF ACCESS

3.2 Toilet with access, for men

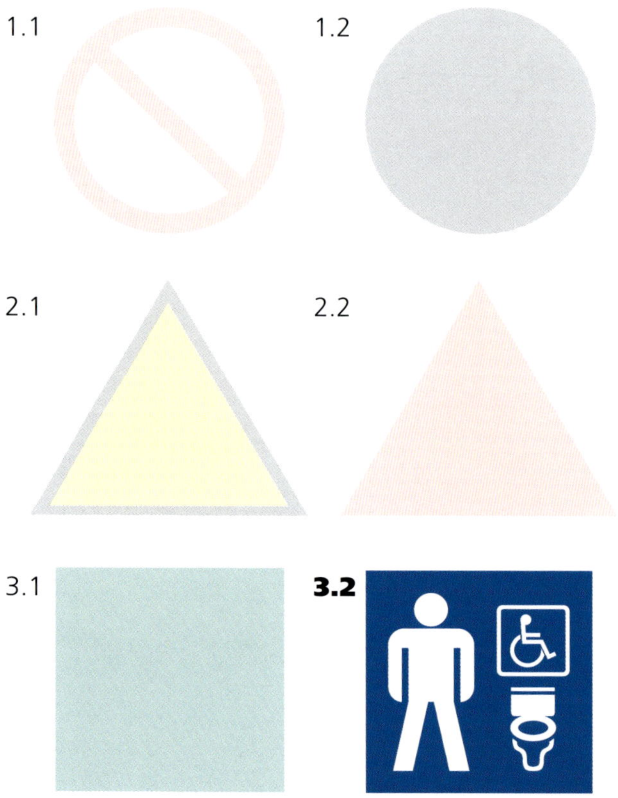

0047

HUMAN FIGURE, WOMAN, TOILET

3.2 Toilet for women

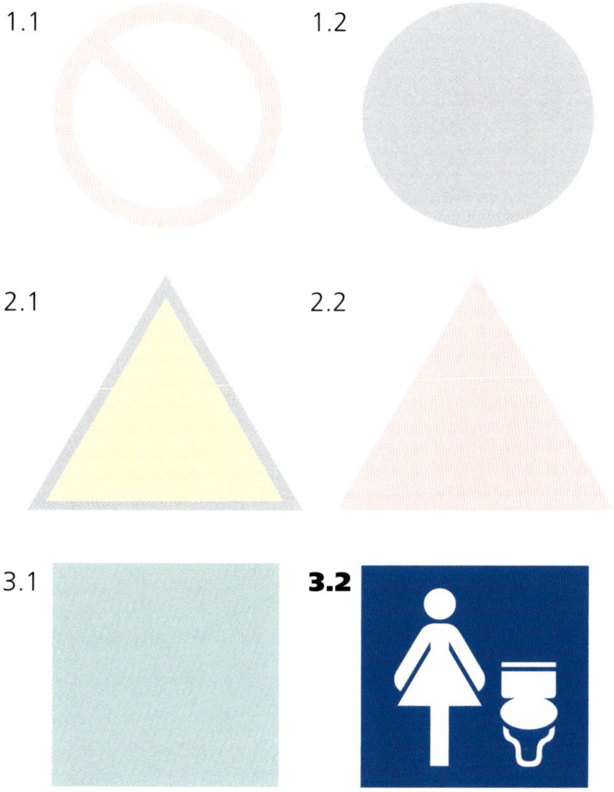

0048

WOMAN, TOILET, SYMBOL OF ACCESS

3.2 Toilet with access, for women

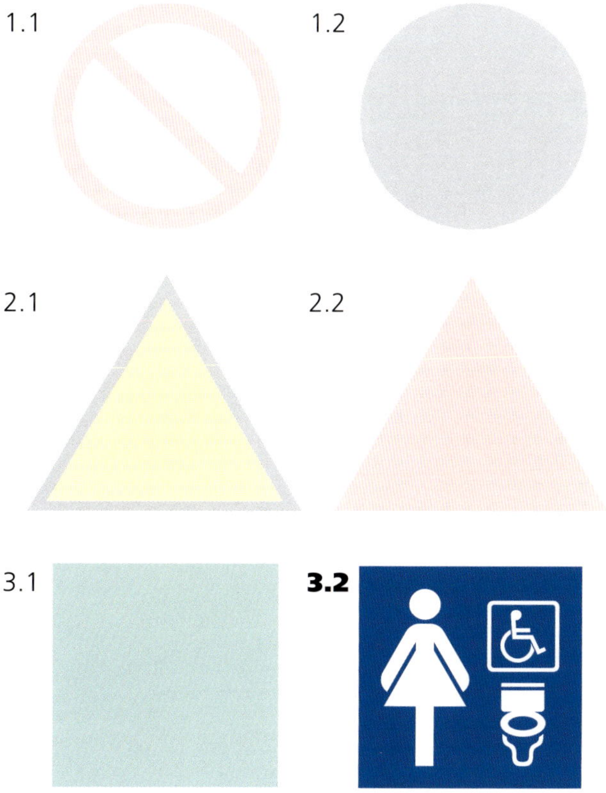

0
1
2
3
4
5
6
7
8
Index

0049

HUMAN FIGURES, MAN & WOMAN, TOILET

3.2 Toilets

1.1

1.2

2.1

2.2

3.1

3.2

0050

MAN & WOMAN, TOILET, SYMBOL OF ACCESS

3.2 Toilet with access

1.1

1.2

2.1

2.2

3.1

3.2

0051

HUMAN FIGURES, MAN & WOMAN, VERTICAL BAR

3.2 Toilets

0052

LOCKERS

3.2 Locker room

0053

HUMAN FIGURE, MAN

1.1 No men allowed

3.2 Man

1.1

1.2

2.1

2.2

3.1

3.2

0054

HUMAN FIGURE, WOMAN

1.1 No women allowed

3.2 Woman

1.1

1.2

2.1

2.2

3.1

3.2

0055

COAT HANGER

3.2 Cloakroom

0056

TELEPHONE HANDSET

3.2 Pay phone

0057

TELEPHONE HANDSET, SHEET OF PAPER

3.2 Fax machine

1.1

1.2

2.1

2.2

3.1

3.2

0058

SHEAF OF PAPERS, ELECTRICAL SYMBOL

3.2 Fax machine

1.1

1.2

2.1

2.2

3.1

3.2

0059

TELEPHONE HANDSET, SOS

3.1 Emergency phone

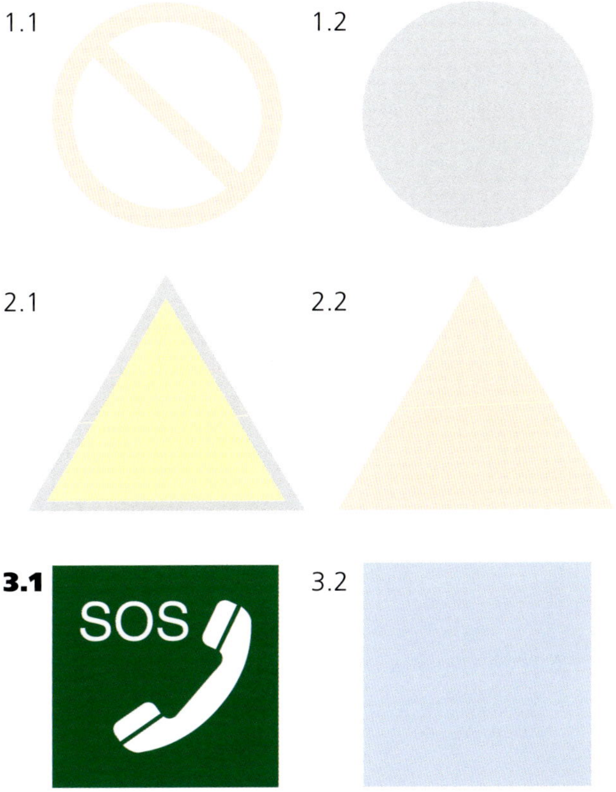

0060

SHIELD (OPTIONAL: SECURITY)

3.2 Security

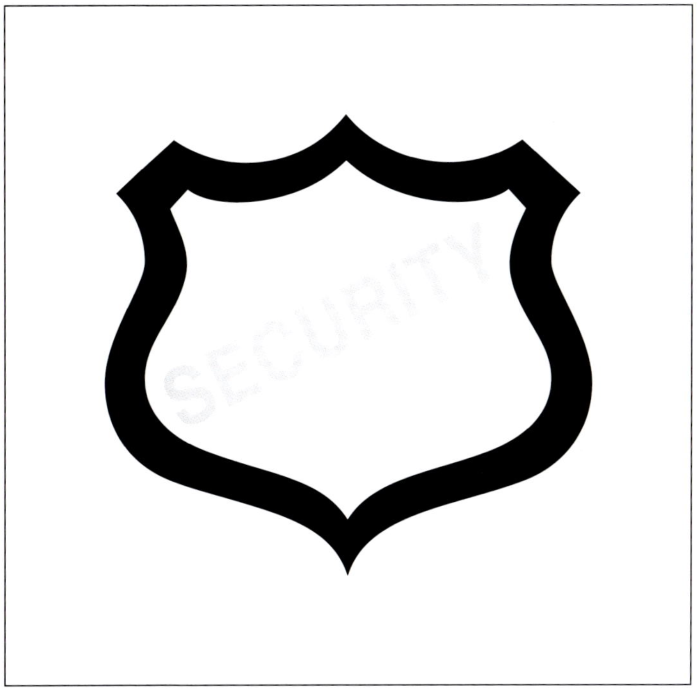

0
1
2
3
4
5
6
7
8
Index

0061

INDEX FINGER, HORIZONTAL BAR

1.1 Do not touch

3.2 Touch

1.1

1.2

2.1

2.2

3.1

3.2

0062

FINGER PUSHING THE BUTTON, FLAMES

3.1 Fire alarm (ISO)

1.1

1.2

2.1

2.2

3.1

3.2

0063

DISC, CONCENTRIC ARCS, HAMMER, FLAMES

3.1 Fire alarm

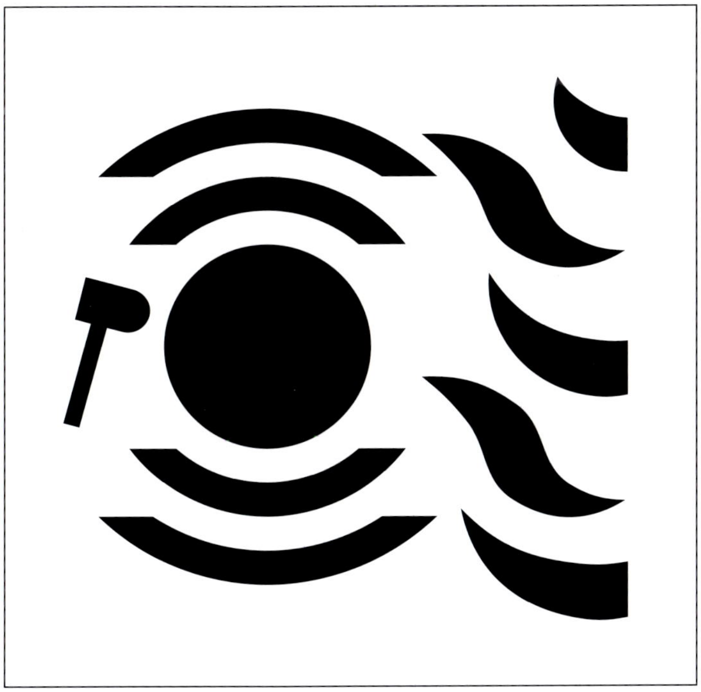

1.1

1.2

2.1

2.2

3.1

3.2

0064

FIRE-PULL MECHANISM, FLAMES

3.1 Fire alarm

1.1

1.2

2.1

2.2

3.1

3.2

0
1
2
3
4
5
6
7
8
Index

0065

EXTINGUISHER, FLAMES

3.1 Fire extinguisher

1.1

1.2

2.1

2.2

3.1

3.2

0066

HYDRANT, FLAMES

3.1 Fire hydrant

1.1

1.2

2.1

2.2

3.1

3.2

0067

COILED HOSE, FLAMES

3.1 Fire hose

1.1

1.2

2.1

2.2

3.1

3.2

0068

FOLDED HOSE, FLAMES

3.1 Fire hose

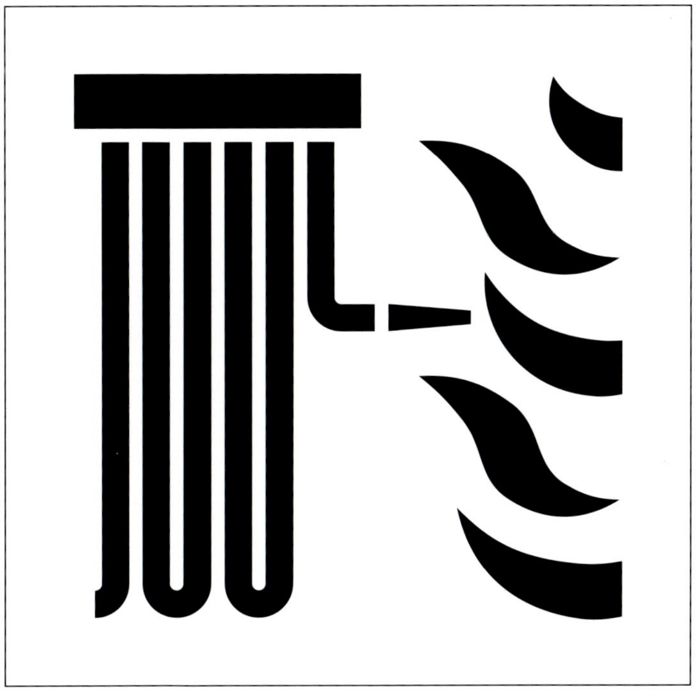

1.1

1.2

2.1

2.2

3.1

3.2

0069

EXIT

3.1 Exit

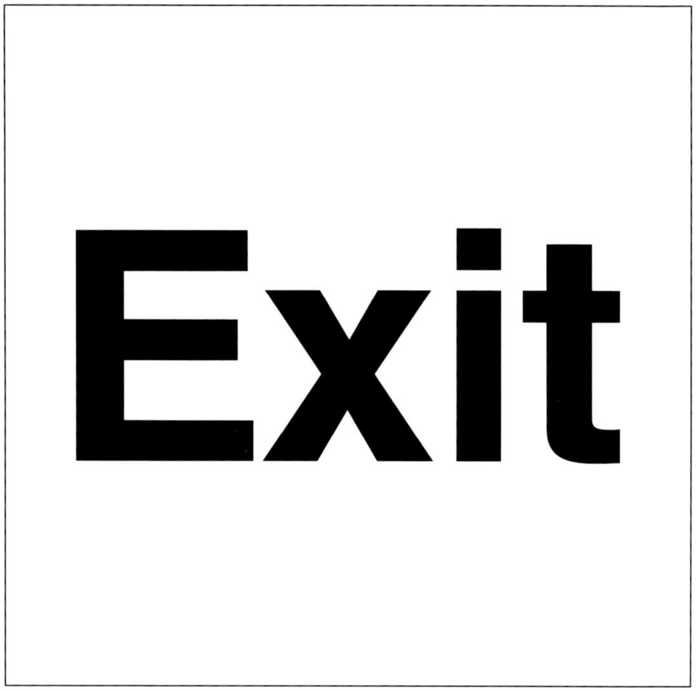

1.1

1.2

2.1

2.2

3.1

3.2

0070

HUMAN FIGURE, EXIT, IN TRIANGULAR SHAPE

3.1 Emergency exit

1.1

1.2

2.1

2.2

3.1

3.2

0071

FLAMES, HUMAN FIGURE (WALKING)

3.1 Fire exit

1.1

1.2

2.1

2.2

3.1

3.2

0072

FLAMES, HUMAN FIGURE (RUNNING)

3.1 Fire exit

1.1

1.2

2.1

2.2

3.1

3.2

0073

FIRE AXE, FLAMES

3.1 Fire axe

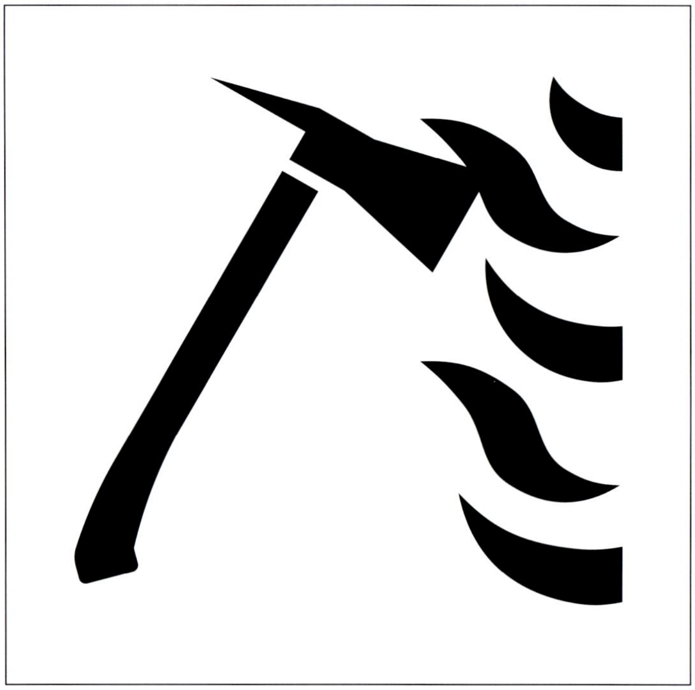

1.1

1.2

2.1

2.2

3.1

3.2

0074

FIREFIGHTER'S HAT, FLAMES

3.1 Firefighter's access, elevator

1.1

1.2

2.1

2.2

3.1

3.2

0075

GREEK CROSS
3.1 Emergency

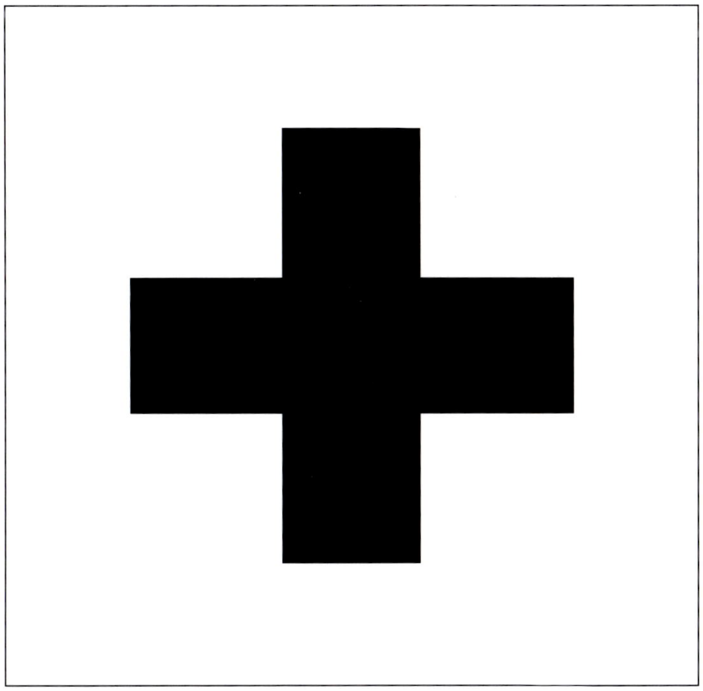

1.1

1.2

2.1

2.2

3.1

3.2

0076

GREEK CROSS, BANDAGED HAND
3.1 First aid

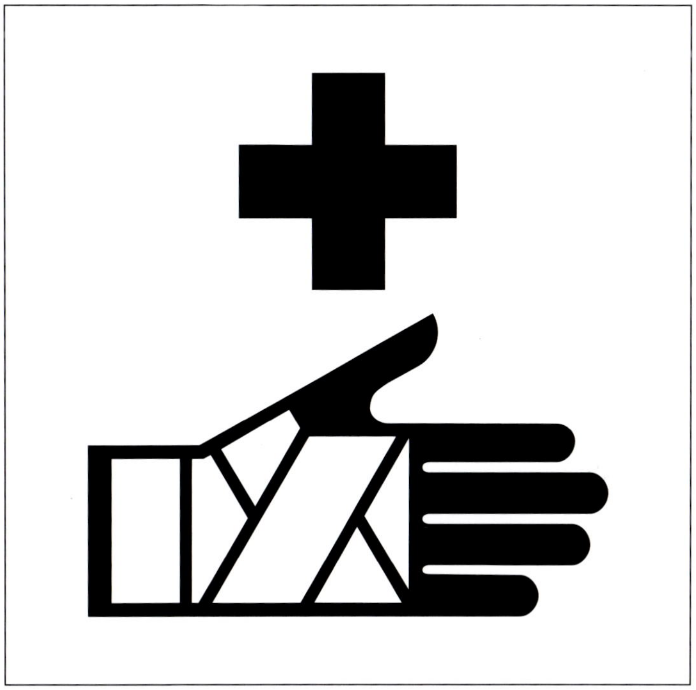

1.1

1.2

2.1

2.2

3.1

3.2

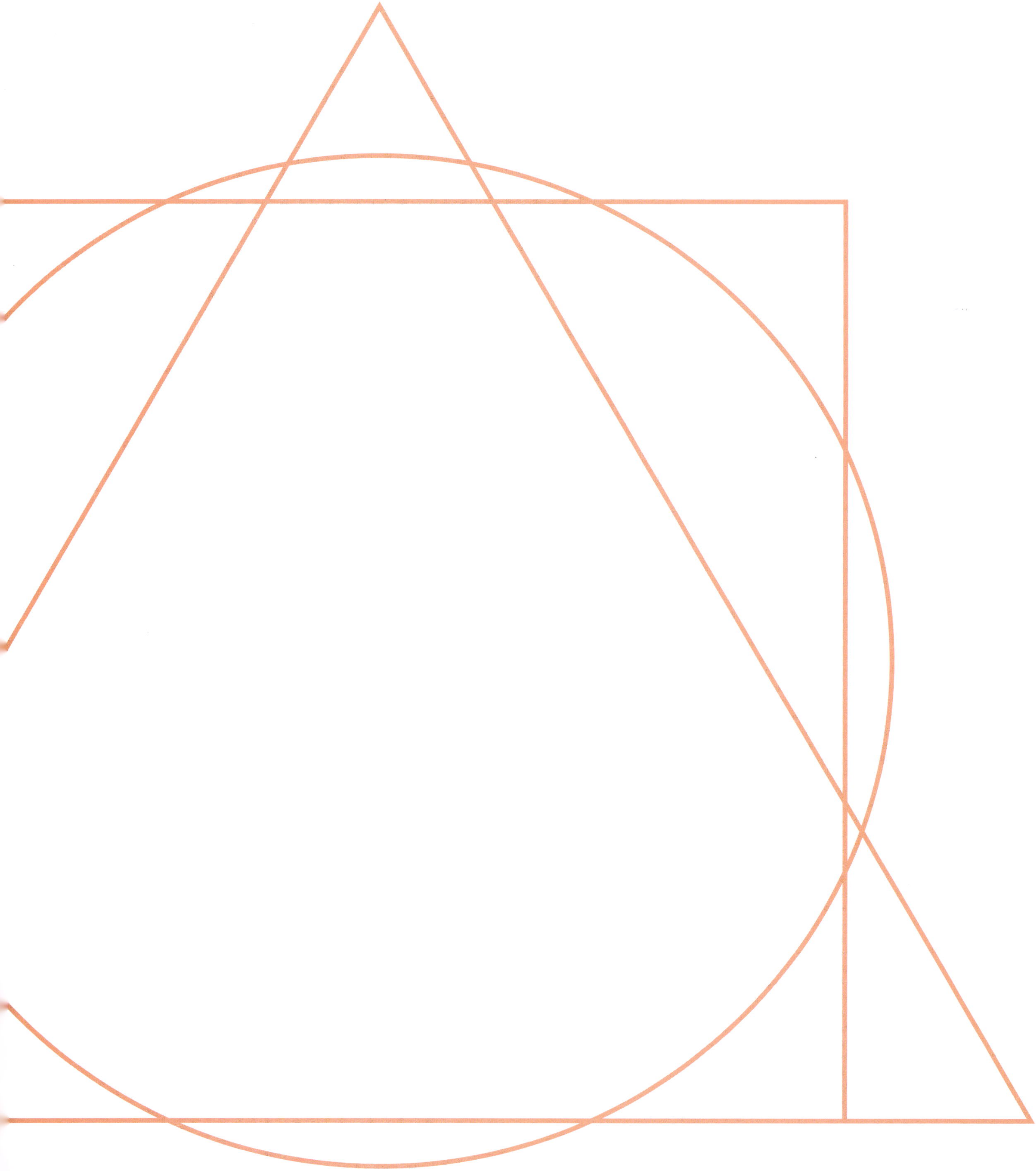

Series 1 – Pictographs for base building

1001

MOTOR VEHICLE, BETWEEN TWO BARS

3.2 Garage

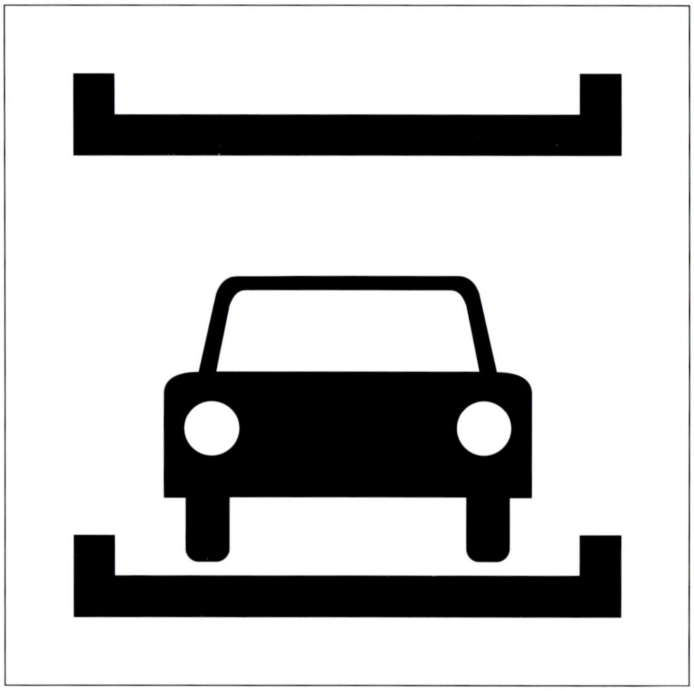

1.1

1.2

2.1

2.2

3.1

3.2

1002

MOTOR VEHICLE, FRONT VIEW

1.1 No motor vehicles allowed

2.1 Caution! Motor vehicles

3.2 Motor vehicles allowed

1.1

1.2

2.1

2.2

3.1

3.2

1003

MOTOR VEHICLE, SIDE VIEW

1.1 No motor vehicles allowed
2.1 Caution! Motor vehicles
3.2 Motor vehicles allowed

1.1

1.2

2.1

2.2

3.1

3.2

1004

BICYCLE, IN THE RACK

1.1 No bicycle parking
3.2 Bicycle rack

1.1

1.2

2.1

2.2

3.1

3.2

1005

KEY

1.1 Do not start

1.2 Lock up

3.2 Keys

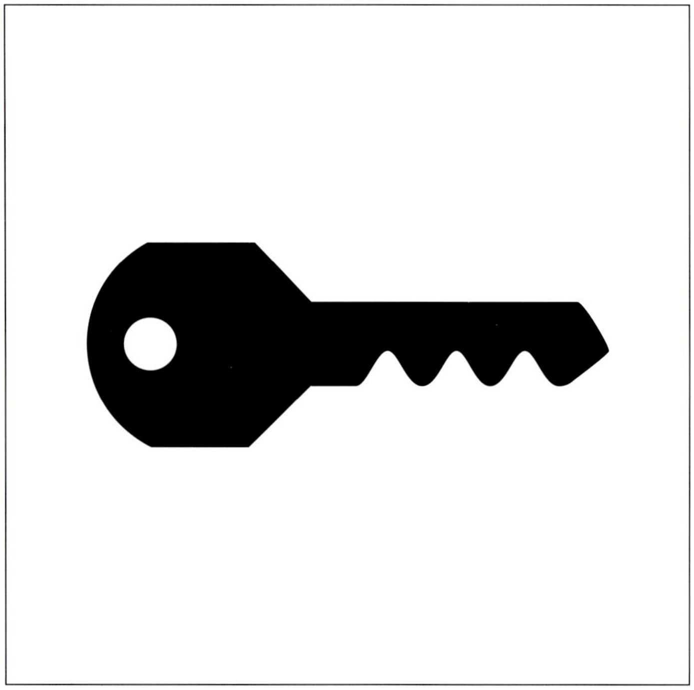

1.1

1.2

2.1

2.2

3.1

3.2

1006

LOCK, ARROW POINTING DOWN

1.1 Do not lock

1.2 Lock up

1.1

1.2

2.1

2.2

3.1

3.2

1007

DISC, ARROW POINTING UP, HORIZONTAL BAR

1.2 This way up

1008

DISC, ARROW POINTING UP, OVER PLANE

1.2 This way up

1009

COMPASS

3.2 Identification of direction, this way

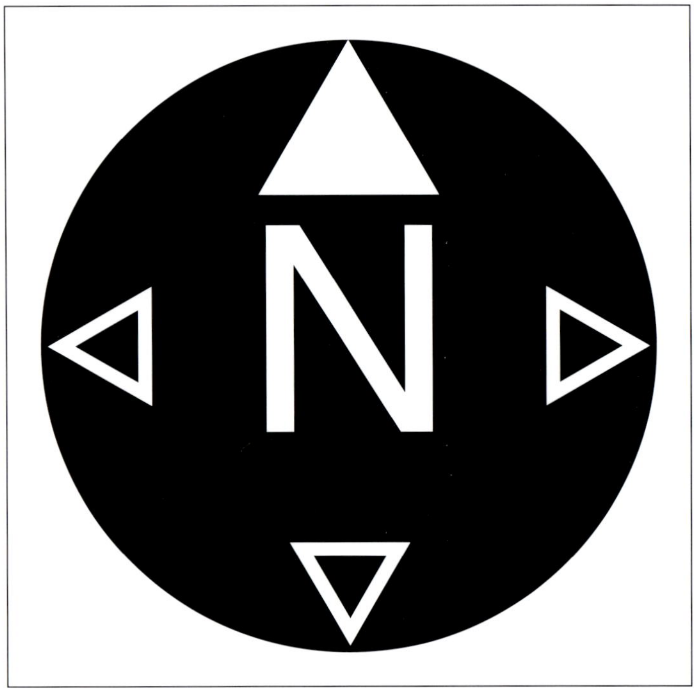

3.2

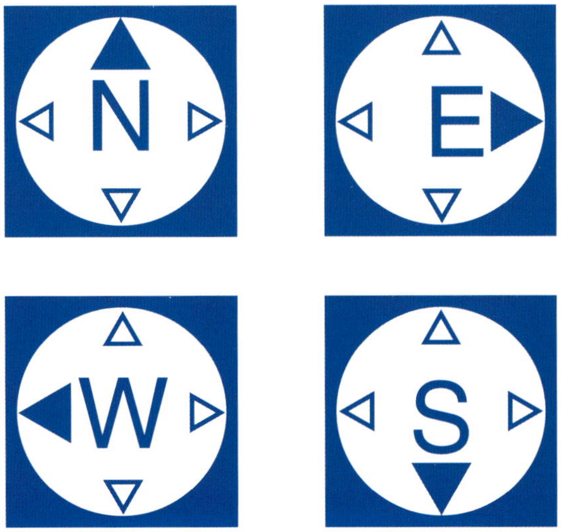

1010

FOUR ARROWS CONVERGING TO CENTRAL POINT

3.2 Meeting place

1.1

1.2

2.1

2.2

3.1

3.2

1011

HUMAN FIGURE, HORIZONTAL BAR

3.2 Reception

1.1

1.2

2.1

2.2

3.1

3.2

1012

PENCIL

3.2 Admitting, registration

1.1

1.2

2.1

2.2

3.1

3.2

1013

PIGEONHOLES, COILED PAPER

3.2 Messages

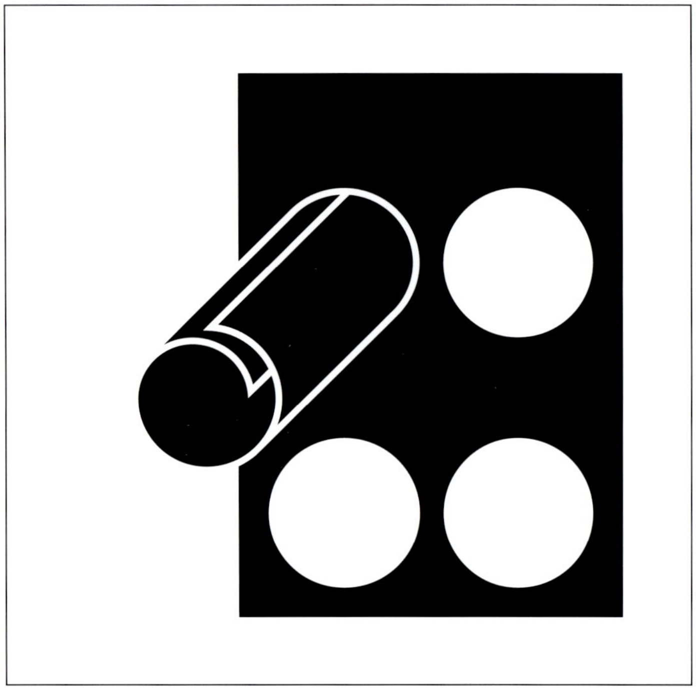

1.1

1.2

2.1

2.2

3.1

3.2

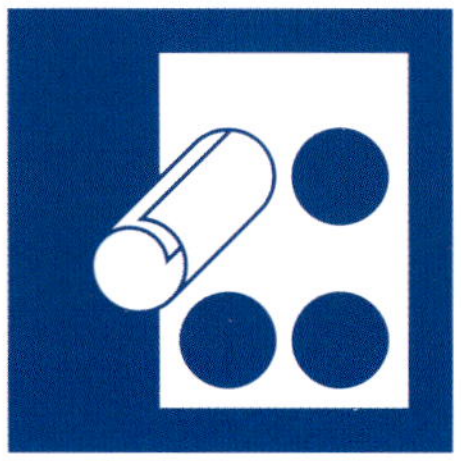

1014

KEY, ENVELOPE IN BOX

3.2 Mailbox

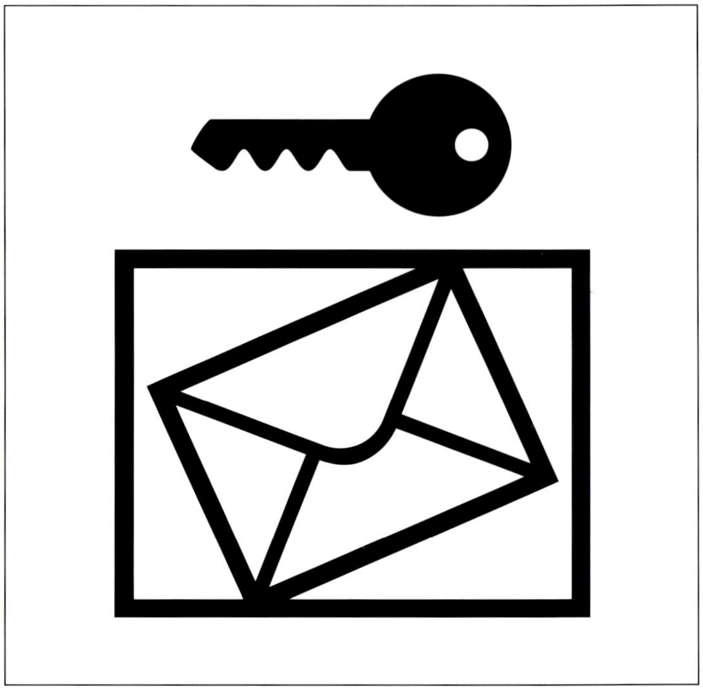

1.1

1.2

2.1

2.2

3.1

3.2

1015

ENVELOPE, ENTERING SLOT

3.2 Mail (room)

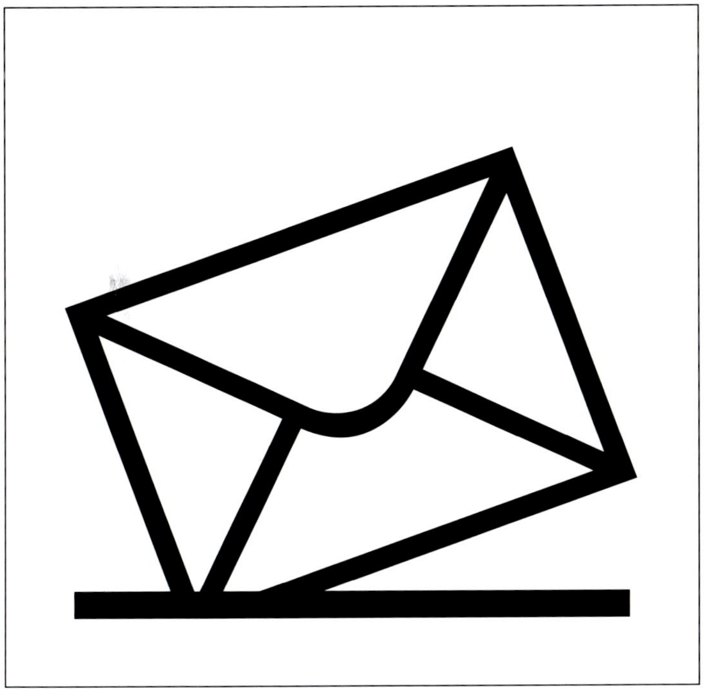

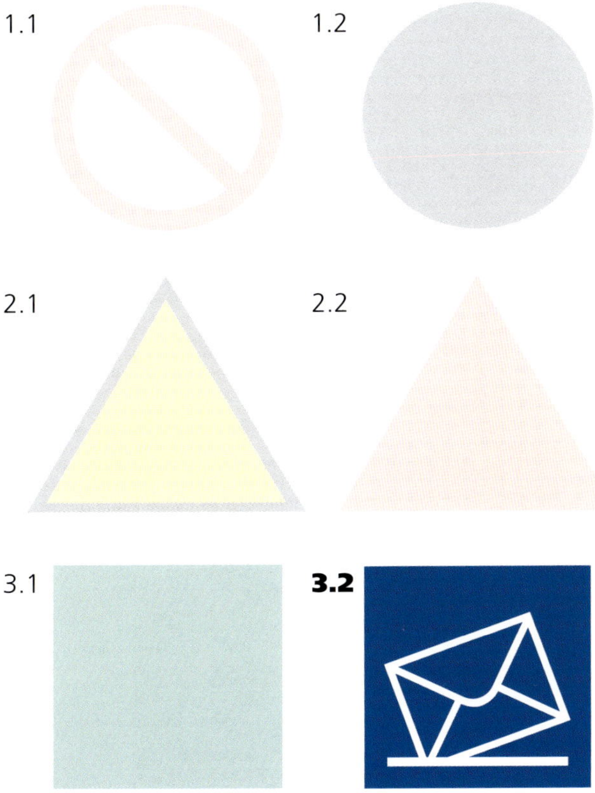

1016

E, ENVELOPE

3.2 e-mail (electronic mail)

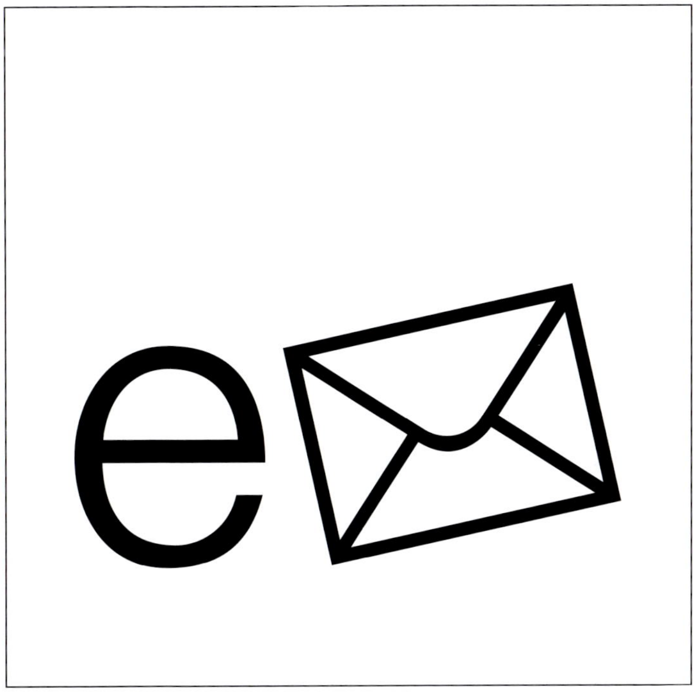

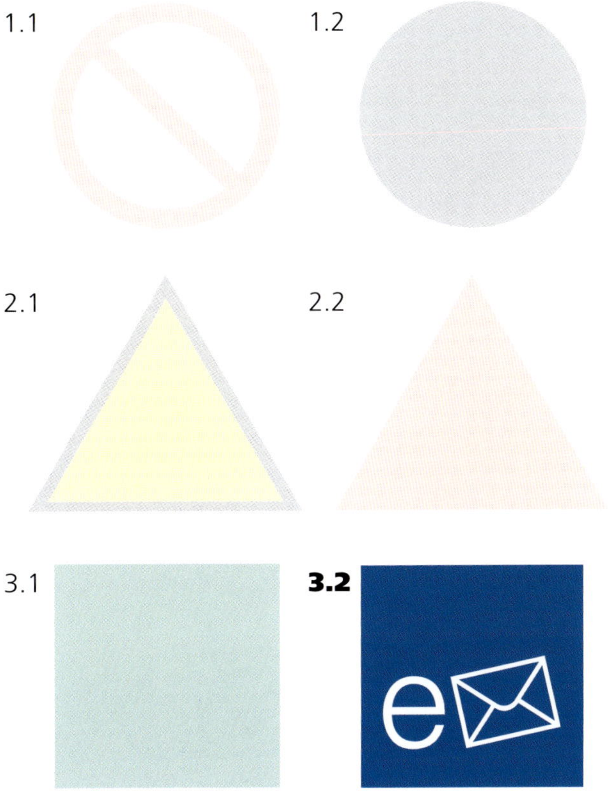

0
1
2
3
4
5
6
7
8
Index

1017

HUMAN FIGURE, COMPUTER OR LAPTOP

3.2 Office

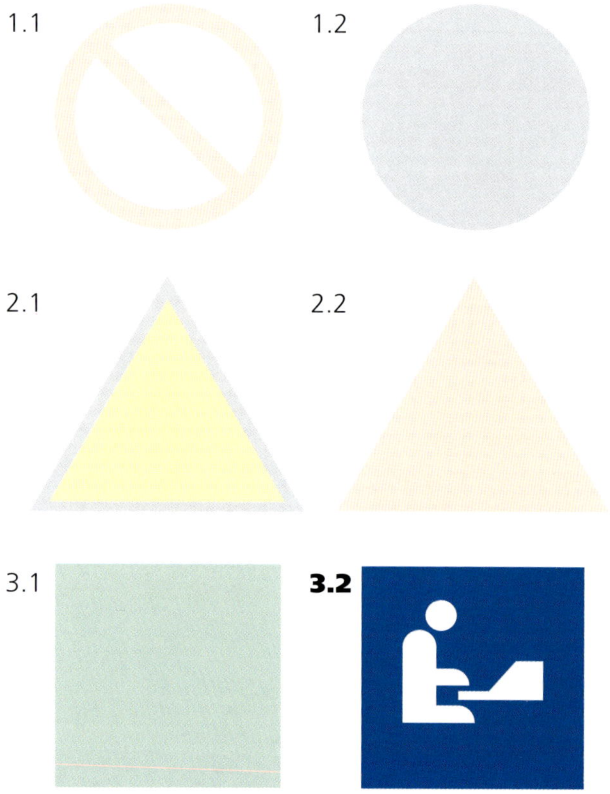

1018

MONITOR, KEYBOARD, COMPUTER

3.2 Computer room, resource center

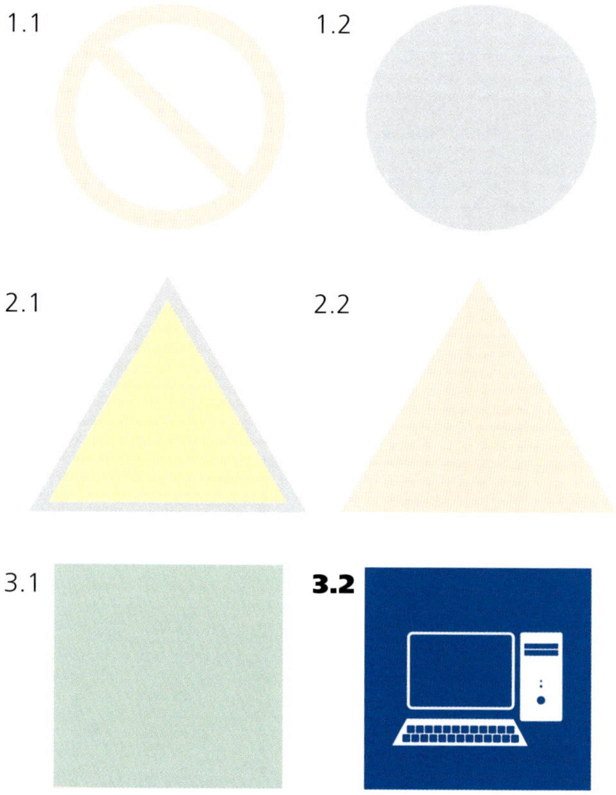

1019

HUMAN FIGURE, OPEN BOOK

3.2 Library, reading room

1.1

1.2

2.1

2.2

3.1

3.2

1020

HUMAN FIGURES, OVERHEAD PROJECTOR, VIDEO

3.2 Screening room

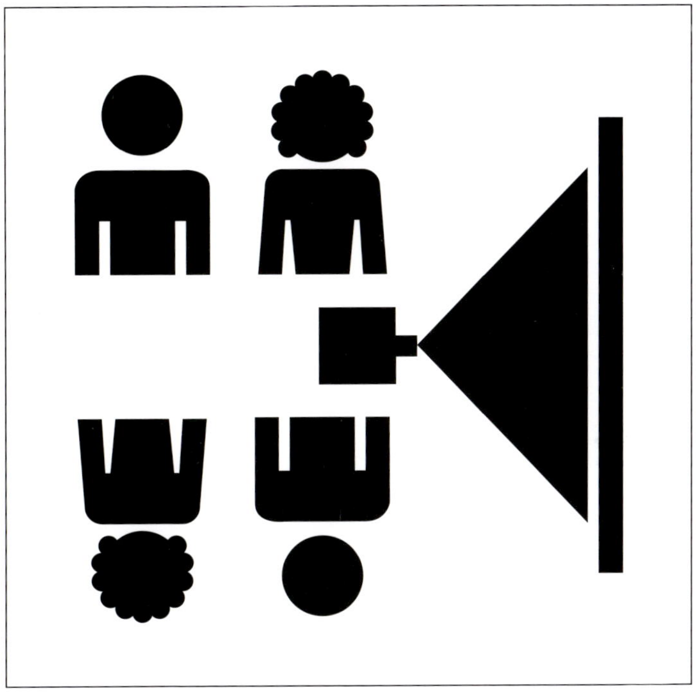

1.1

1.2

2.1

2.2

3.1

3.2

1021

PAPER SHEETS, X

1.1 Do not copy

3.2 Copier room, reproduction

1.1

1.2

2.1

2.2

3.1

3.2

1022

SHEET OF PAPER, BEING SHREDDED

1.1 Do not shred

3.2 Shredder

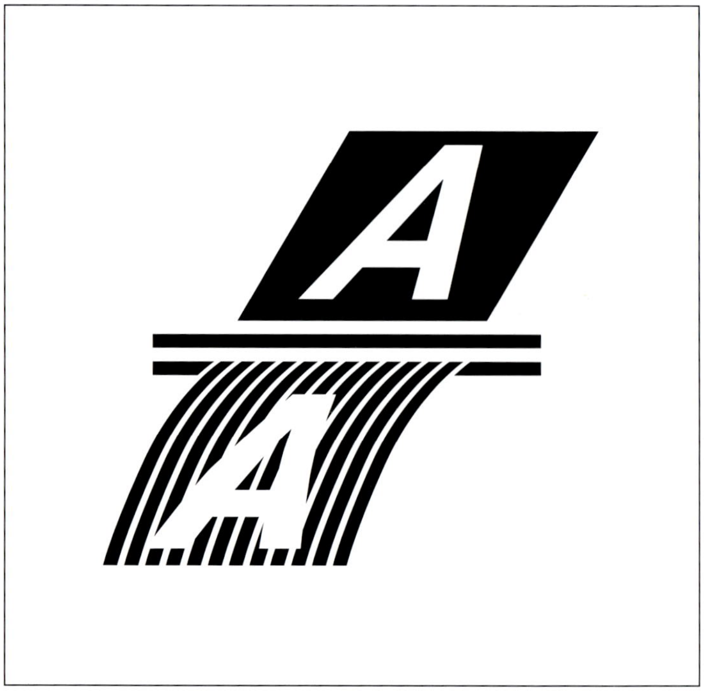

1.1

1.2

2.1

2.2

3.1

3.2

1023

FILING CABINET
3.2 File (room)

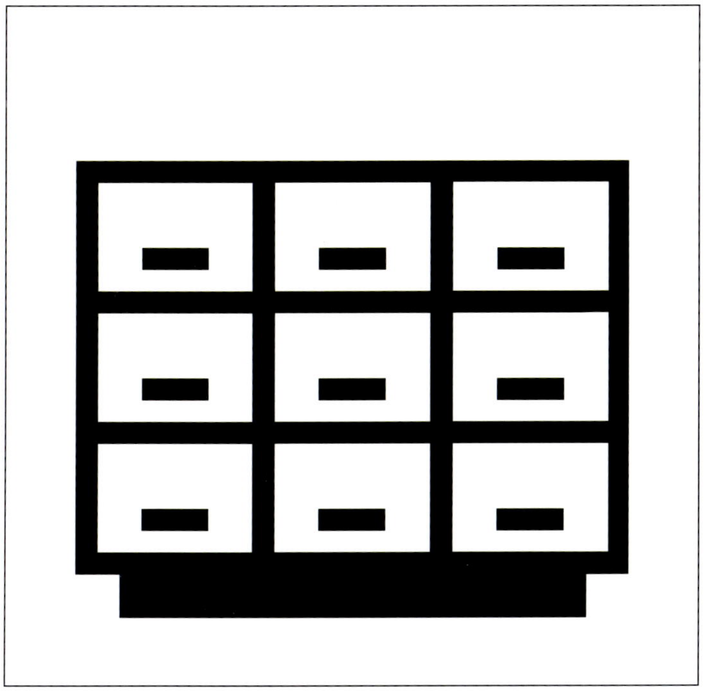

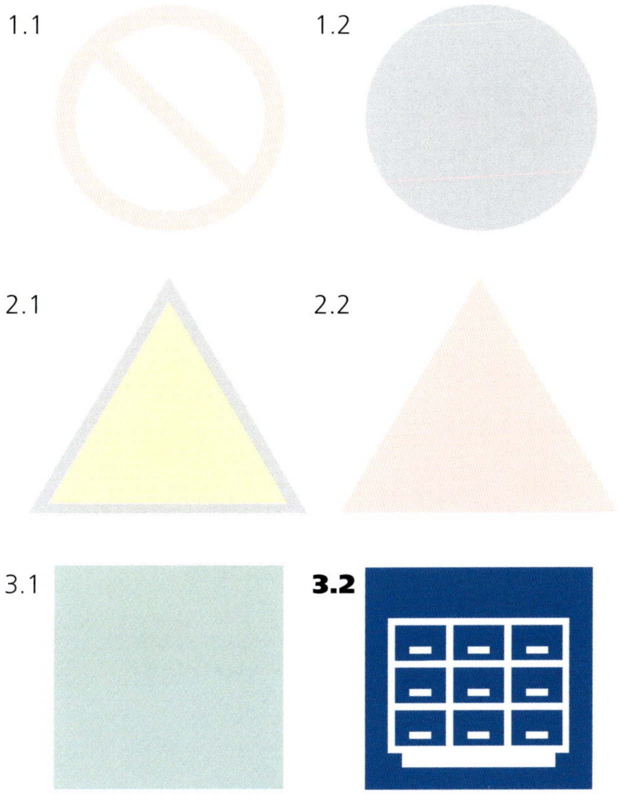

1024

MILK, EGG, BREAD, APPLE
3.2 Kitchenette

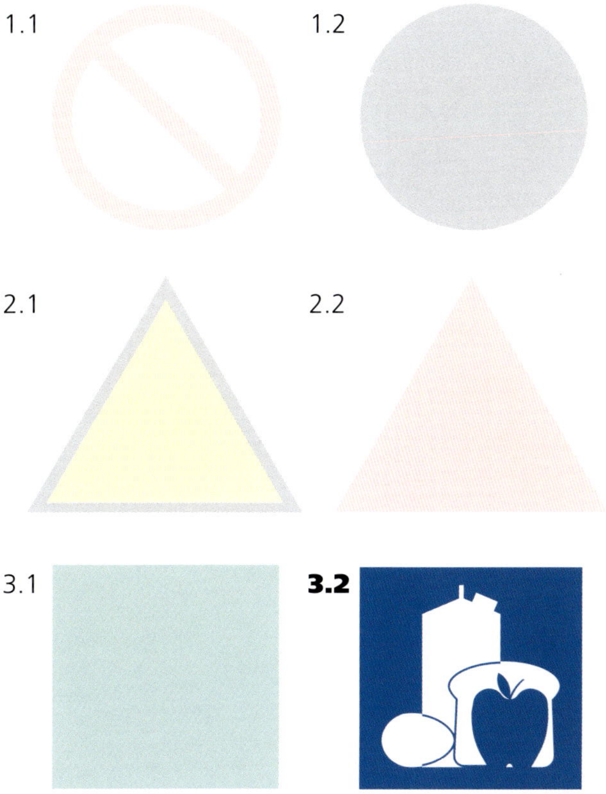

1025

SLOT, COIN, SODA CAN, SANDWICHES

3.2 Vending machine

1.1

1.2

2.1

2.2

3.1

3.2

1026

HUMAN FIGURES, FACING EACH OTHER, HORIZONTAL BAR BETWEEN

3.2 Interview room

1.1

1.2

2.1

2.2

3.1

3.2

1027

HUMAN FIGURES, BROKEN VERTICAL BAR BETWEEN

3.2 Courthouse interview room

1.1

1.2

2.1

2.2

3.1

3.2

1028

HUMAN FIGURES, AROUND A TABLE

3.2 Meeting room

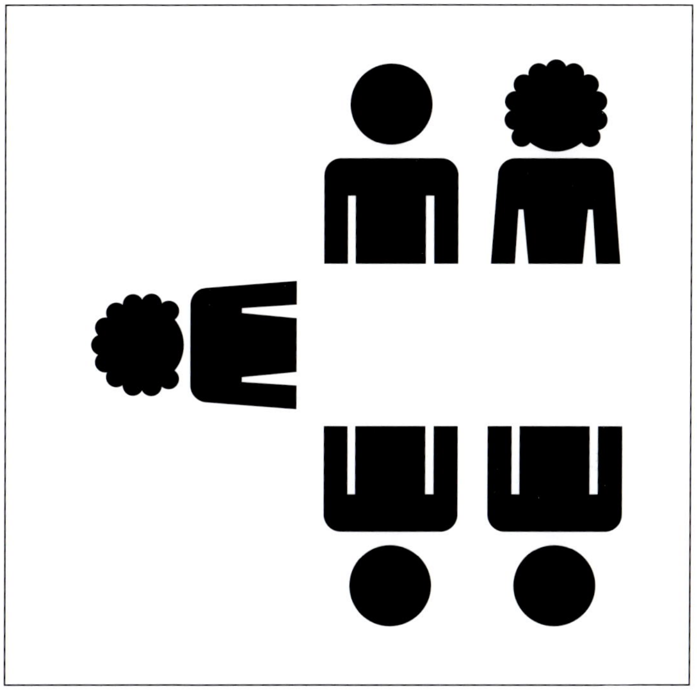

1.1

1.2

2.1

2.2

3.1

3.2

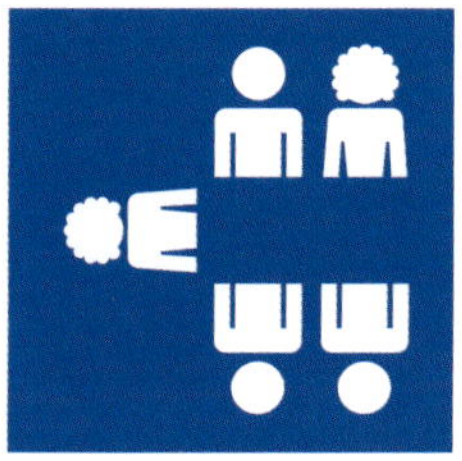

1029

HUMAN FIGURE, MICROPHONES

3.2 Media room

1.1

1.2

2.1

2.2

3.1

3.2

1030

HUMAN FIGURES, AT DESKS

3.2 Conference hall

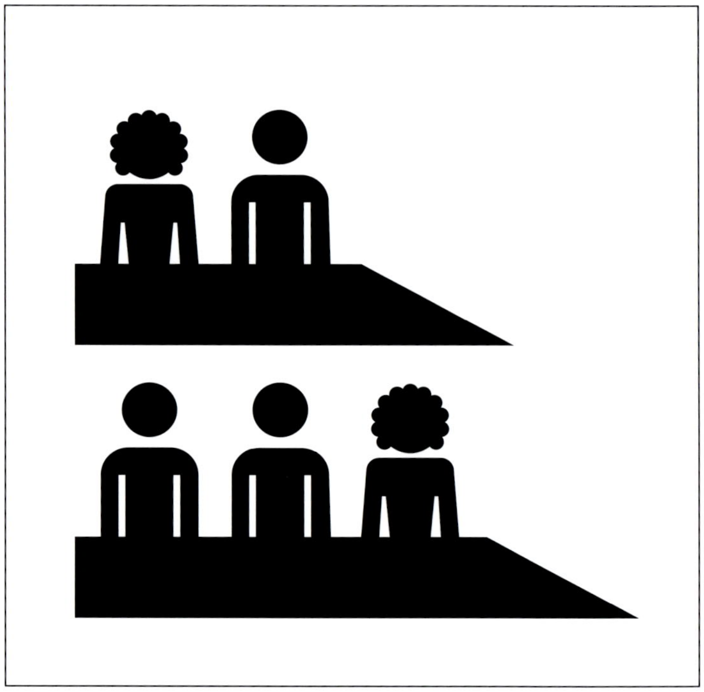

1.1

1.2

2.1

2.2

3.1

3.2

1031

HUMAN FIGURES, IN THREE ROWS

3.2 Conference hall

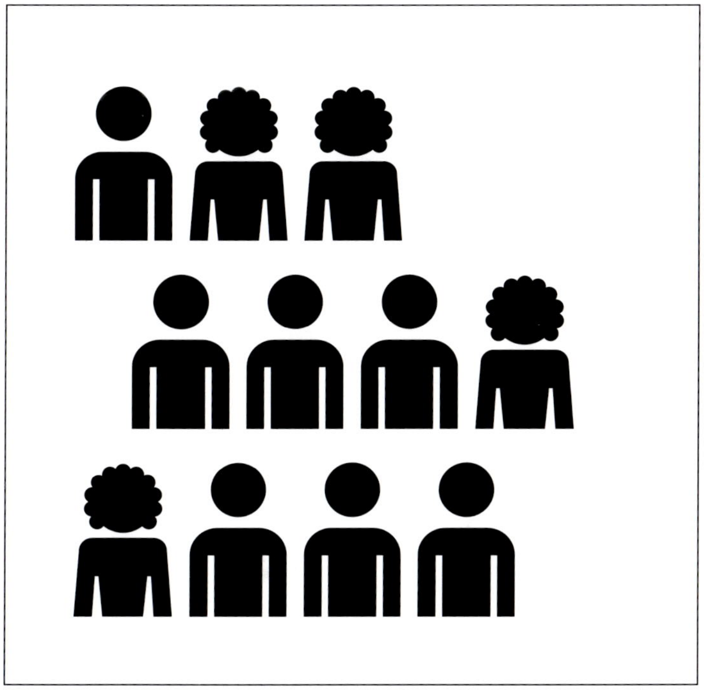

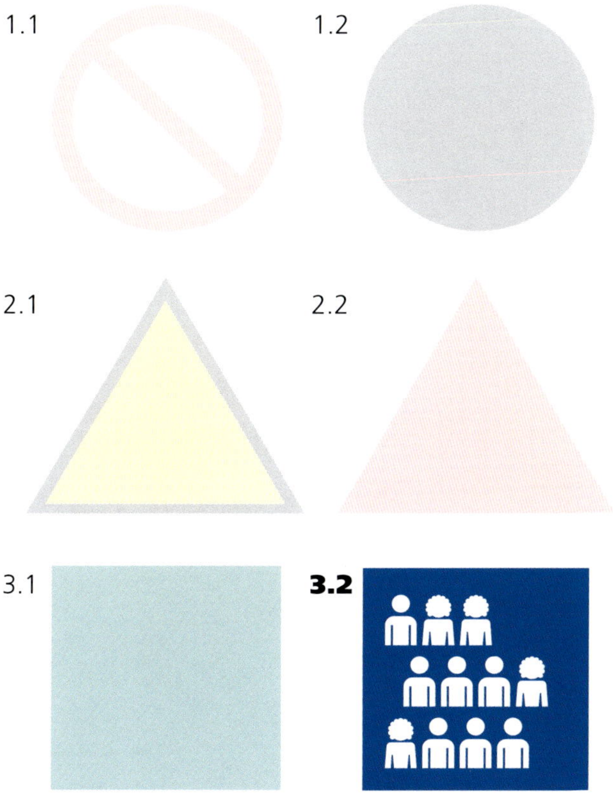

1032

HUMAN FIGURES, SEATED ON STEPS

3.2 Auditorium

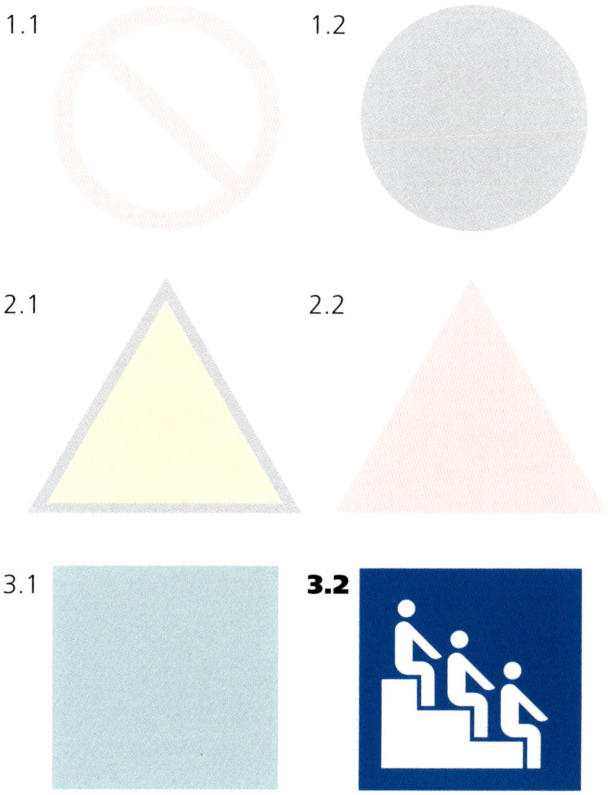

0
1
2
3
4
5
6
7
8
Index

1033

GAVEL, OVER HORIZONTAL BAR

3.2 Court (room)

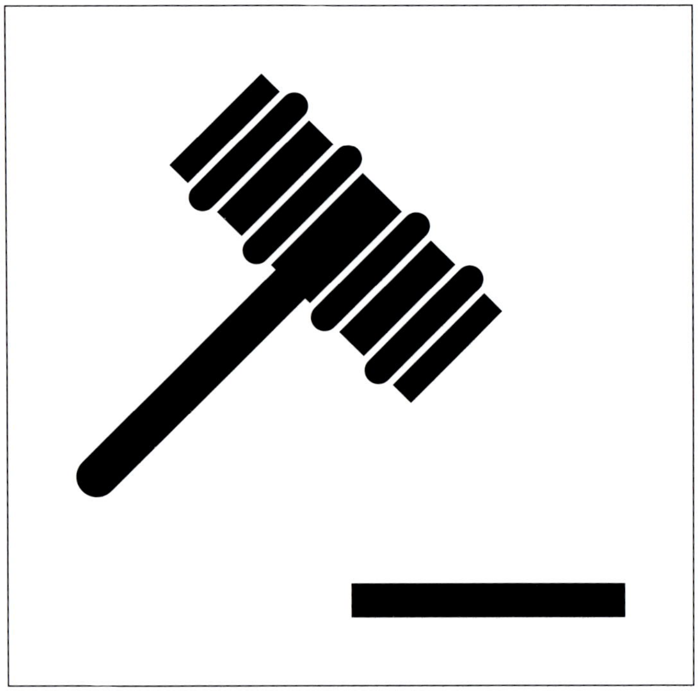

1034

SHOWER HEAD, WATER DROPS

3.2 Shower

1035

BROOM

3.2 Broom closet, janitor

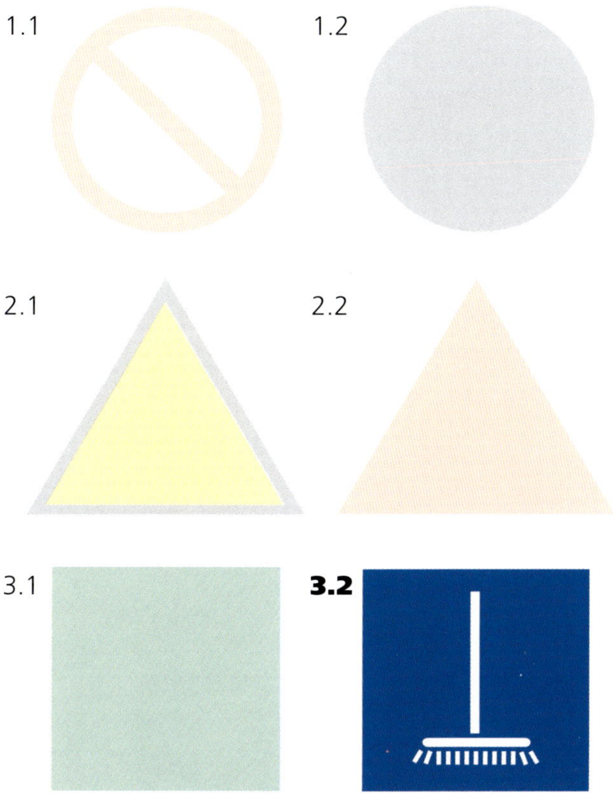

1036

CRATES

1.1 No storage allowed

3.2 Storage (area)

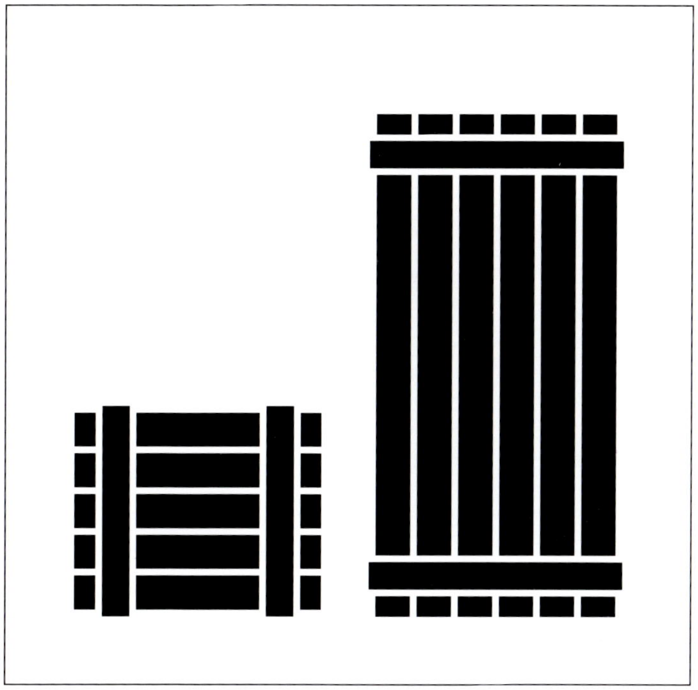

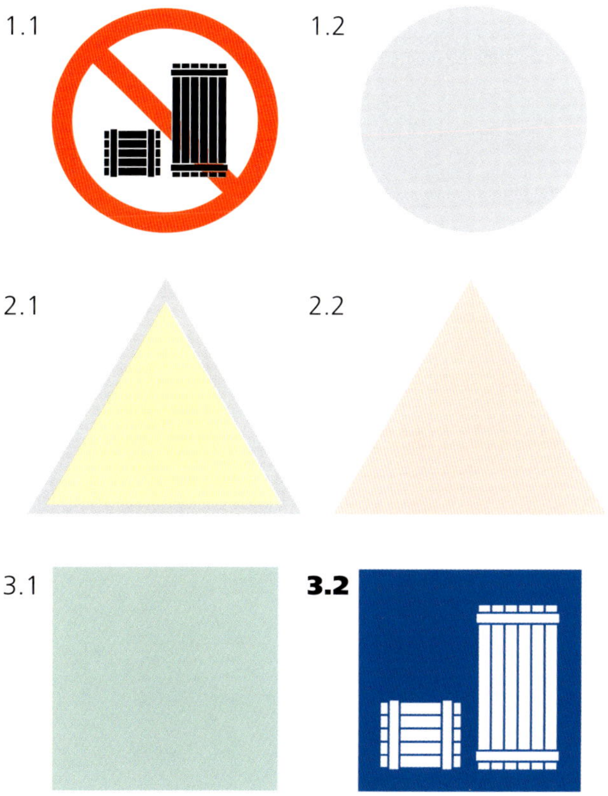

1037

ELECTRICITY SYMBOL

2.1 Caution! Power line

2.2 Danger! Electricity

3.2 Electrical room

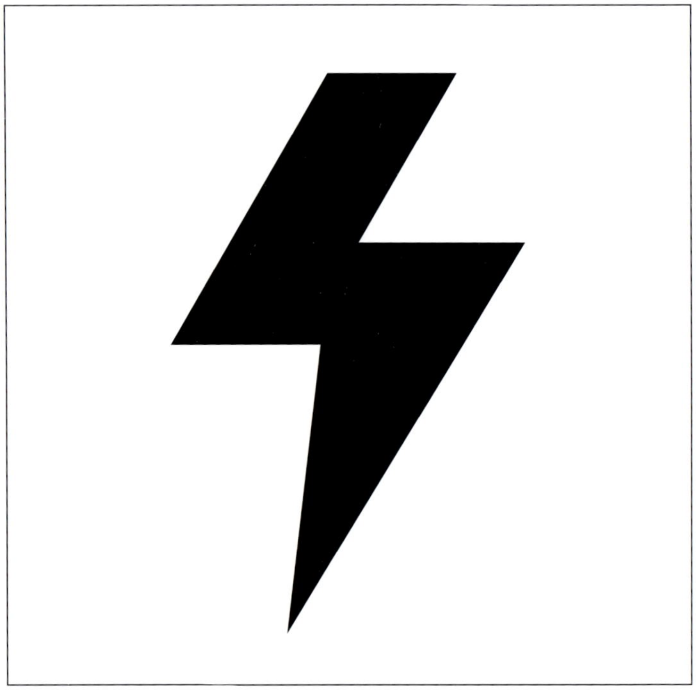

1.1

1.2

2.1

2.2

3.1

3.2

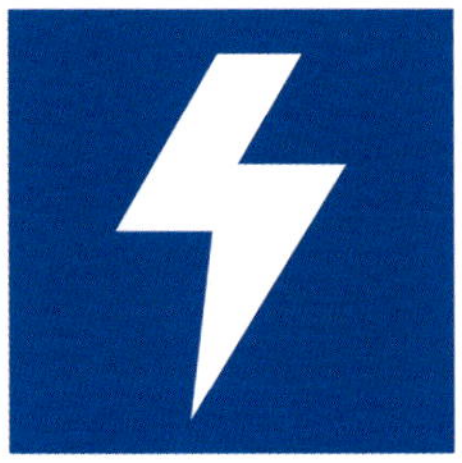

1038

FAN BLADES, OVER COIL

3.2 Mechanical (room)

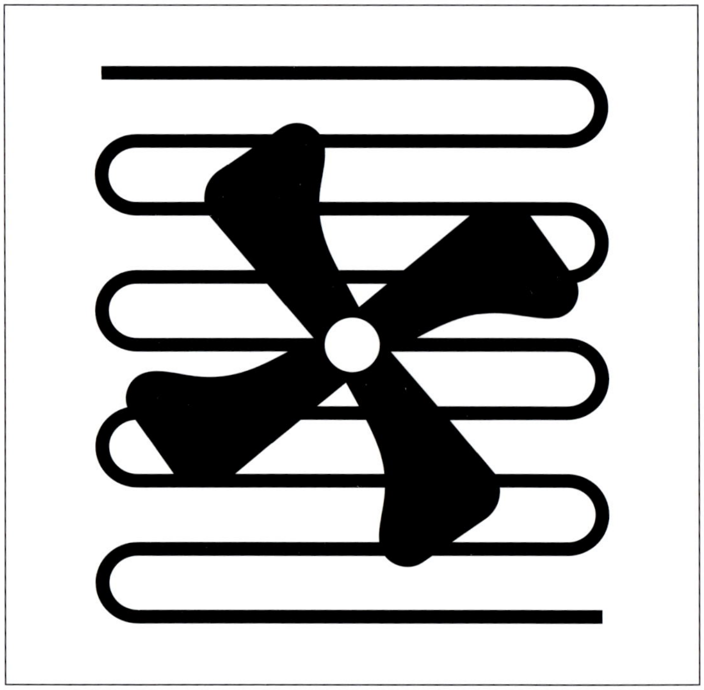

1.1

1.2

2.1

2.2

3.1

3.2

1039

GEARS

3.2 Mechanical (room)

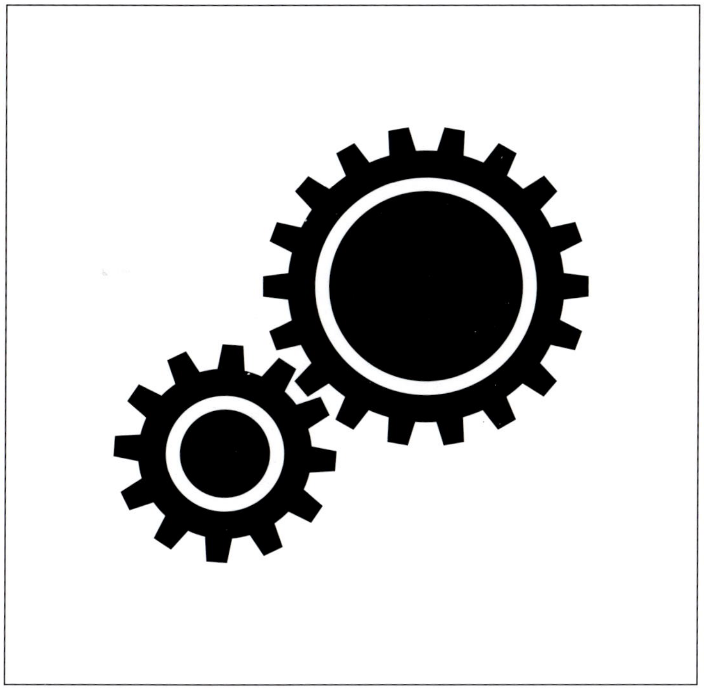

1.1

1.2

2.1

2.2

3.1

3.2

1040

SNOWFLAKE

3.2 Winter, air conditioning

1.1

1.2

2.1

2.2

3.1

3.2

1041

S-DRAIN TRAP, WATER DROPS

3.2 Drain

1042

VALVE

3.2 Valve, international engineering sign

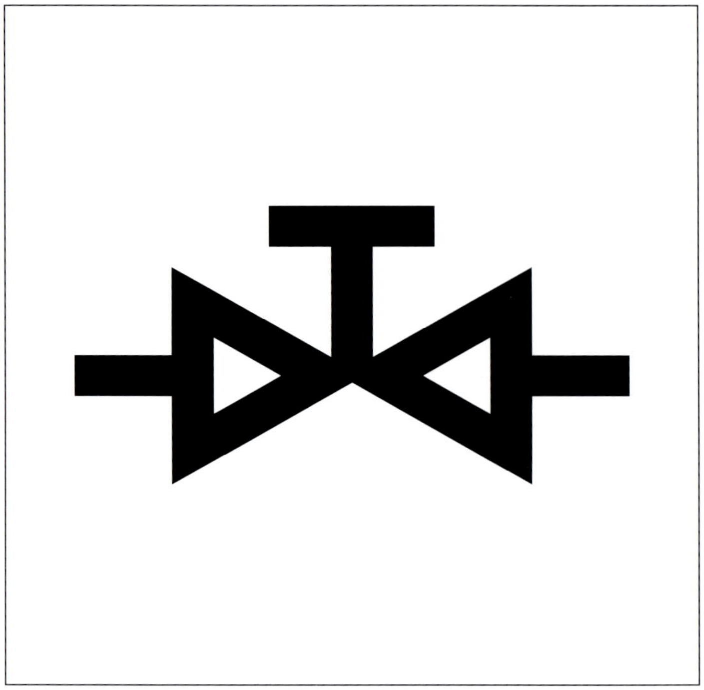

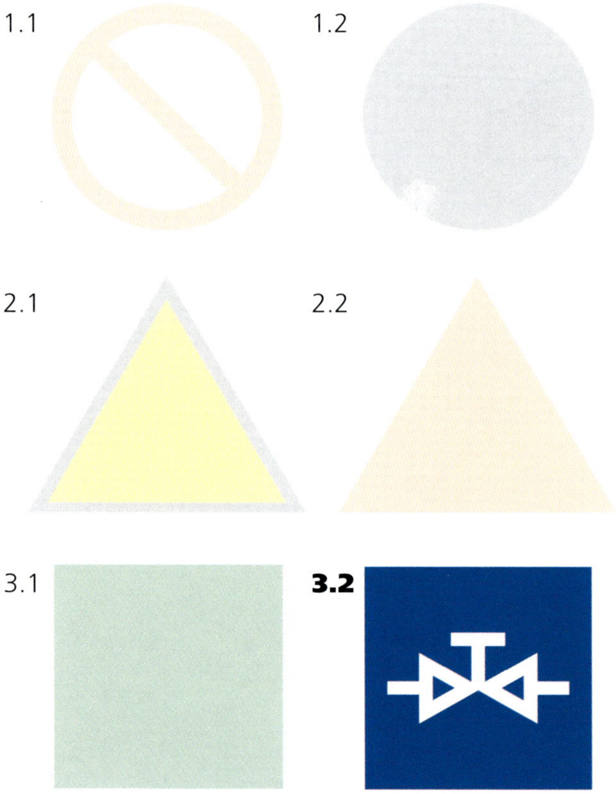

1043

ROLLERBLADE

1.1 No rollerblading

1.1

1.2

2.1

2.2

3.1

3.2

1044

SKATEBOARD

1.1 No skateboarding

1.1

1.2

2.1

2.2

3.1

3.2

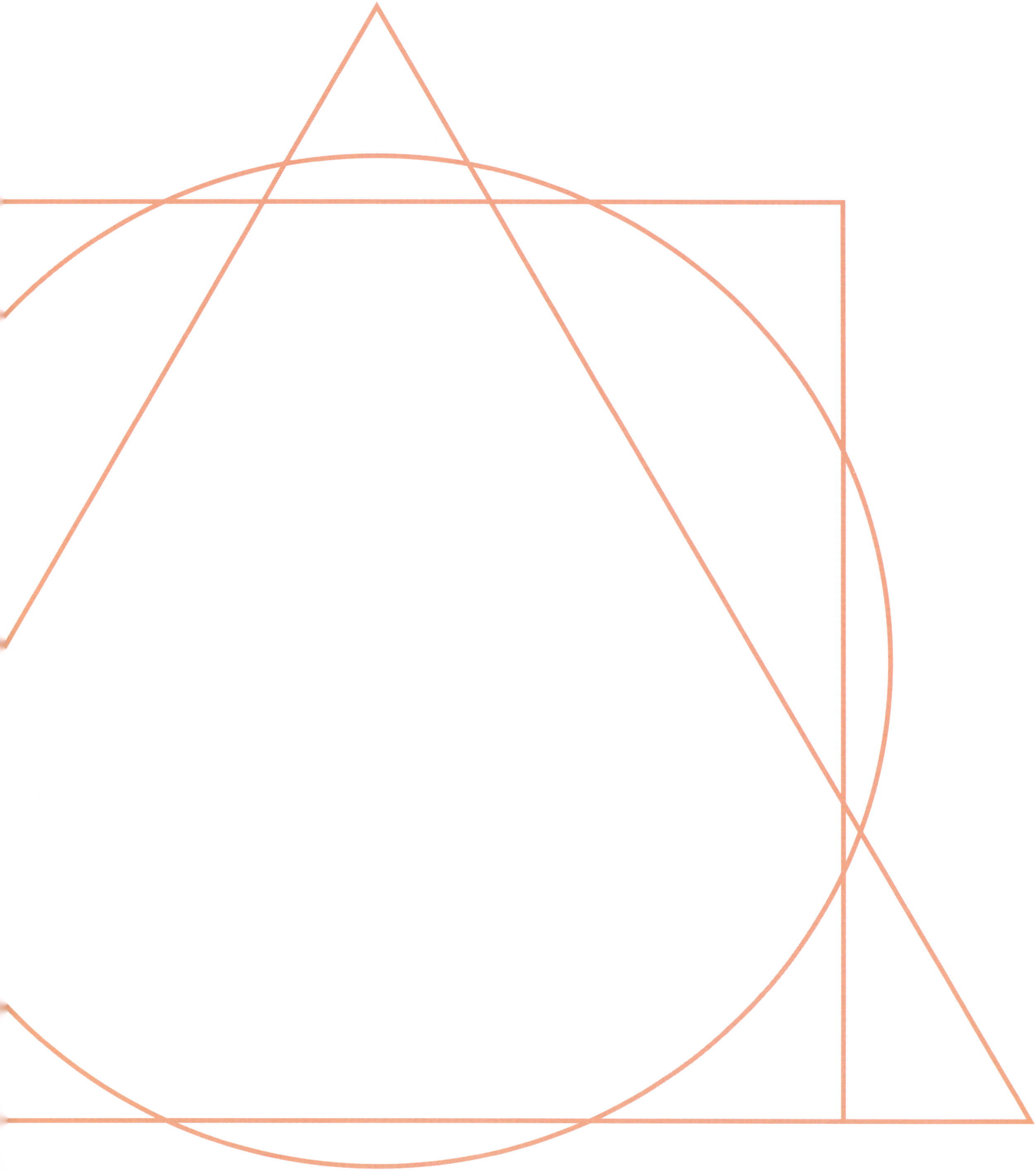

2001

WIRE GROCERY CART

1.1 No grocery carts allowed

3.2 Grocery store, supermarket

1.1

1.2

2.1

2.2

3.1

3.2

2002

APPLE

3.2 Apple, fruit, fruit market

1.1

1.2

2.1

2.2

3.1

3.2

2003

CARROTS, TOMATO, PEPPERS

3.2 Produce (store), farmers' market

1.1

1.2

2.1

2.2

3.1

3.2

2004

LIQUOR AND WINE BOTTLES

1.1 Don't drink and drive, no liquor allowed

3.2 Liquor store

1.1

1.2

2.1

2.2

3.1

3.2

2005

RECEPTACLE, ICE CUBES

3.2 Ice, ice machine

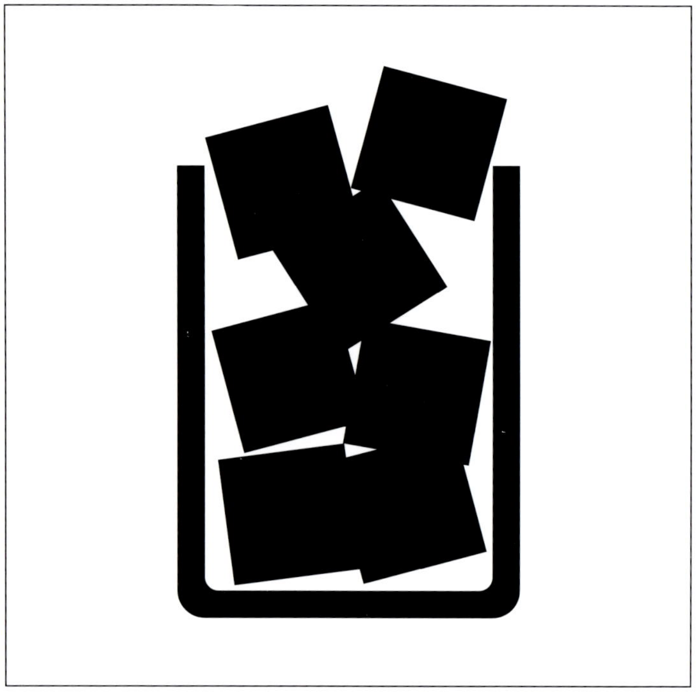

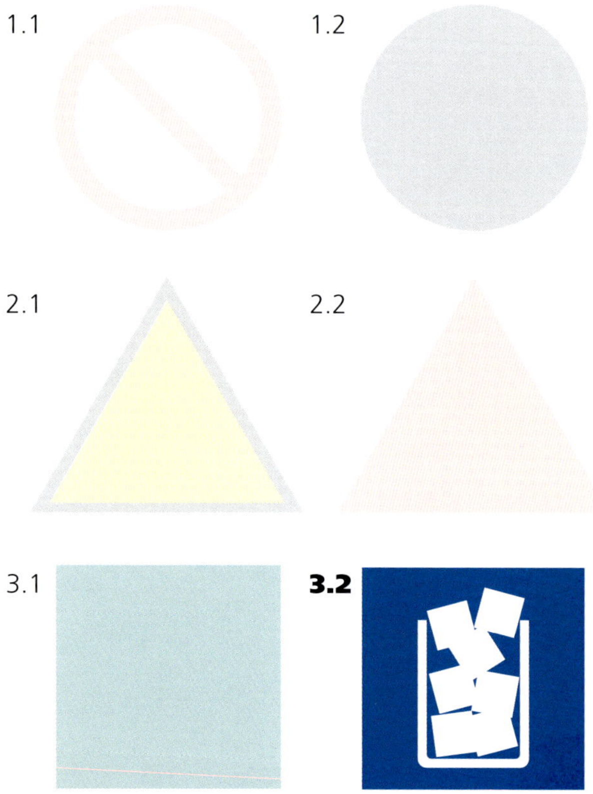

2006

LADLE, KITCHEN KNIFE, WHISK

3.2 Kitchen equipment (store)

2007

FLOWER

3.2 Flowers, flower shop

2008

FLOWERS

3.2 Flowers, nursery

2009

BABY, UNWRAPPED DIAPER

3.2 Diaper change station

1.1

1.2

2.1

2.2

3.1

3.2

2010

CHILD

1.1 No children allowed

3.2 Children

1.1

1.2

2.1

2.2

3.1

3.2

2011

HUMAN FIGURES, ADULT, INFANT

3.2 Day care, baby-sitting

2012

BABY CARRIAGE

1.1 No carriages allowed

3.2 Baby store

2013

BABY, IN STROLLER

1.1 No strollers allowed

1.2 Keep infants under control

3.2 Strollers

1.1

1.2

2.1

2.2

3.1

3.2

2014

ROCKING HORSE

3.2 Toy (store)

1.1

1.2

2.1

2.2

3.1

3.2

2015

INFANT, WITH BOOK

3.2 Children's books

1.1 1.2

2.1 2.2

3.1 **3.2**

2016

BOOK

3.2 Bookstore, library

1.1 1.2

2.1 2.2

3.1 **3.2**

2017

MAGNIFYING GLASS, OVER BOOK

3.2 Large-print books

2018

NEWSPAPER

3.2 Newspapers, newsstand

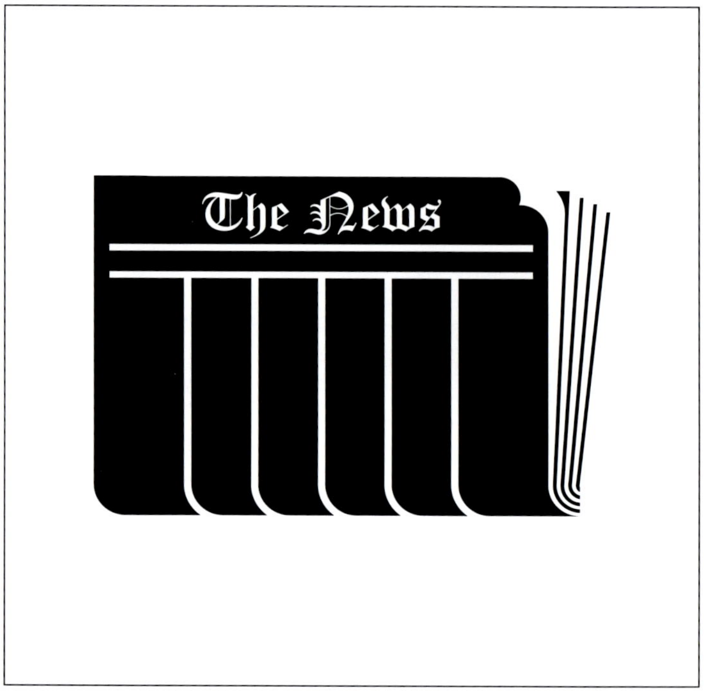

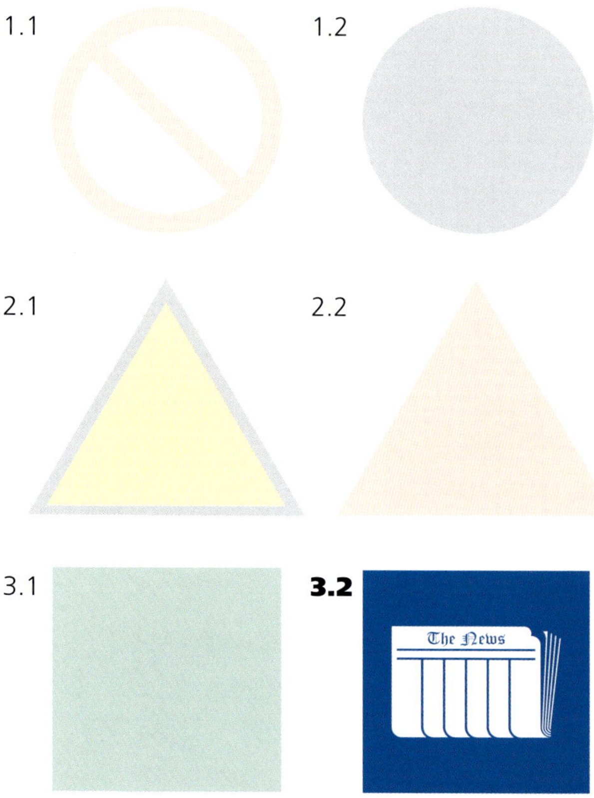

2019

HOUSE

3.2 Home, home furnishings

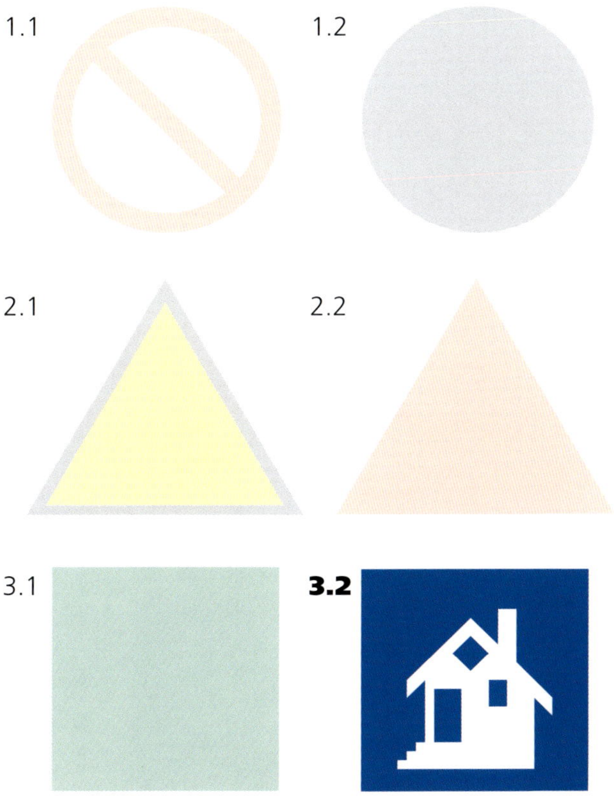

2020

CHAIR, TABLE

3.2 Furniture (store)

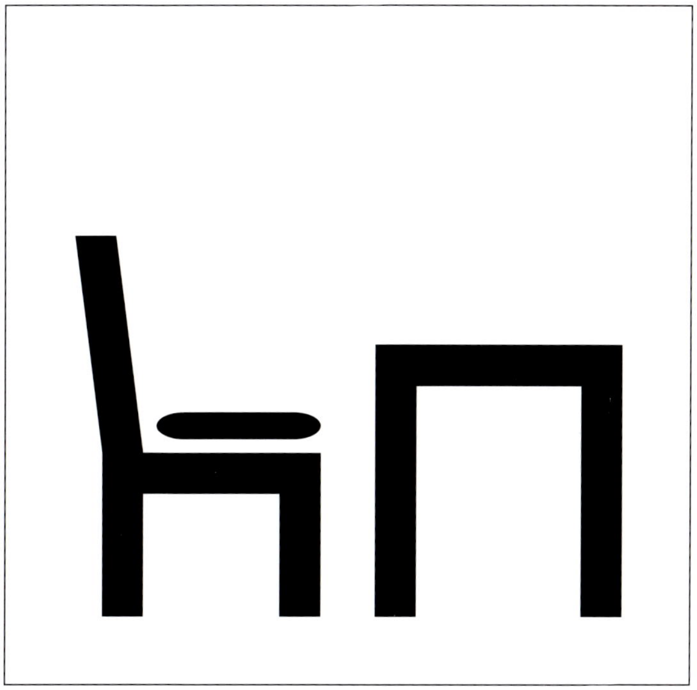

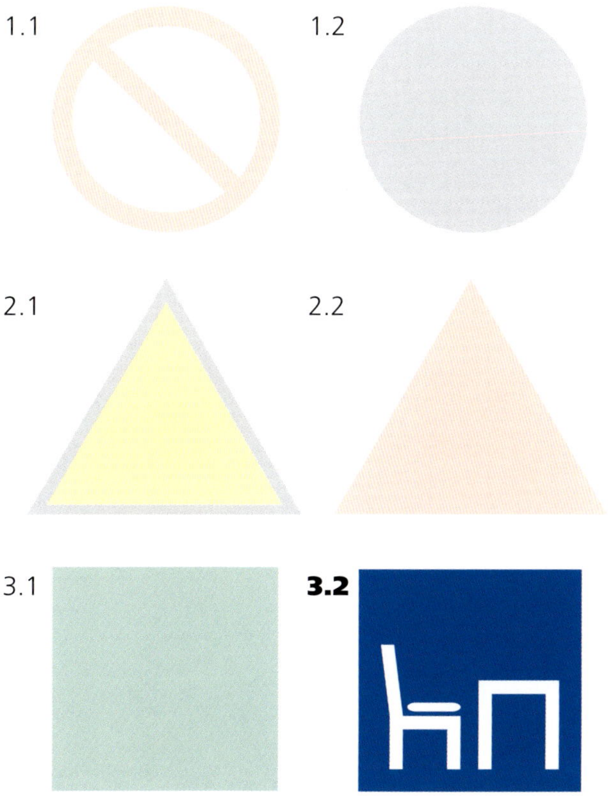

2021

KEY

3.2 Keys, keys made here

1.1 1.2

2.1 2.2

3.1 **3.2**

2022

LOCK

3.2 Locks, hardware store, locksmith

1.1 1.2

2.1 2.2

3.1 **3.2**

2023

SAW, HAMMER

3.2 Hardware store

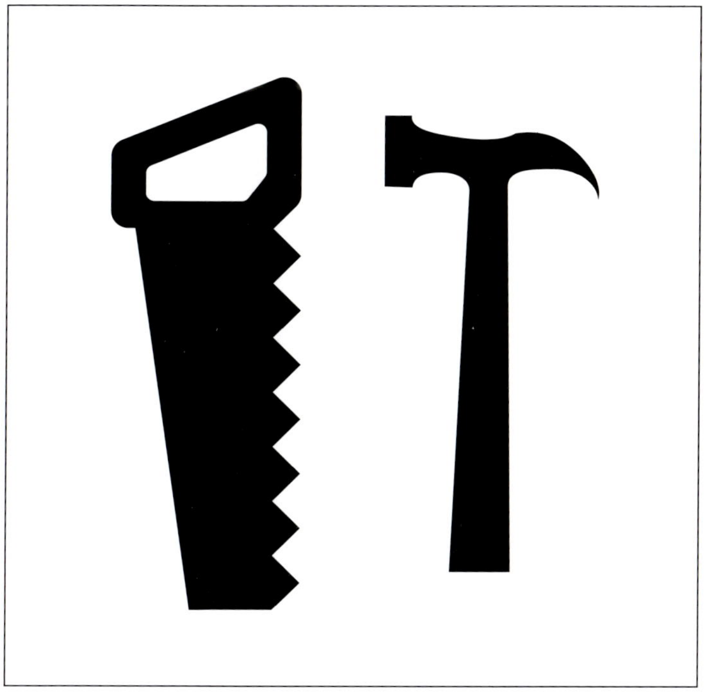

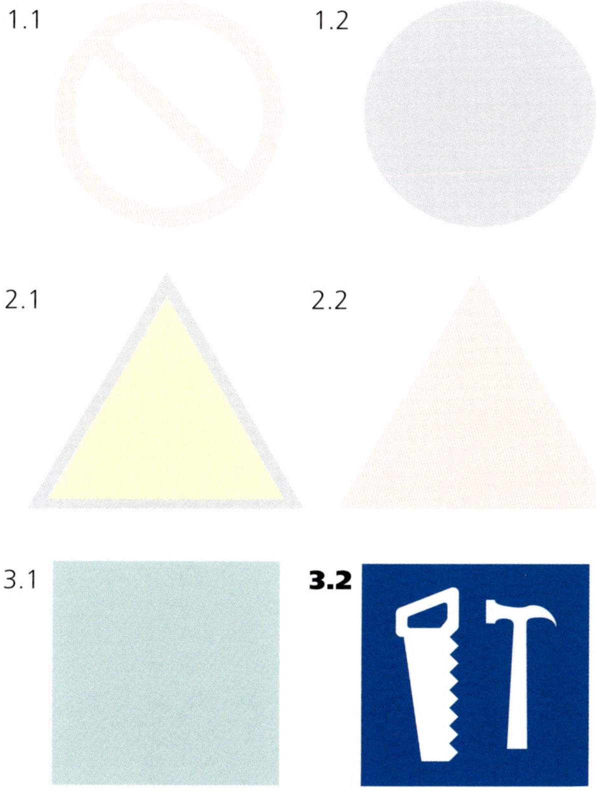

2024

DRESS

3.2 Dresses (store)

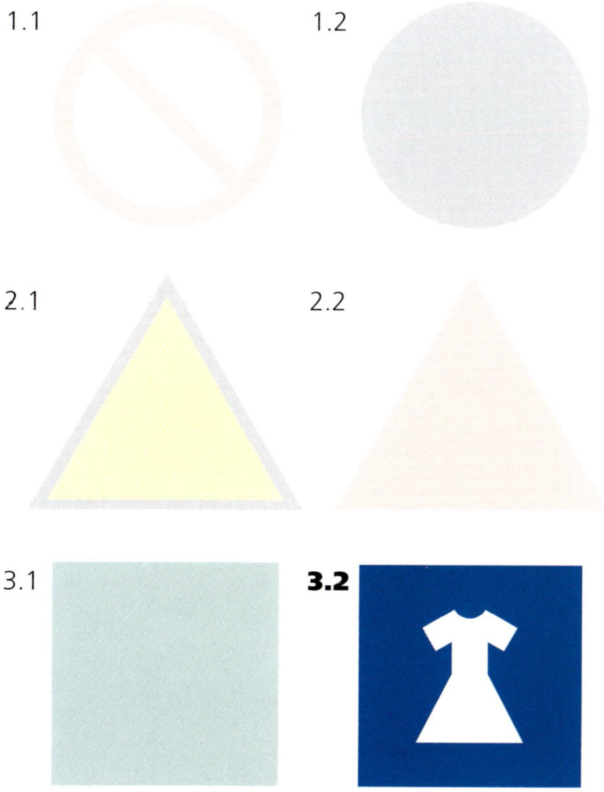

2025

SHOES

3.2 Shoe store

1.1

1.2

2.1

2.2

3.1

3.2

2026

THIMBLE, SCISSORS, SPOOL OF THREAD

3.2 Sewing supplies (store)

1.1

1.2

2.1

2.2

3.1

3.2

2027

UMBRELLA

1.2 Keep dry

3.2 Umbrellas (store)

2028

MUSICAL NOTES

3.2 Music store

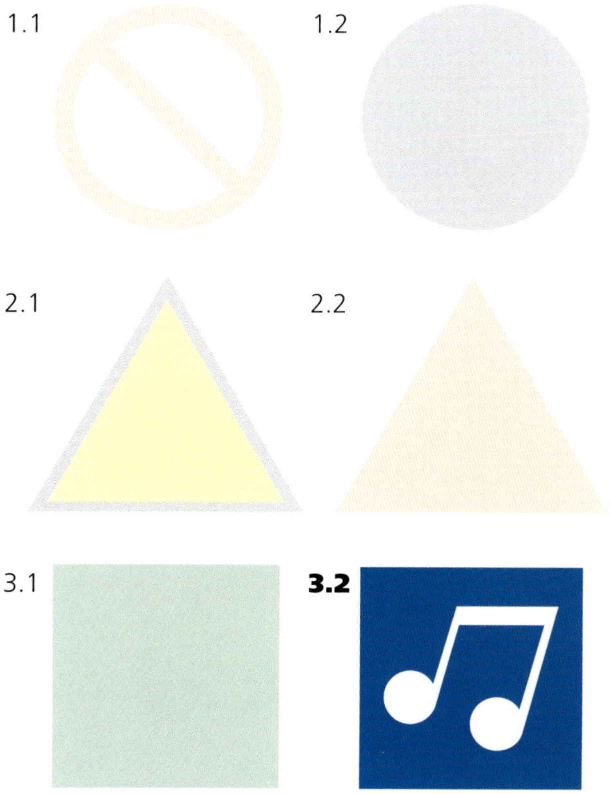

2029

CELLULAR PHONE

1.1 No cellular phones allowed

3.2 Cellular phones (store)

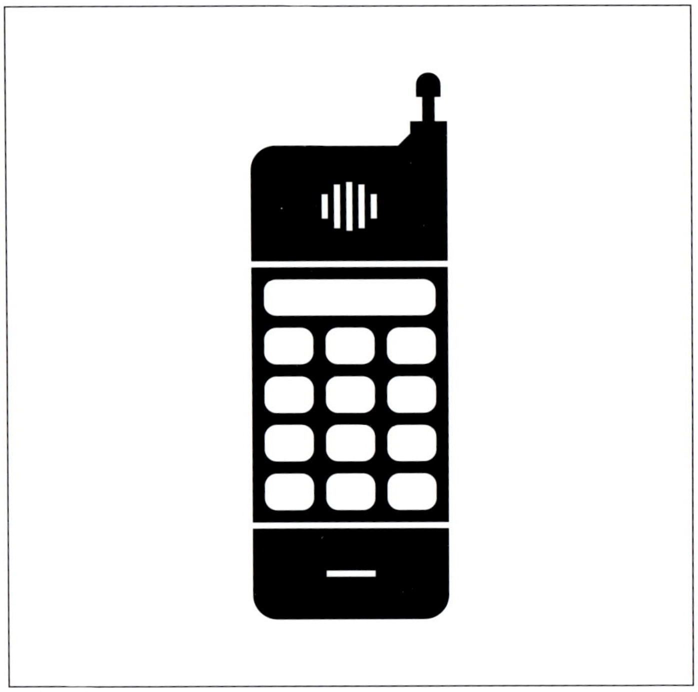

1.1

1.2

2.1

2.2

3.1

3.2

2030

WALKIE-TALKIE

1.1 No wireless devices allowed

3.2 Wireless (store)

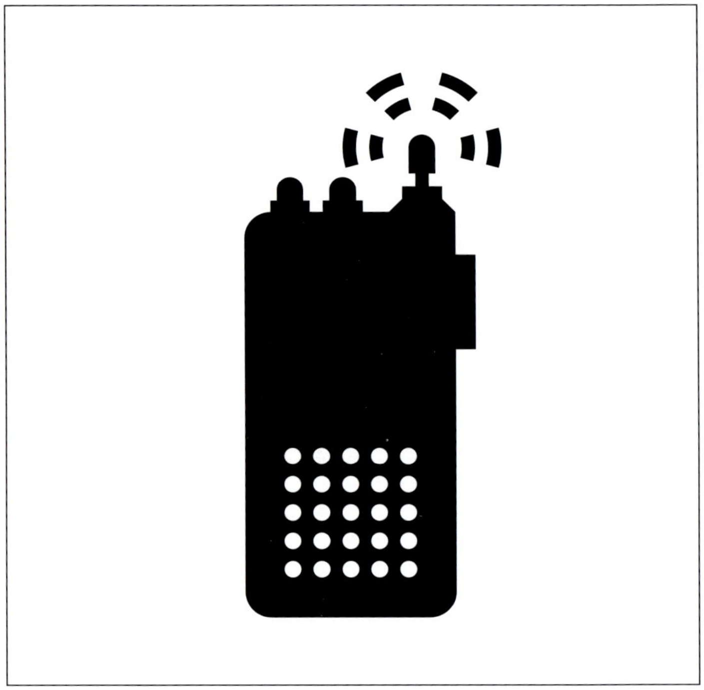

1.1

1.2

2.1

2.2

3.1

3.2

2031

FILM, CAMERA

3.2 Cameras (store), photo supplies

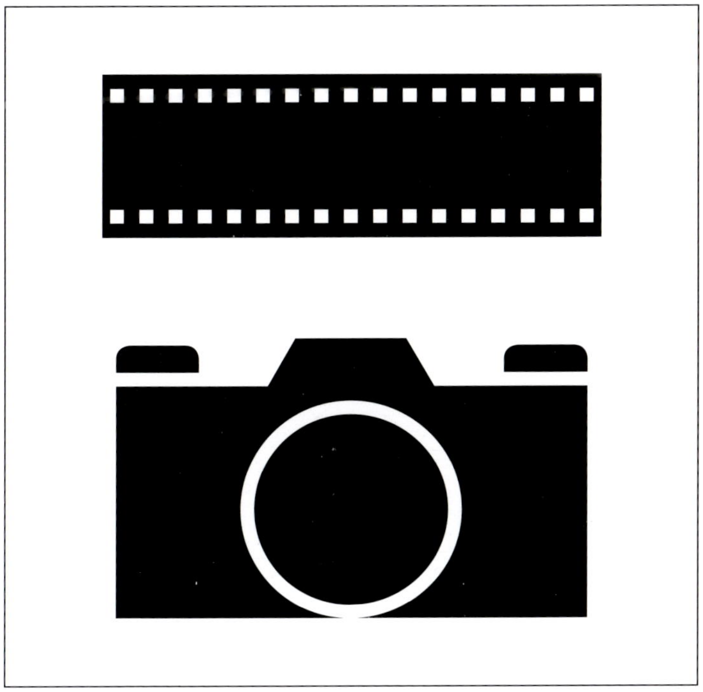

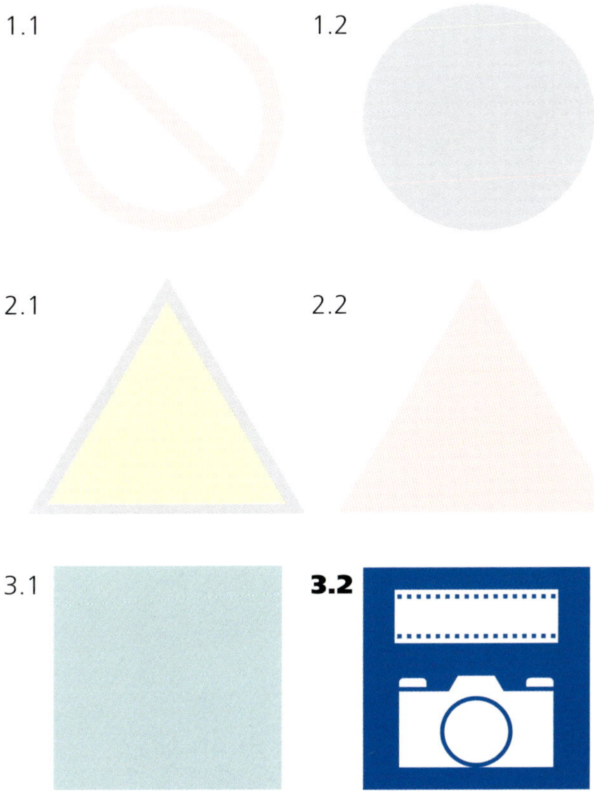

2032

STEMWARE GLASS

1.2 Fragile

3.2 Stemware glass (store)

2033

PEN NIB, PAPER CLIP

3.2 Stationery (store)

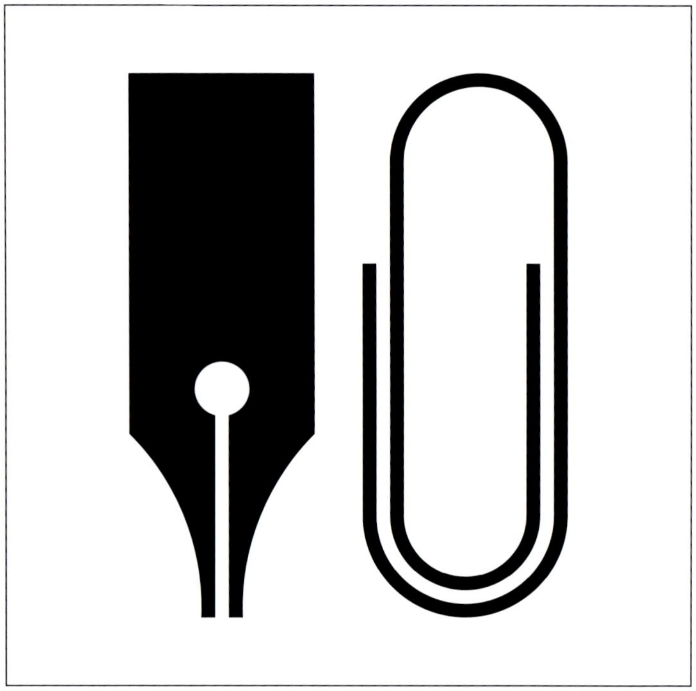

1.1

1.2

2.1

2.2

3.1

3.2

2034

BRUSHES, PAINT TUBE, MARKER

3.2 Art supplies (store)

1.1

1.2

2.1

2.2

3.1

3.2

2035

BALLOONS

3.2 Balloons, party supplies (store), toy store

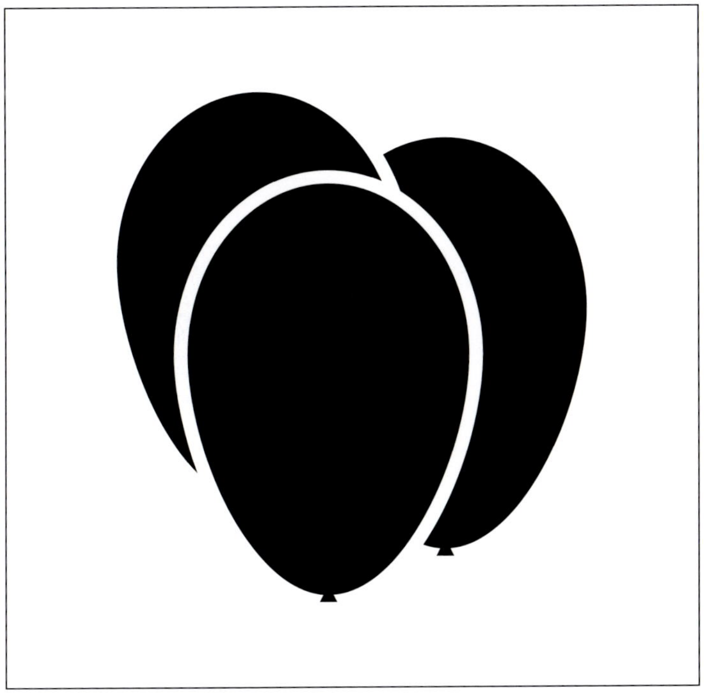

1.1

1.2

2.1

2.2

3.1

3.2

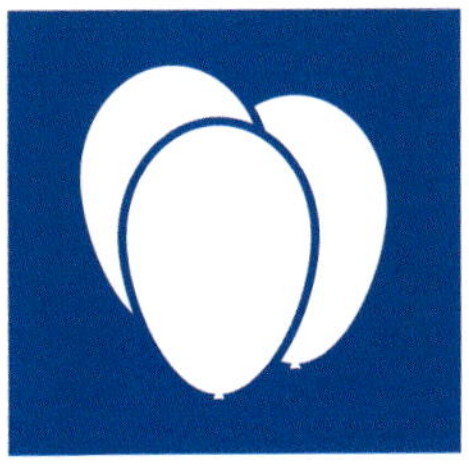

2036

BASKET

3.2 Basketwork, gift baskets

1.1

1.2

2.1

2.2

3.1

3.2

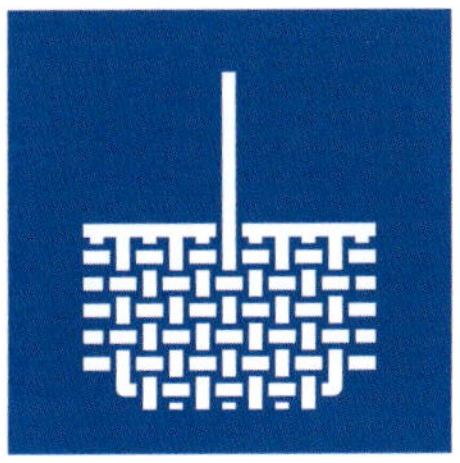

2037

SNOWFLAKE

3.2 Winter, air conditioning

1.1

1.2

2.1

2.2

3.1

3.2

2038

EVERGREEN TREE

3.2 Christmas trees

1.1

1.2

2.1

2.2

3.1

3.2

2039

RIFLE

1.1 No weapons, firearms allowed

3.2 Rifle, firearms, weapons (store)

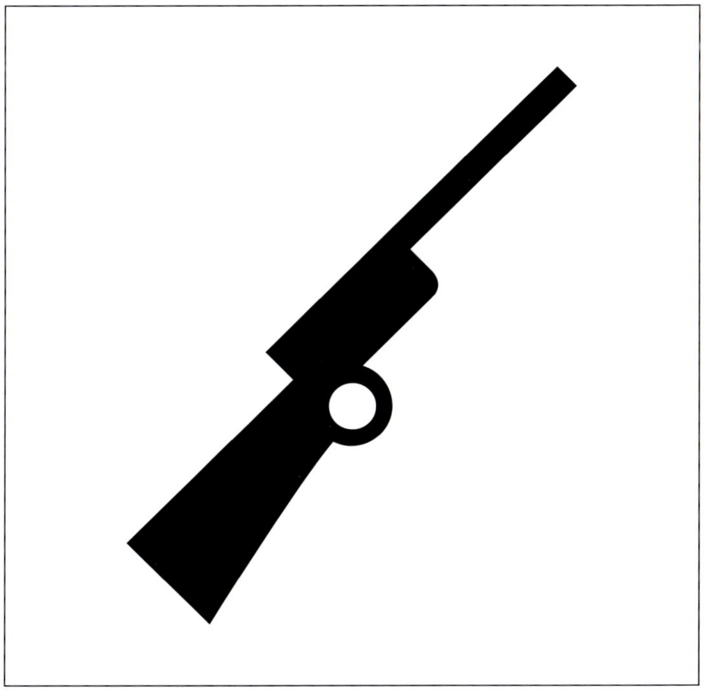

1.1

1.2

2.1

2.2

3.1

3.2

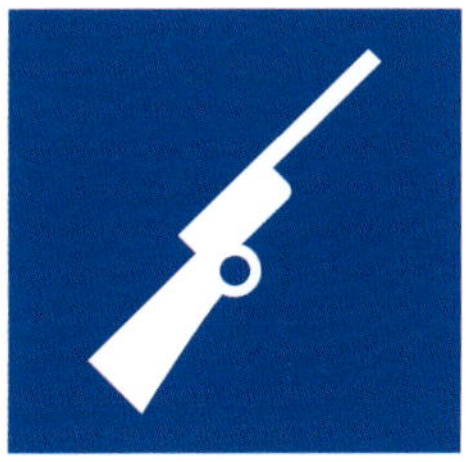

2040

DIAMOND SHAPE, WITH CROSSED LINES

3.2 Other goods and services

1.1

1.2

2.1

2.2

3.1

3.2

2041

BOX, WRAPPED WITH RIBBON, BOW ON TOP

3.2 Gift wrapping, gift shop

2042

BOX, WRAPPED IN PAPER

3.2 Parcels, courier service

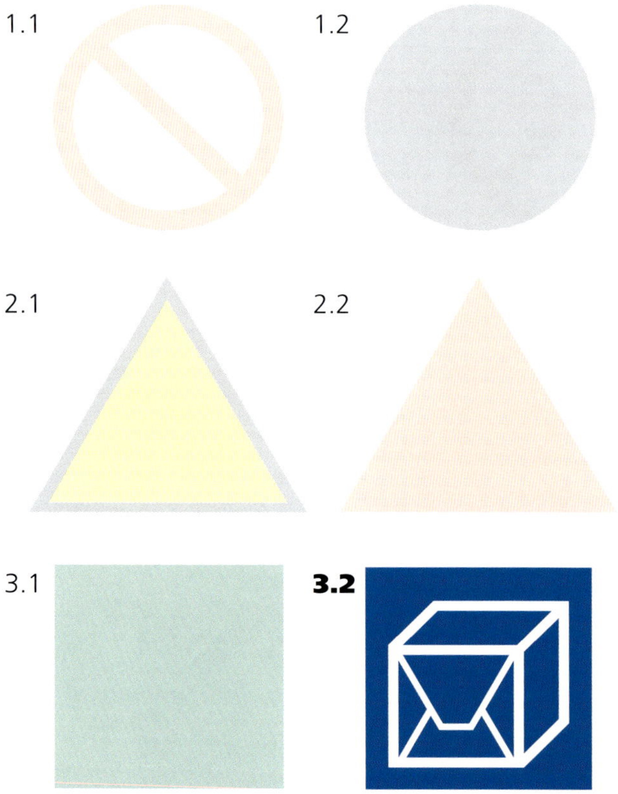

2043

ENVELOPES, SPEEDING FLASHES

3.2 Express mail, courier service

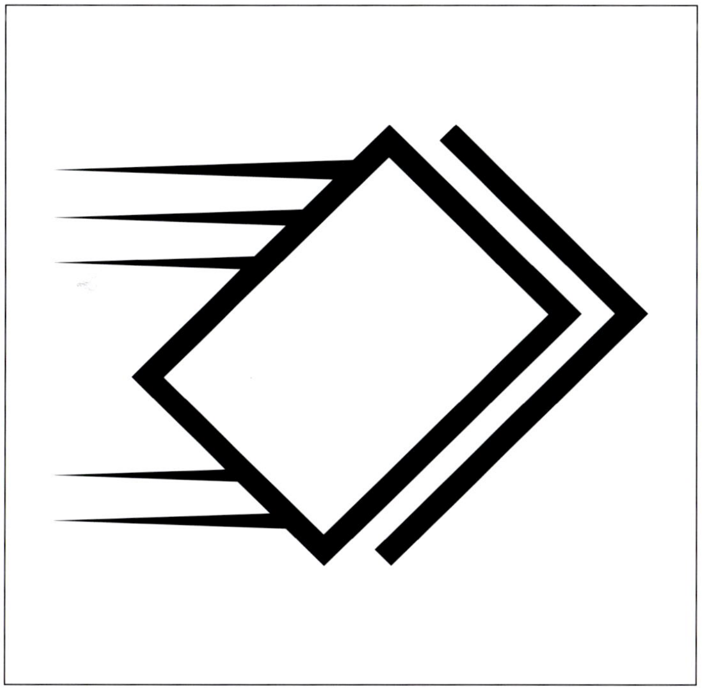

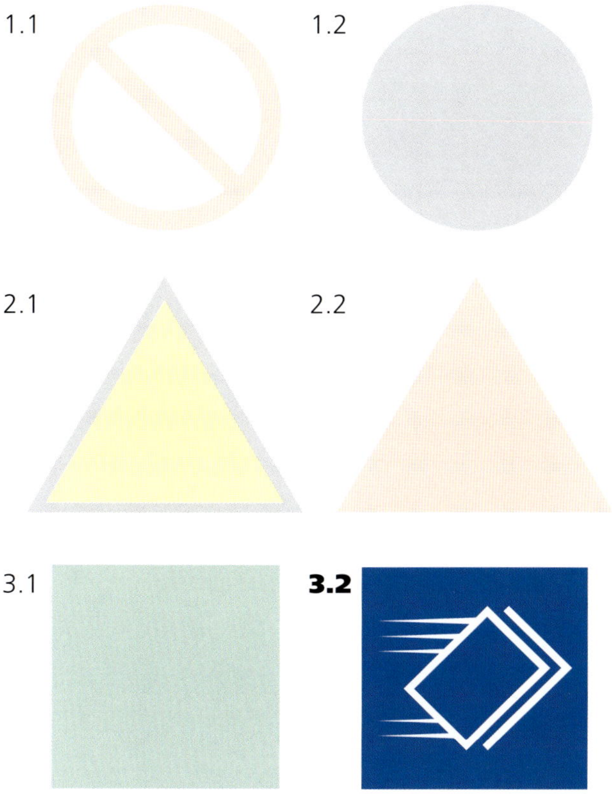

2044

STAMP, SQUIGGLY LINES

3.2 Stamps, post office

2045

MAGNIFYING GLASS, OVER STAMP

3.2 Stamp collecting, philately

2046

KEY, OVER ENVELOPE, IN BOX

3.2 Mailbox

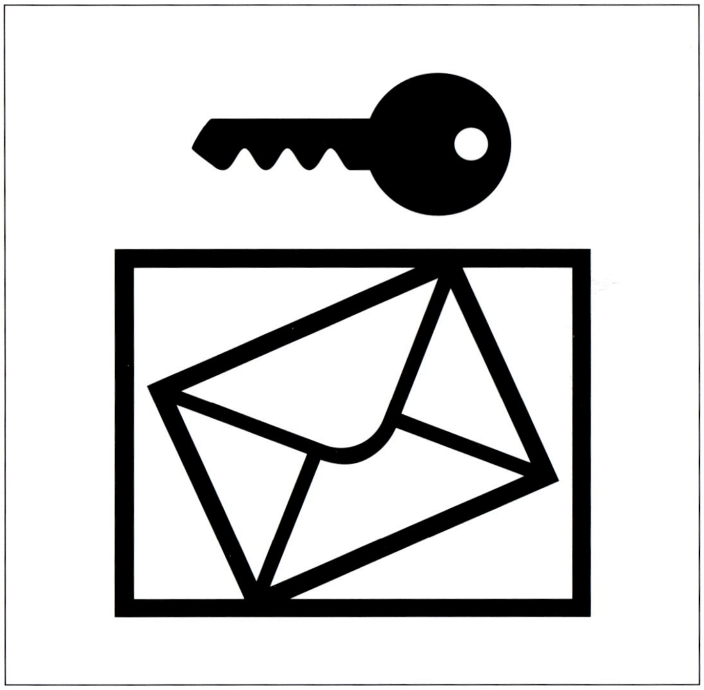

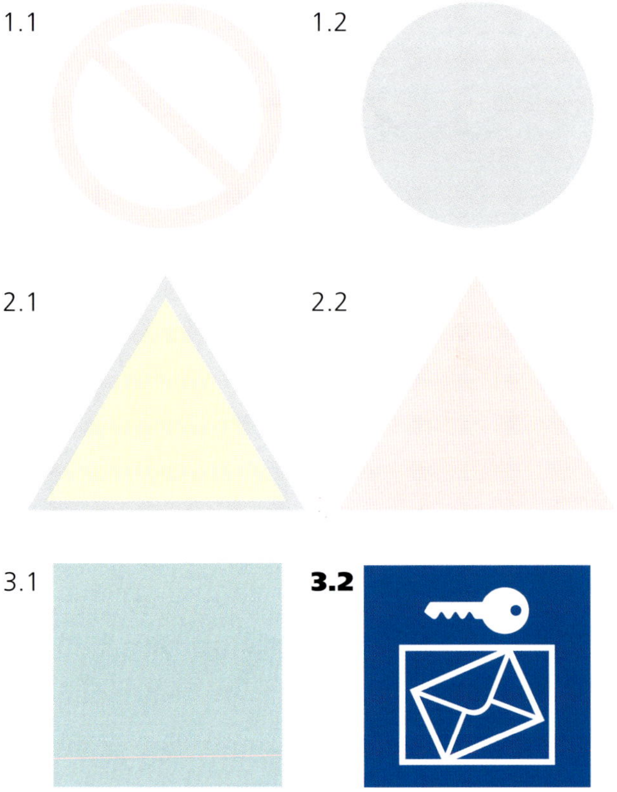

2047

HUMAN FIGURE, MAN, SCISSORS, COMB
3.2 Barbershop

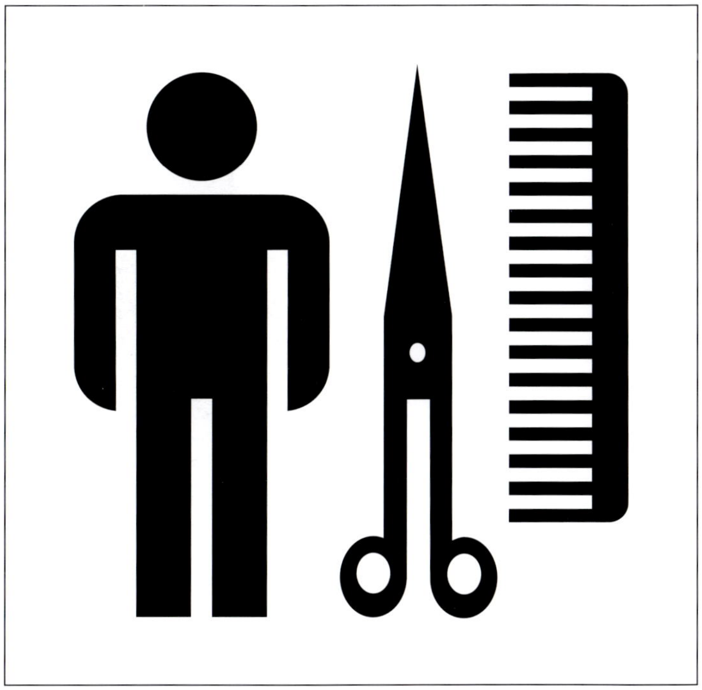

1.1

1.2

2.1

2.2

3.1

3.2
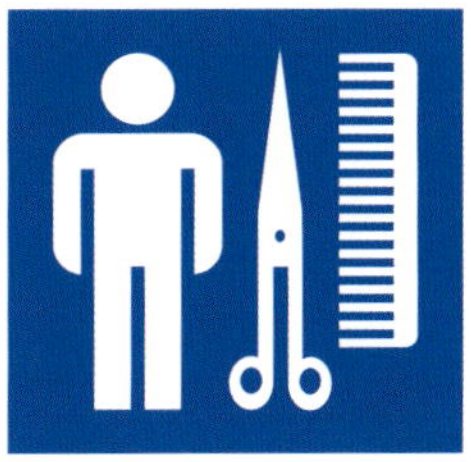

2048

HUMAN FIGURE, WOMAN, SCISSORS, COMB
3.2 Beauty salon

1.1

1.2

2.1

2.2

3.1

3.2

0
1
2
3
4
5
6
7
8
Index

2049

HUMAN FIGURES, MAN, WOMAN, SCISSORS

3.2 Unisex hair salon

1.1 1.2

2.1 2.2

3.1 **3.2**

2050

LAUNDRY WASHING MACHINE

3.2 Laundry (room), self-service laundry

1.1 1.2

2.1 2.2

3.1 **3.2**

2051

FOOTPRINT

1.1 No bare feet allowed

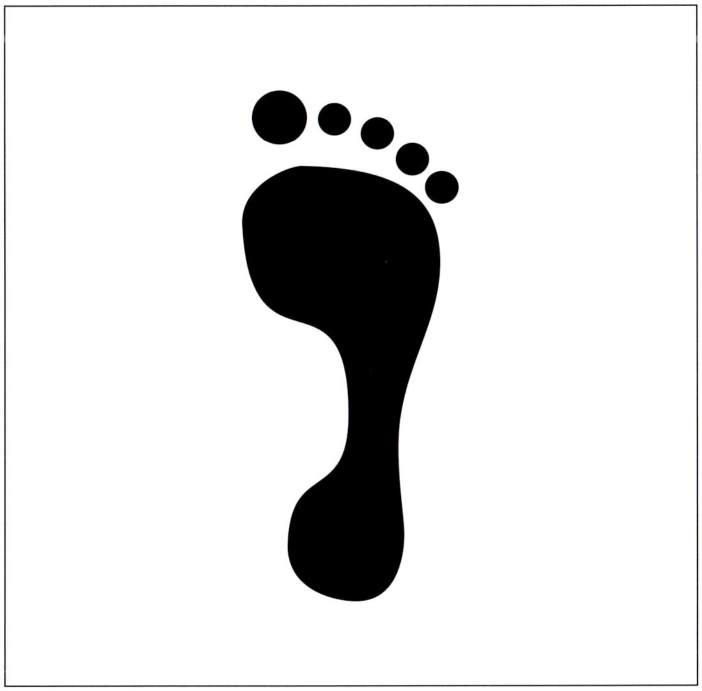

1.1

1.2

2.1

2.2

3.1

3.2

2052

DOG, LEASH (OPTIONAL)

1.1 No dogs allowed

1.2 Dogs must be on leash

3.2 Pets, pet supplies (store)

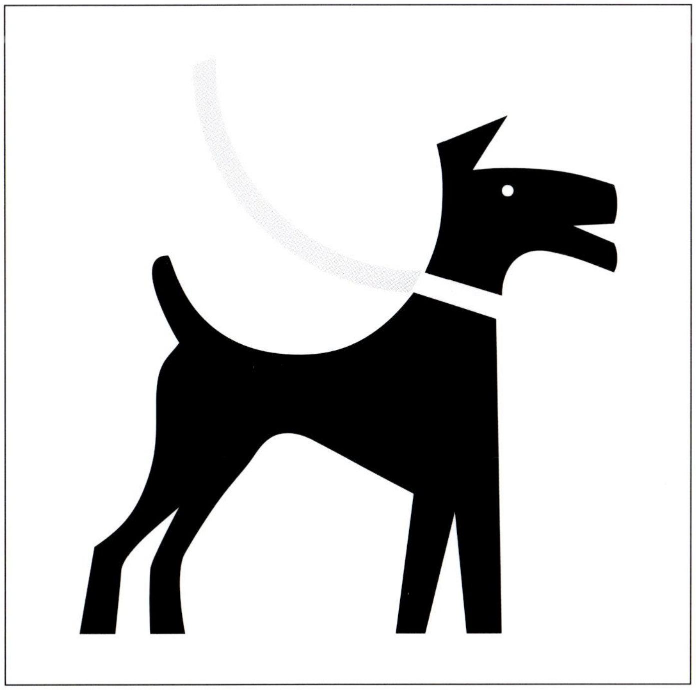

1.1

1.2

2.1

2.2

3.1

3.2

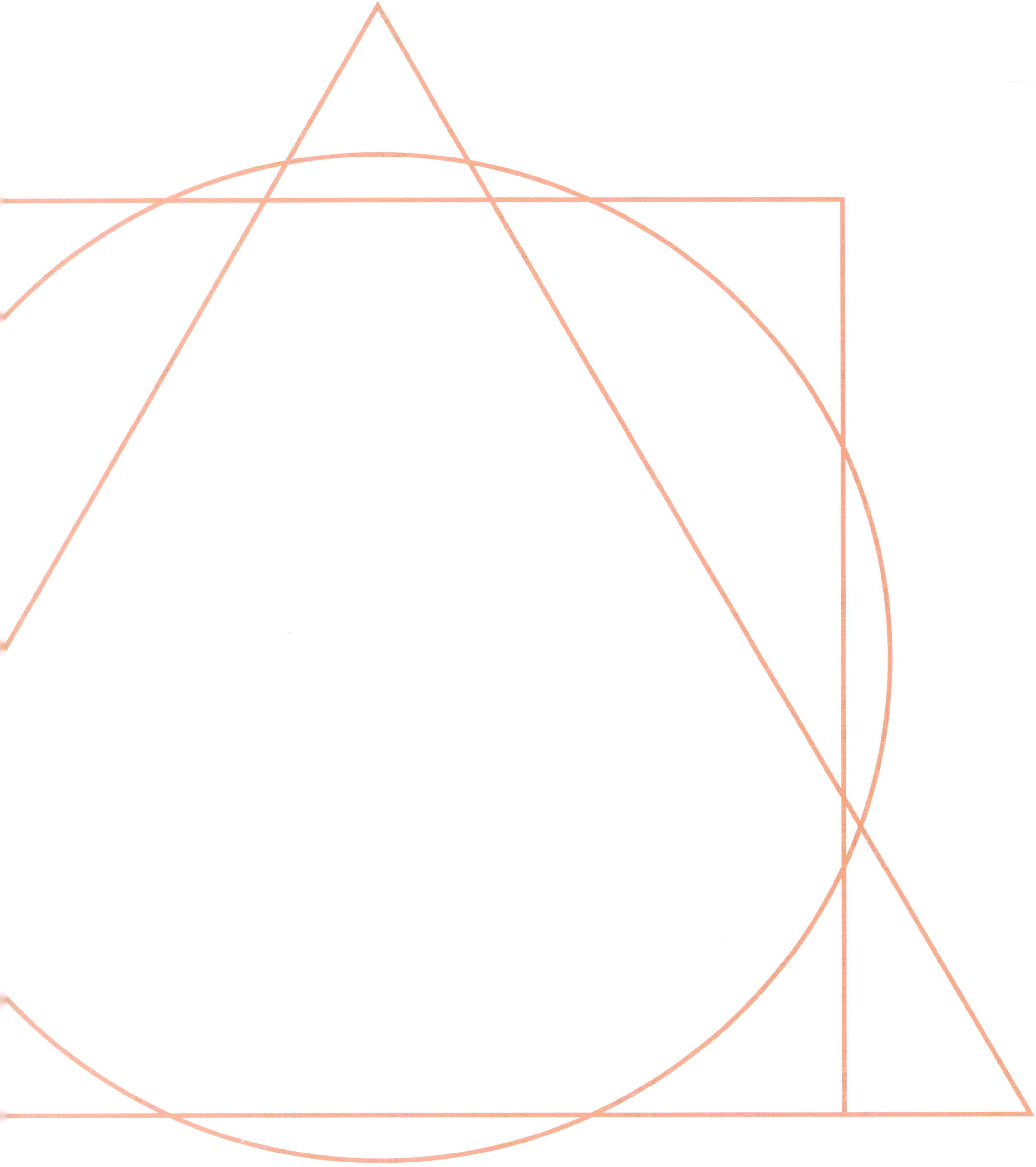

3001

HUMAN FIGURE, DANCING

3.2 Ballet

1.1

1.2

2.1

2.2

3.1

3.2

3002

HUMAN FIGURES, DANCING TOGETHER

3.2 Dance, ballroom dancing

1.1

1.2

2.1

2.2

3.1

3.2

3003

HUMAN FIGURES, DANCING APART

3.2 Disco

1.1 1.2 

2.1  2.2 

3.1  **3.2** 

3004

BILLIARD BALLS RACK

3.2 Billiards, pool, snooker (hall)

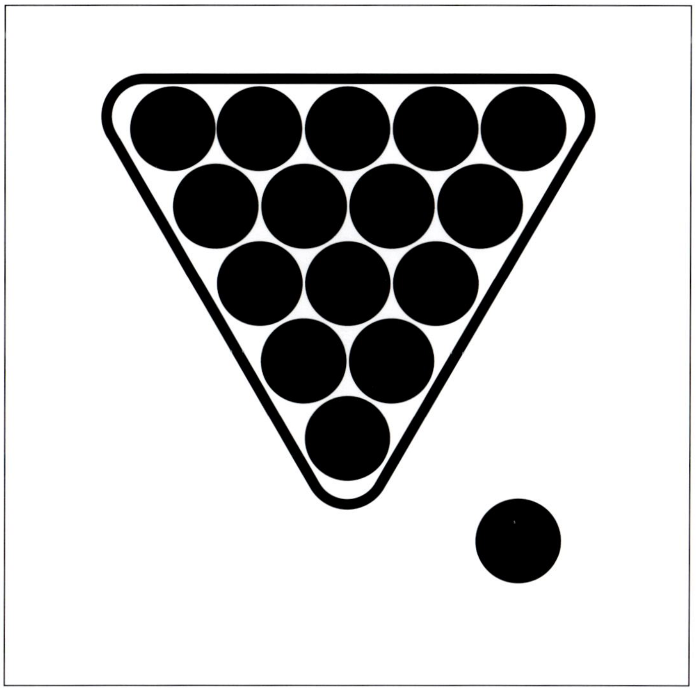

1.1 1.2 

2.1  2.2 

3.1  **3.2** 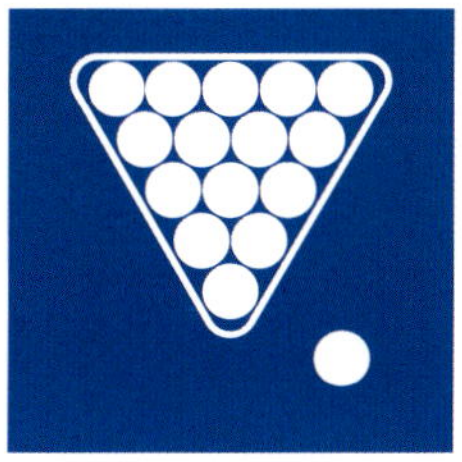

3005

BISHOP CHESS PIECE

3.2 Chess club

1.1

1.2

2.1

2.2

3.1

3.2

3006

PLAYING CARDS

3.2 Playing cards, games

1.1

1.2

2.1

2.2

3.1

3.2

3007

MASKS, COMIC AND TRAGIC

3.2 Theater

1.1 1.2

2.1 2.2

3.1 **3.2**

3008

MOVIE PROJECTOR

3.2 Movie theater

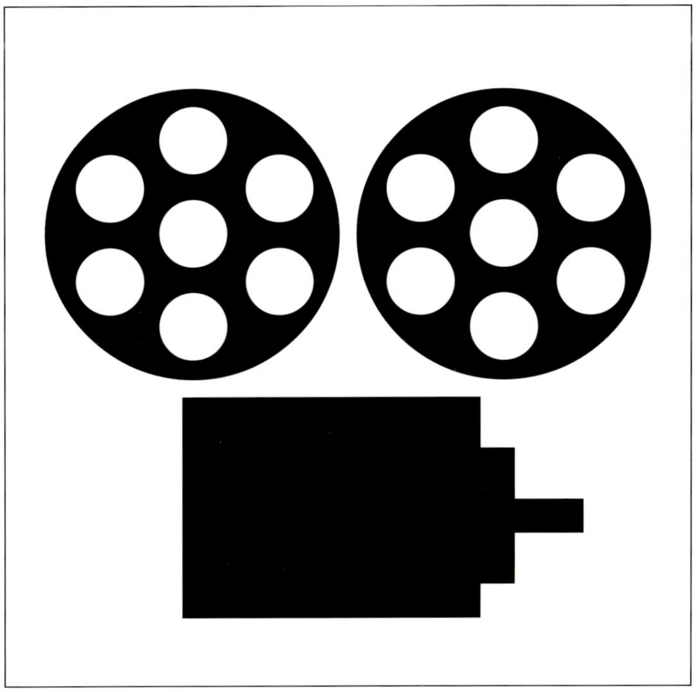

1.1 1.2

2.1 2.2

3.1 **3.2**

3009

MUSICAL NOTES

1.1 No music playing

3.2 Music (room)

1.1

1.2

2.1

2.2

3.1

3.2

3010

TELEVISION SET

3.2 Television (room)

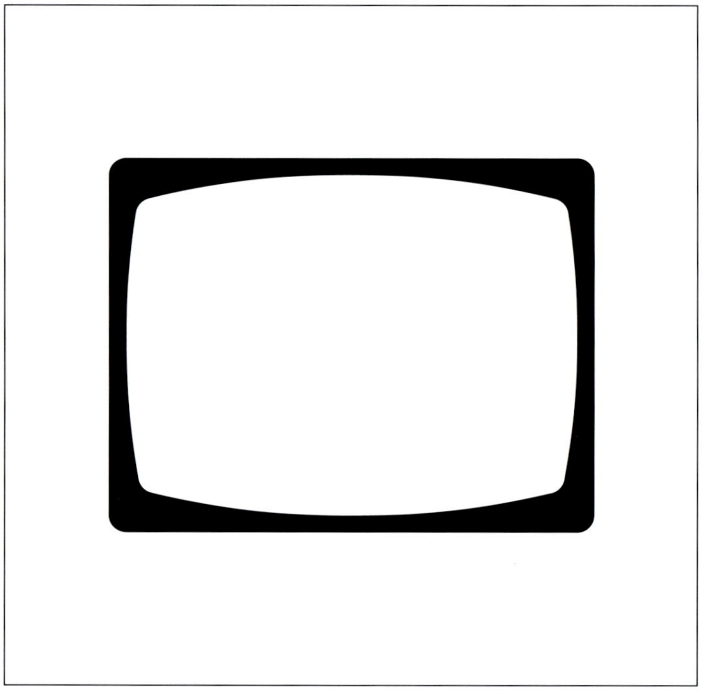

1.1

1.2

2.1

2.2

3.1

3.2

3011

VAN, BOOK SYMBOL, STOP

3.2 Bookmobile stop

1.1

1.2

2.1

2.2

3.1

3.2

3012

PLANET

3.2 Planetarium

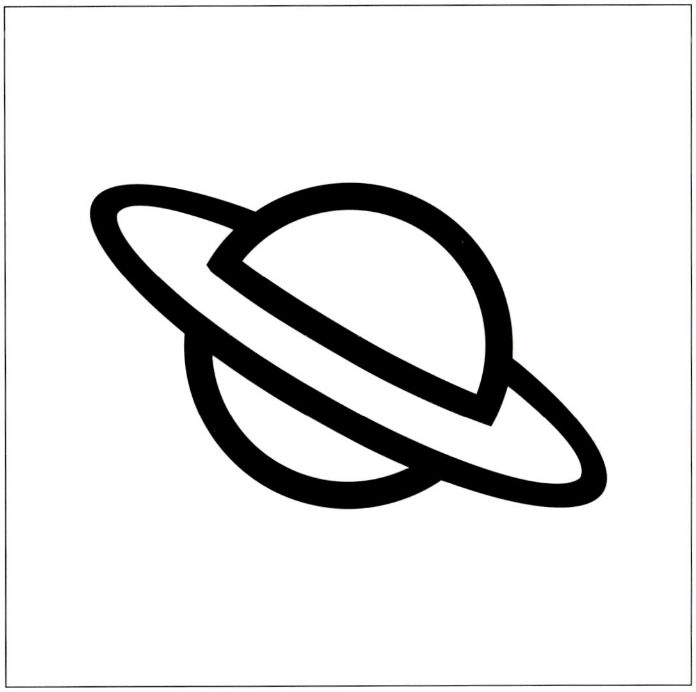

1.1

1.2

2.1

2.2

3.1

3.2

3013

BRUSH, PALETTE

3.2 Visual arts

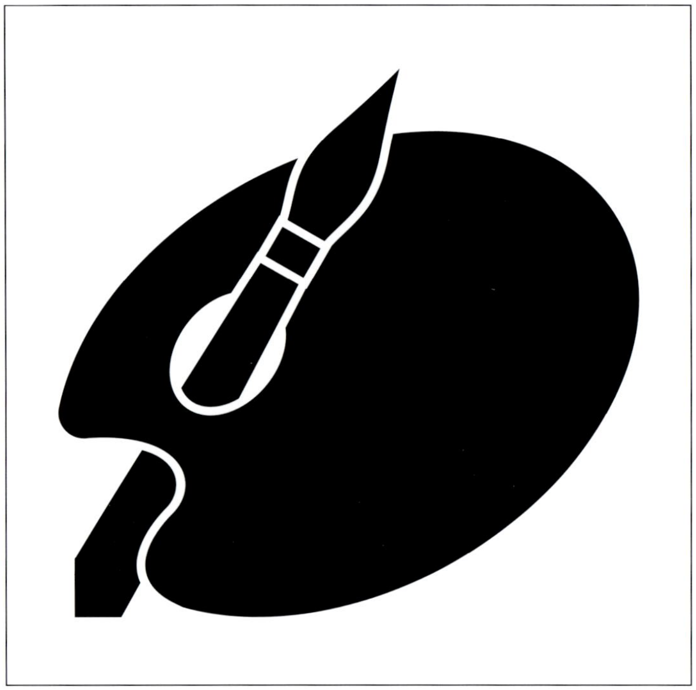

1.1

1.2

2.1

2.2

3.1

3.2

3014

HAND, LAYING UP COILS OF MATERIAL

3.2 Arts and crafts, ceramics (store)

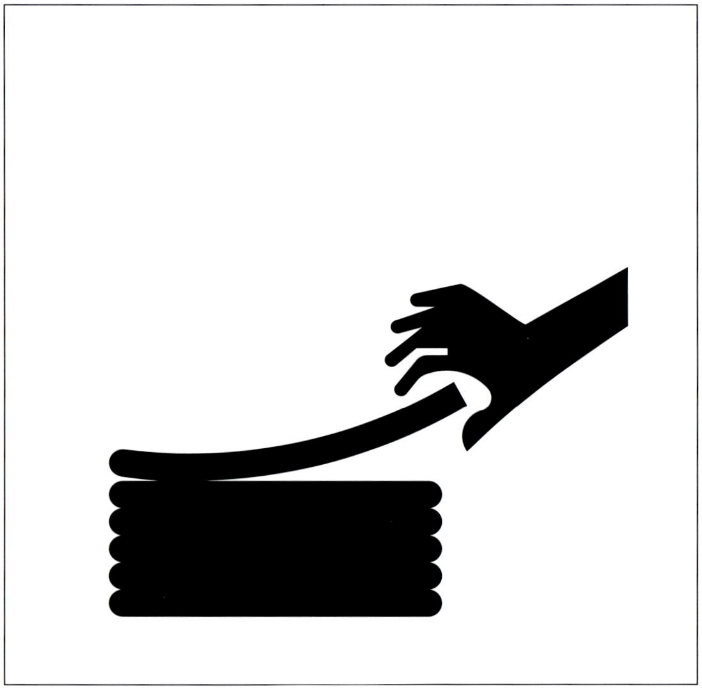

1.1

1.2

2.1

2.2

3.1

3.2

3015

HUMAN FIGURE, READING A BOOK

3.2 Library, reading room

1.1

1.2

2.1

2.2

3.1

3.2

3016

SUN

3.2 Sun tanning

1.1

1.2

2.1

2.2

3.1

3.2

3017

HAND, HOLDING KEY, INSERTED IN THE SLOT

3.2 Locker(s)

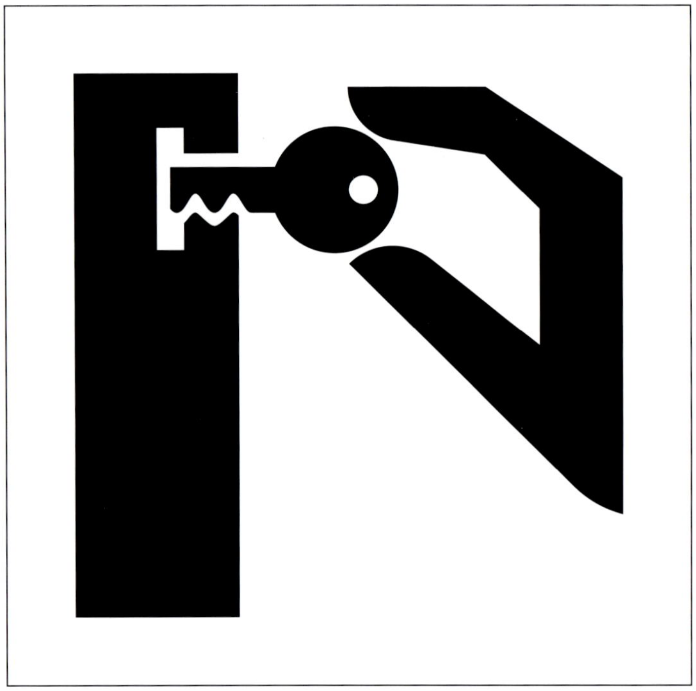

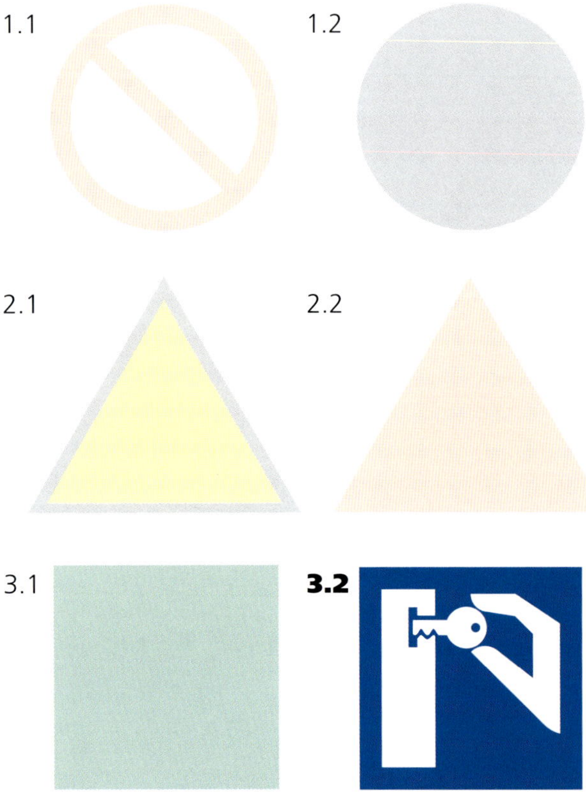

3018

ANCHOR

1.1 No anchoring

3.2 Anchorage, marine supplies, marina

3019

CANOE, OVER WATER

1.1 No canoeing

3.2 Canoeing

1.1

1.2

2.1

2.2

3.1

3.2

3020

PADDLE, OVER WATER

1.1 No canoeing

3.2 Canoeing

1.1

1.2

2.1

2.2

3.1

3.2

3021

OAR BLADE, OVER WATER

1.1 No rowing

3.2 Rowing

1.1

1.2

2.1

2.2

3.1

3.2

3022

RUDDER, STERN, TILLER, SAIL, OVER WATER

1.1 No sailing

3.2 Sailing

1.1

1.2

2.1

2.2

3.1

3.2

3023

SAILBOAT, OVER WATER

1.1 No sailing

3.2 Sailing

1.1

1.2

2.1

2.2

3.1

3.2

3024

MOTOR BOAT, ON TRAILER, ASCENDING RAMP, OVER WATER

1.1 No boat launching

3.2 Boat launching ramp

1.1

1.2

2.1

2.2

3.1

3.2

3025

MOTOR BOAT, OVER WATER

1.1 No motor boats allowed

3.2 Boat (marina)

1.1

1.2

2.1

2.2

3.1

3.2

3026

LARGER MOTOR BOAT, OVER WATER

1.1 No tour boats allowed

3.2 Tour boat

1.1

1.2

2.1

2.2

3.1

3.2

3027

HUMAN FIGURE, OVER STEEP WEDGE

2.1 Caution! Steep slope

1.1

1.2

2.1

2.2

3.1

3.2

3028

LEG, HIKING BOOT, ON UNEVEN GROUND

1.1 No hiking

3.2 Nature path, hiking

1.1

1.2

2.1

2.2

3.1

3.2

3029

HUMAN FIGURE, CLIMBING, SAFETY ROPE

1.1 No climbing

1.2 Safety rope mandatory

3.2 Climbing

1.1

1.2

2.1

2.2

3.1

3.2

3030

HUMAN FIGURE, CLIMBING

1.1 No climbing

3.2 Climbing wall

1.1

1.2

2.1

2.2

3.1

3.2

3031

HUMAN FIGURE, WITH RIFLE

1.1 No hunting, shooting

2.1 Caution! Shooting range

3.2 Hunting, shooting range

1.1

1.2

2.1

2.2

3.1

3.2

3032

ROLLER SKATE

1.1 No roller-skating

3.2 Roller-skating rink

1.1

1.2

2.1

2.2

3.1

3.2

3033

ROLLERBLADE

1.1 No rollerblading

3.2 Rollerblading rink

1.1

1.2

2.1

2.2

3.1

3.2

3034

SKATEBOARD

1.1 No skateboarding

3.2 Skateboard rink

1.1

1.2

2.1

2.2

3.1

3.2

3035

TIP OF SKATE, TIP OF BOOT

1.1 No ice skating

3.2 Ice skating, skate sharpening

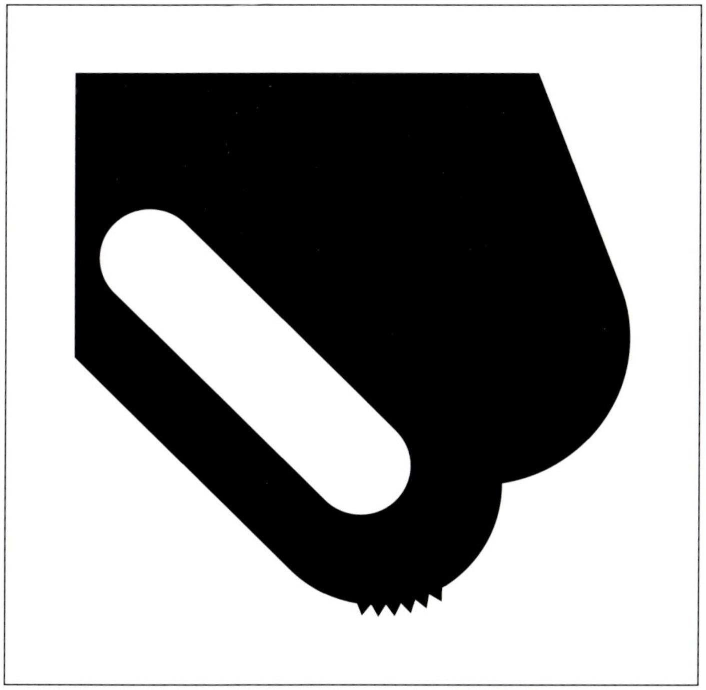

3036

SKATE, WITH BOOT

1.1 No ice skating

3.2 Figure skating

3037

HUMAN FIGURES, ADULT, INFANT, STANDING IN WATER

1.1 No wadding

3.2 Wadding pool

1.1

1.2

2.1

2.2

3.1

3.2

3038

INFANT, STANDING IN WATER

1.1 No wadding

3.2 Wadding pool

1.1

1.2

2.1

2.2

3.1

3.2

3039

CHILD, ON SLIDE

3.2 Play area

1.1

1.2

2.1

2.2

3.1

3.2

3040

INFANTS, ONE SKIPPING, OTHER JUMPING

3.2 Playground

1.1

1.2

2.1

2.2

3.1

3.2

3041

MERRY-GO-ROUND

3.2 Merry-go-round, amusement park

1.1

1.2

2.1

2.2

3.1

3.2

3042

HUMAN FIGURE, DANCING

3.2 Fitness (club), aerobics, dance (studio)

1.1

1.2

2.1

2.2

3.1

3.2

3043

HUMAN FIGURE, IN LOTUS POSITION

3.2 Yoga (studio)

3044

HUMAN FIGURE, MAN, TOP CLOUDED IN STEAM

3.2 Sauna for men

0
1
2
3
4
5
6
7
8
Index

3045

HUMAN FIGURE, WOMAN, TOP CLOUDED IN STEAM

3.2 Sauna for women

1.1

1.2

2.1

2.2

3.1

3.2

3046

HUMAN FIGURE, MAN, IN WATER

3.2 Spa for men

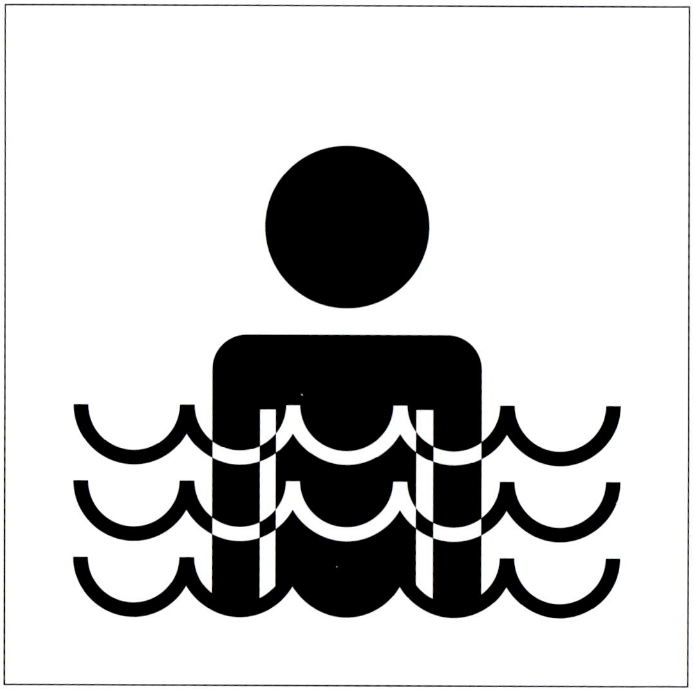

1.1

1.2

2.1

2.2

3.1

3.2

3047

HUMAN FIGURE, WOMAN, IN WATER

3.2 Spa for women

1.1

1.2

2.1

2.2

3.1

3.2

3048

SKIER

1.1 No skiing

2.1 Caution! Skiing

3.2 Downhill skiing

1.1

1.2

2.1

2.2

3.1

3.2

3049

HUMAN FIGURE, WITH SKIS, ON SKI LIFT

2.1 Caution! Ski lift

3.2 Ski lift

1.1

1.2

2.1

2.2

3.1

3.2

3050

HUMAN FIGURE, WITH SKIS, IN HANGING CHAIR

3.2 Ski lift

1.1

1.2

2.1

2.2

3.1

3.2

3051

FOOT, BENT, ON SKI, WITH POLE

1.1 No cross-country skiing

3.2 Cross-country skiing

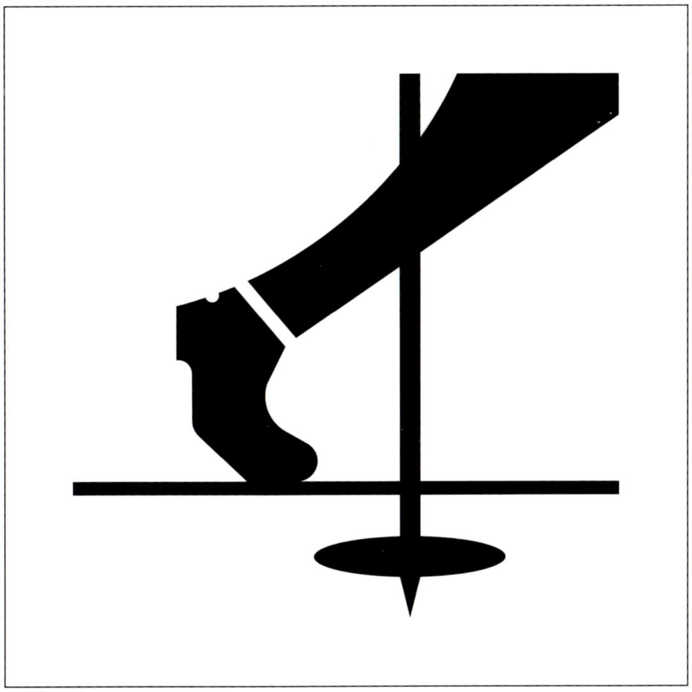

1.1

1.2

2.1

2.2

3.1

3.2

3052

SNOWMOBILE

1.1 No snowmobiles allowed

2.1 Caution! Snowmobiles

3.2 Snowmobiles

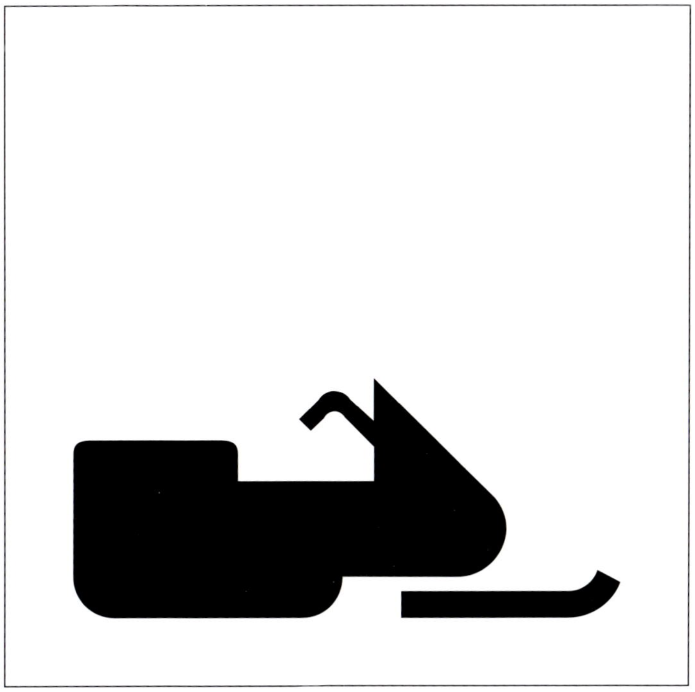

1.1

1.2

2.1

2.2

3.1

3.2

3053

TOBOGGAN

1.1 No tobogganing

2.1 Caution! Tobogganing

3.2 Tobogganing

3054

SNOWFLAKE

3.2 Winter

1.1

1.2

2.1

2.2

3.1

3.2

1.1

1.2

2.1

2.2

3.1

3.2

3055

BICYCLE, WITH RIDER

1.1 No bicycling
2.1 Caution! Bicyclers
3.2 Bicycling

1.1

1.2

2.1

2.2

3.1

3.2

3056

BULLSEYE, ARROW

1.1 No archery allowed
2.1 Caution! Archery
3.2 Archery

1.1

1.2

2.1

2.2

3.1

3.2

0
1
2
3
4
5
6
7
8
Index

3057

HOCKEY STICK, PUCK

1.1 No hockey playing

3.2 Hockey

1.1

1.2

2.1

2.2

3.1

3.2

3058

HOCKEY STICK, TENNIS BALL ABOVE

1.1 No floor hockey playing

3.2 Floor hockey

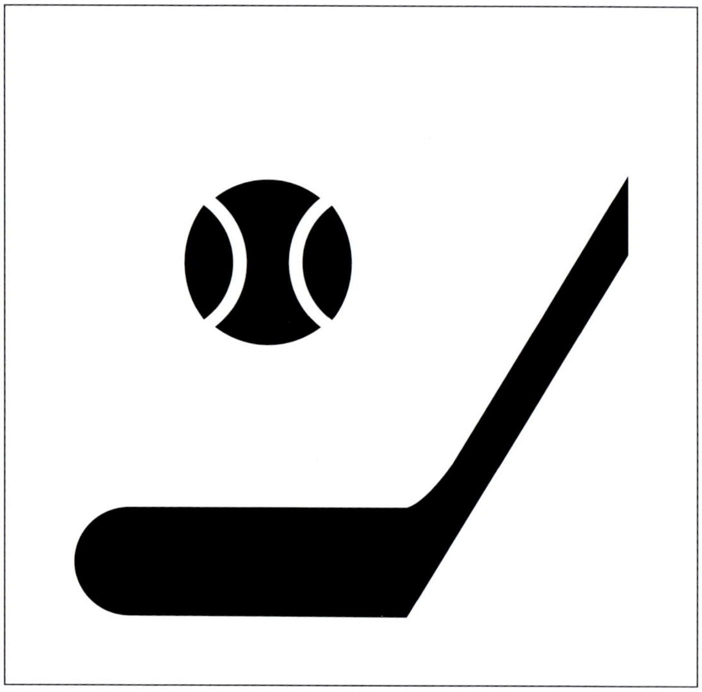

1.1

1.2

2.1

2.2

3.1

3.2

3059

BALL, OVER BASKET

3.2 Basketball

1.1

1.2

2.1

2.2

3.1

3.2

3060

FOOTBALL, RUGBY

1.1 No football allowed

3.2 Football, rugby

1.1

1.2

2.1

2.2

3.1

3.2

3061

SOCCER, FOOTBALL

1.1 No soccer, football allowed

3.2 Soccer, Football

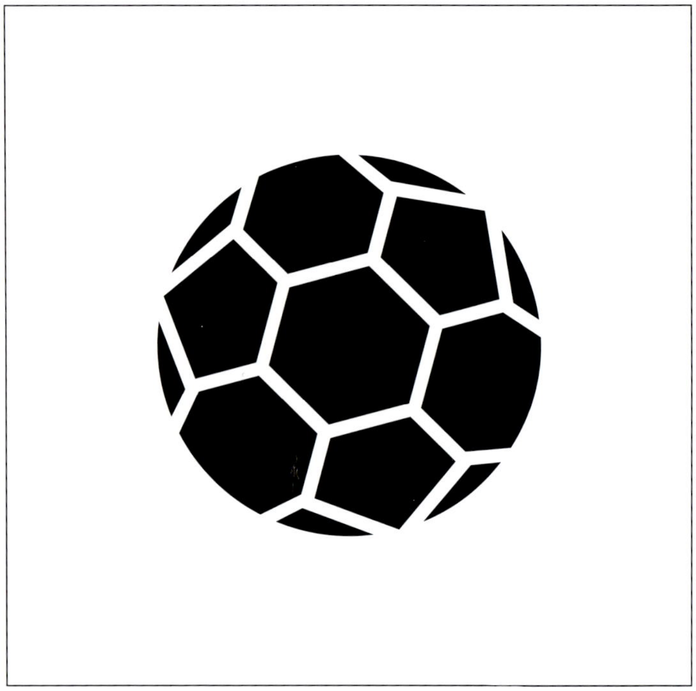

1.1

1.2

2.1

2.2

3.1

3.2

3062

POLO BALL, OVER WATER

1.1 No water polo allowed

3.2 Water polo

1.1

1.2

2.1

2.2

3.1

3.2

3063

VOLLEY BALL, OVER NET

3.2 Volleyball

1.1

1.2

2.1

2.2

3.1

3.2

3064

BASEBALL, BAT

1.1 No baseball allowed

3.2 Baseball

1.1

1.2

2.1

2.2

3.1

3.2

3065

CRICKET BAT, BALL, WICKET

1.1 No cricket allowed

3.2 Cricket (game of)

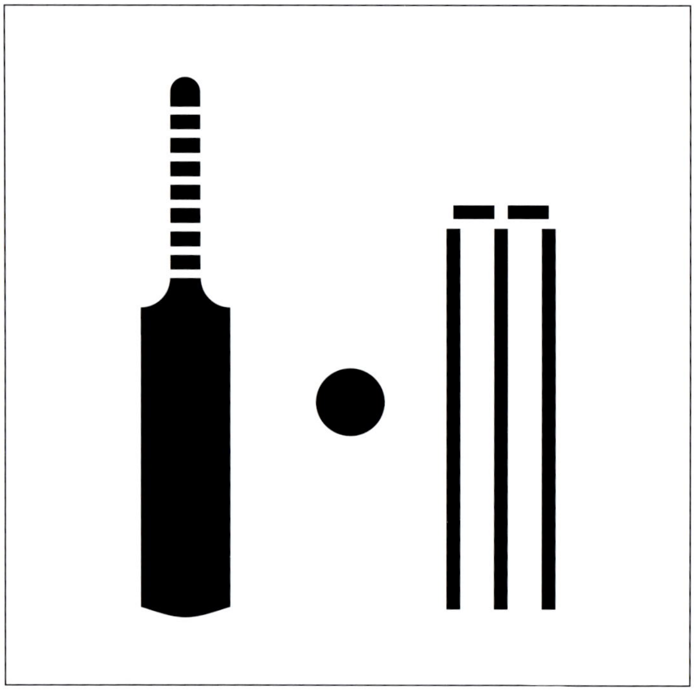

1.1

1.2

2.1

2.2

3.1

3.2

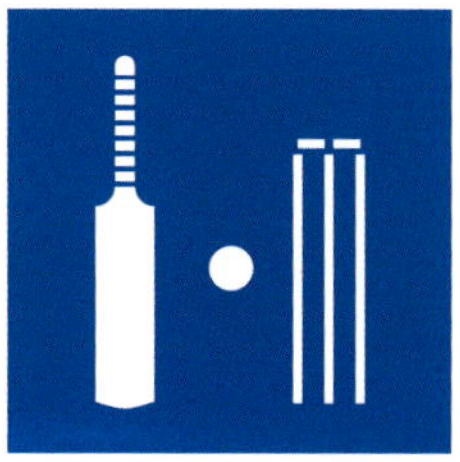

3066

BOXING GLOVE

3.2 Boxing

1.1

1.2

2.1

2.2

3.1

3.2

3067

HUMAN FIGURE, IN AGGRESSIVE STANCE

3.2 Martial arts (studio)

1.1

1.2

2.1

2.2

3.1

3.2

3068

HUMAN FIGURE, OVER HORIZONTAL BAR

3.2 Gymnastics

1.1

1.2

2.1

2.2

3.1

3.2

0
1
2
3
4
5
6
7
8
Index

3069

GOLF CART

1.1 No golf carts allowed

2.1 Caution! Golf carts

3.2 Golf carts

1.1

1.2

2.1

2.2

3.1

3.2

3070

GOLF CLUB, BALL, TEE

1.1 No golfing

2.1 Caution! Golfers

3.2 Golf

1.1

1.2

2.1

2.2

3.1

3.2

3071

ARM, RAISING WEIGHTS

3.2 Weight lifing

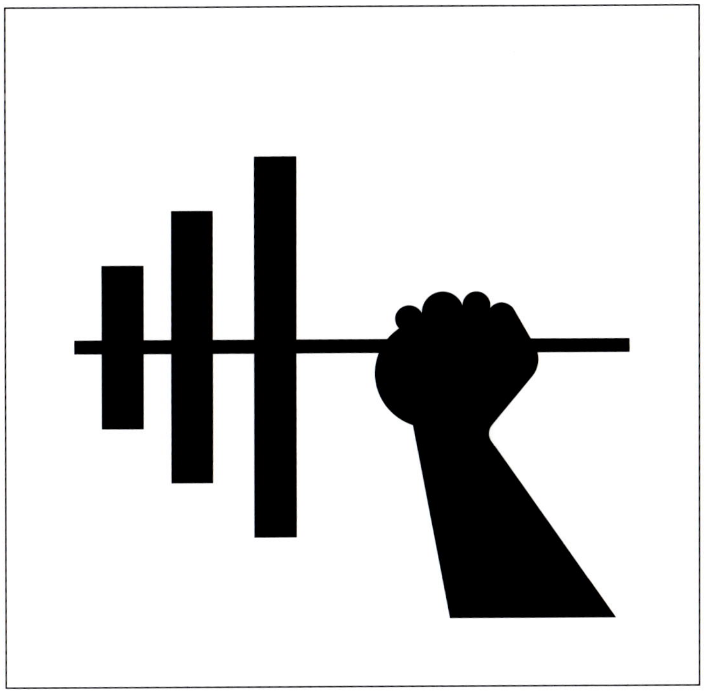

1.1

1.2

2.1

2.2

3.1

3.2

3072

HUMAN FIGURE, ARMS OUTSTRETCHED, HOLDING WEIGHTS

3.2 Weights

1.1

1.2

2.1

2.2

3.1

3.2

3073

BOWLING BALL, PINS

3.2 Bowling

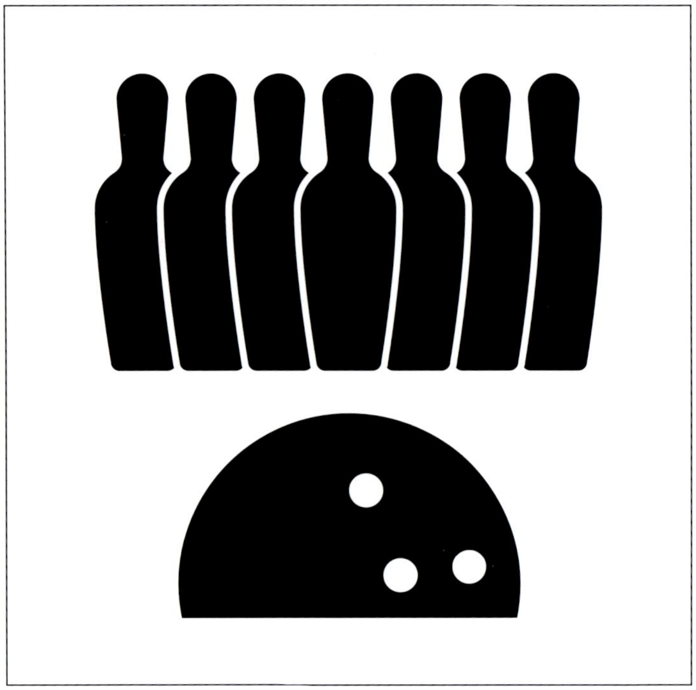

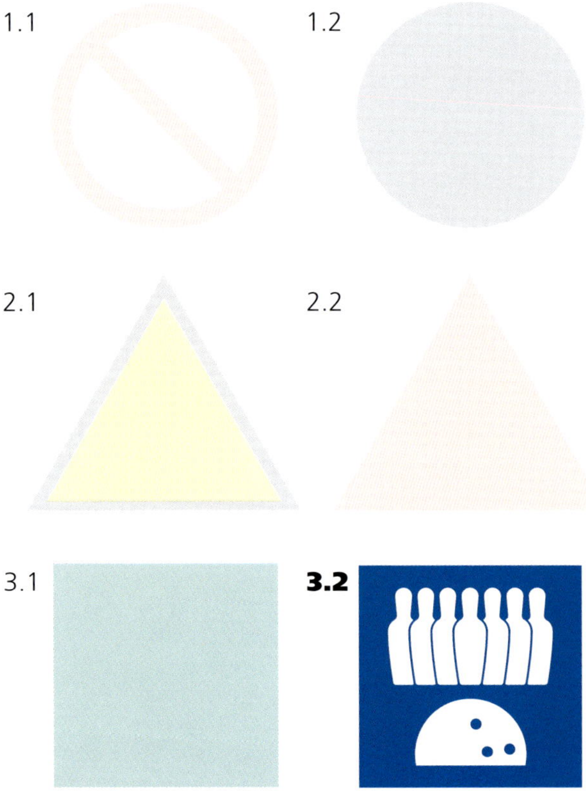

3074

BOWLING BALL, ON GRASS

1.1 No lawn bowling

3.2 Lawn bowling

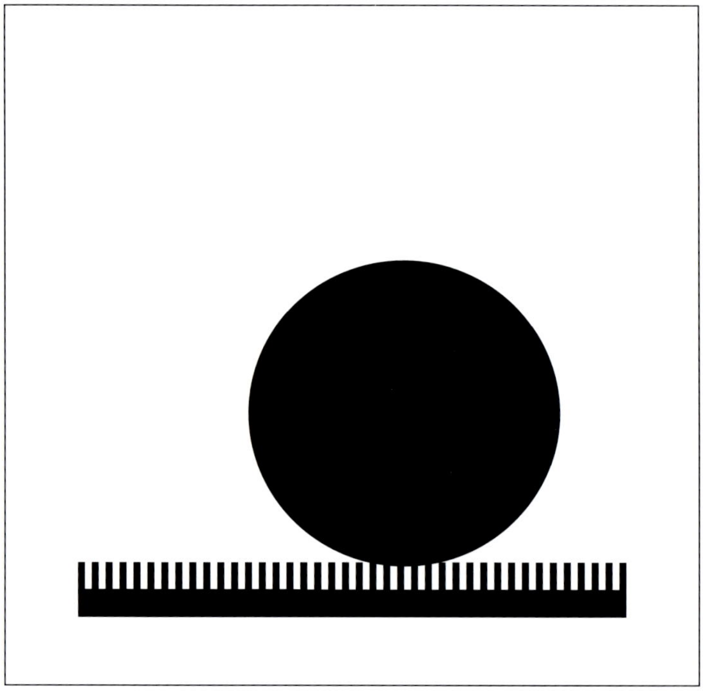

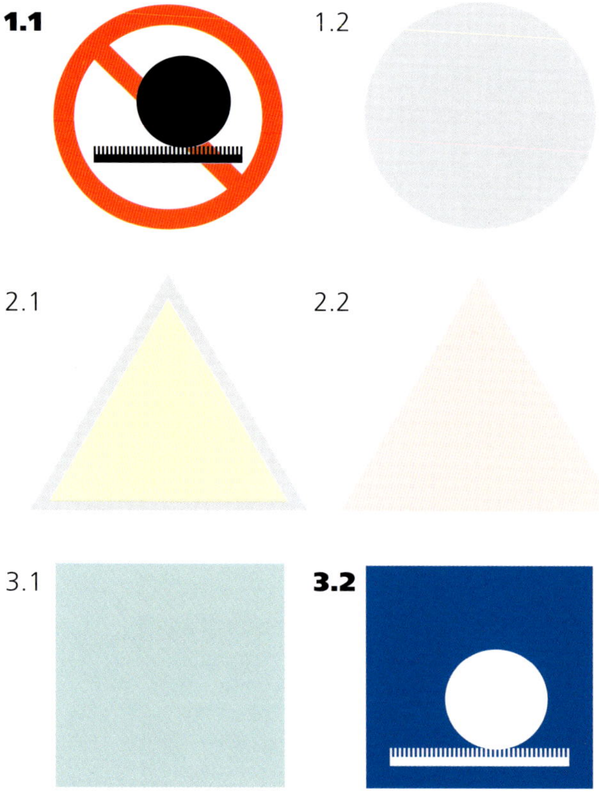

3075

CURLING STONE

1.1 No curling

3.2 Curling

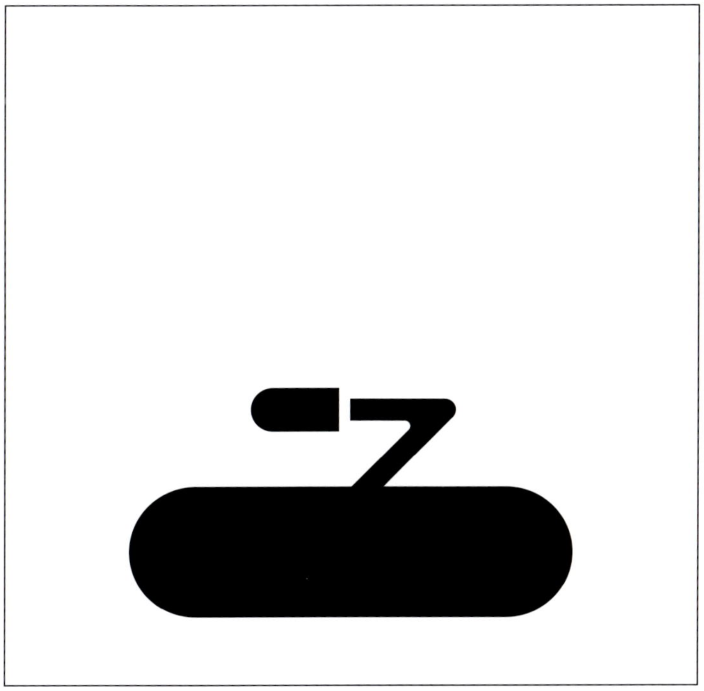

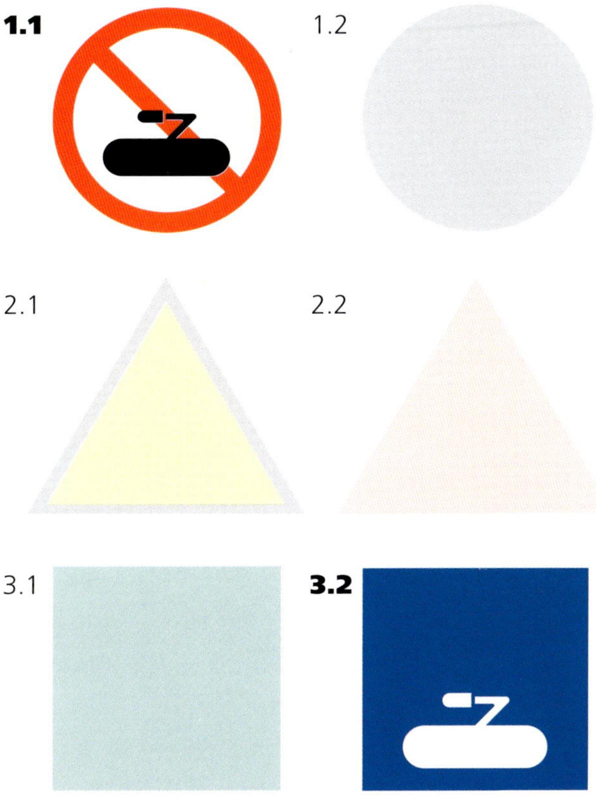

3076

HUMAN FIGURE, JOGGING

1.1 No jogging

2.1 Caution! Jogging

3.2 Jogging, running track

3077

LACROSSE STICK, BALL

1.1 No lacrosse allowed

3.2 Lacrosse, sports supplies

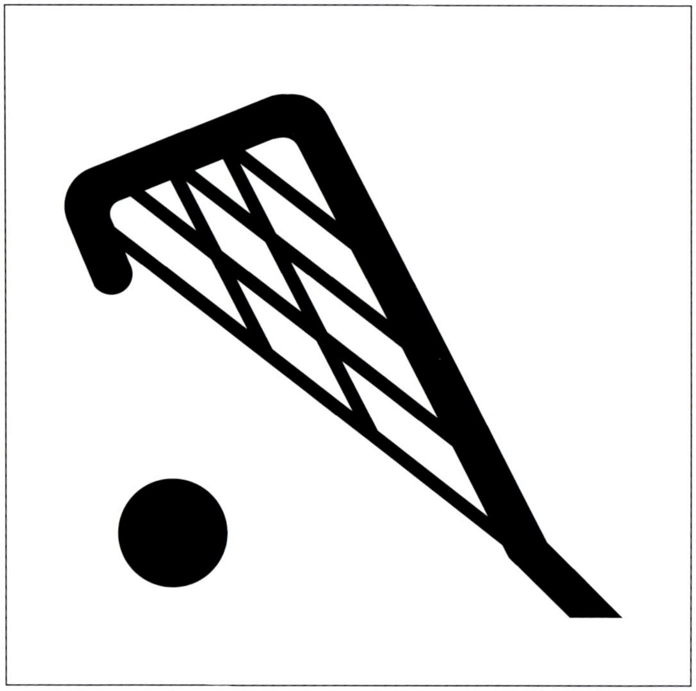

1.1

1.2

2.1

2.2

3.1

3.2
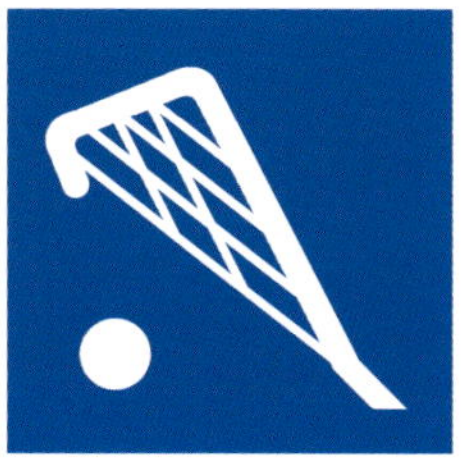

3078

SHUTTLECOCK, BADMINTON RACKET

1.1 No badminton allowed

3.2 Badminton

1.1

1.2

2.1

2.2

3.1

3.2

3079

TENNIS BALL, OVER RACKET

1.1 No tennis allowed

3.2 Tennis court

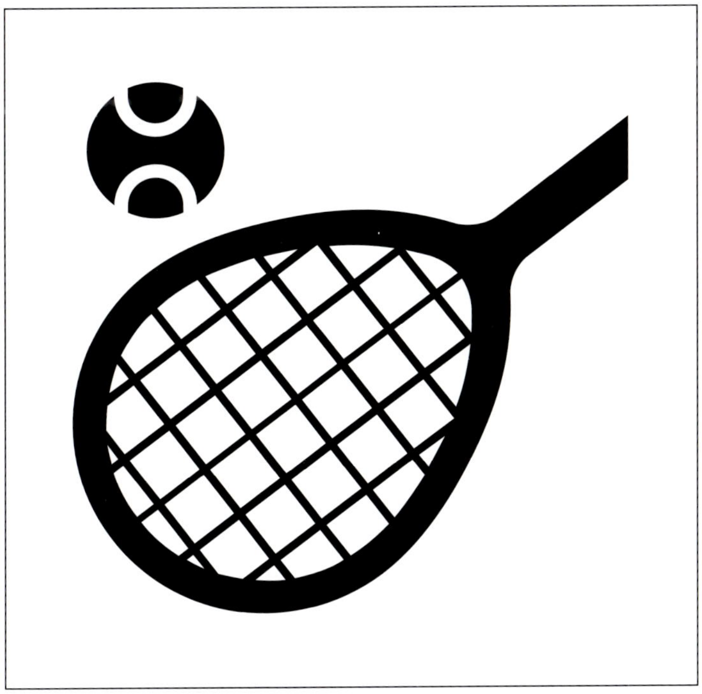

3080

TWO RACKETS, BALL, OVER NET

3.2 Table tennis, Ping-Pong

0
1
2
3
4
5
6
7
8
Index

3081

FISH, FISH HOOK

1.1 No fishing

3.2 Fishing

1.1

1.2

2.1

2.2

3.1

3.2

3082

SHOE

1.1 No shoes allowed

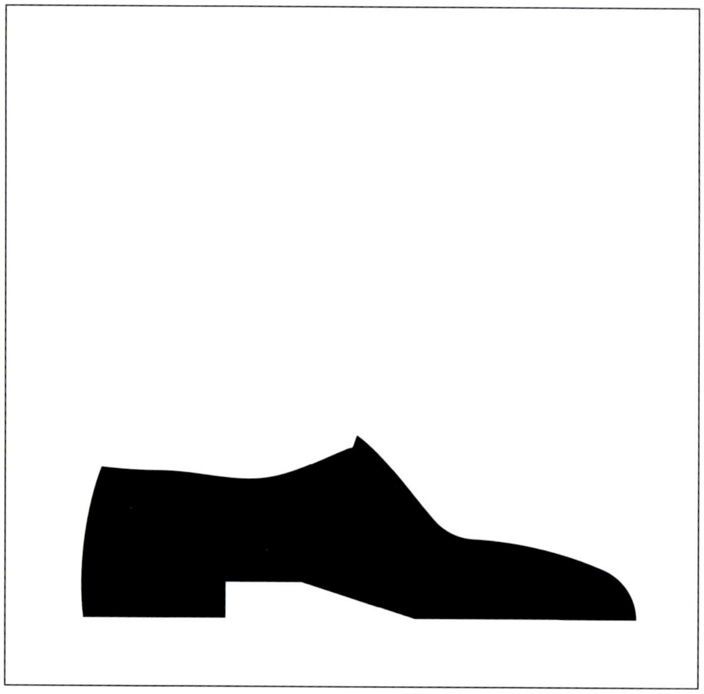

1.1

1.2

2.1

2.2

3.1

3.2

3083

SIX LAYERS OF WATER SYMBOL, OVER HORIZONTAL LINE

2.1 Caution! Deep end

3.2 Pool (deep end)

1.1

1.2

2.1

2.2

3.1

3.2

3084

TWO LAYERS OF WATER SYMBOL, OVER HORIZONTAL LINE

2.1 Caution! Shallow end

3.2 Pool (shallow end)

1.1

1.2

2.1

2.2

3.1

3.2

3085

LIFE PRESERVER, OVER WATER

3.1 Life preserver

1.1

1.2

2.1

2.2

3.1

3.2

3086

HUMAN FIGURE, SEATED ON PLATFORM, OVER WATER

3.2 Beach, lifegard on duty

1.1

1.2

2.1

2.2

3.1

3.2

3087

HUMAN FIGURE, FLOTATION DEVICES, OVER WATER

1.1 No swimming with flotation devices

1.2 Swimming only with flotation devices

3.2 Flotation devices

1.1

1.2

2.1

2.2

3.1

3.2

3088

HUMAN HEAD, SHOULDER, CROOKED ARM, IN WATER

1.1 No swimming

3.2 Swimming

1.1

1.2

2.1

2.2

3.1

3.2

3089

HUMAN FIGURE, DIVING, OVER WATER

1.1 No diving

3.2 Diving

1.1

1.2

2.1

2.2

3.1

3.2

3090

HUMAN FIGURE, TANK ON BACK, UNDER WATER

1.1 No scuba diving

3.2 Scuba diving

1.1

1.2

2.1

2.2

3.1

3.2

3091

HUMAN FIGURE, ON SKI, OVER WATER

1.1 No waterskiing

3.2 Waterskiing

1.1

1.2

2.1

2.2

3.1

3.2

3092

HUMAN FIGURE, ON SURFBOARD, OVER WATER

1.1 No surfing

3.2 Surfing

1.1

1.2

2.1

2.2

3.1

3.2

3093

HUMAN FIGURE, WINDSURFER, SAILBOARD, OVER WATER

1.1 No windsurfing, sailboarding

3.2 Windsurfing, sailboarding

1.1

1.2

2.1

2.2

3.1

3.2

3094

SHUTTLE TRAIN

3.2 Shuttle train station

1.1

1.2

2.1

2.2

3.1

3.2

3095

PICNIC BENCH

1.1 No picnicking

3.2 Picnicking

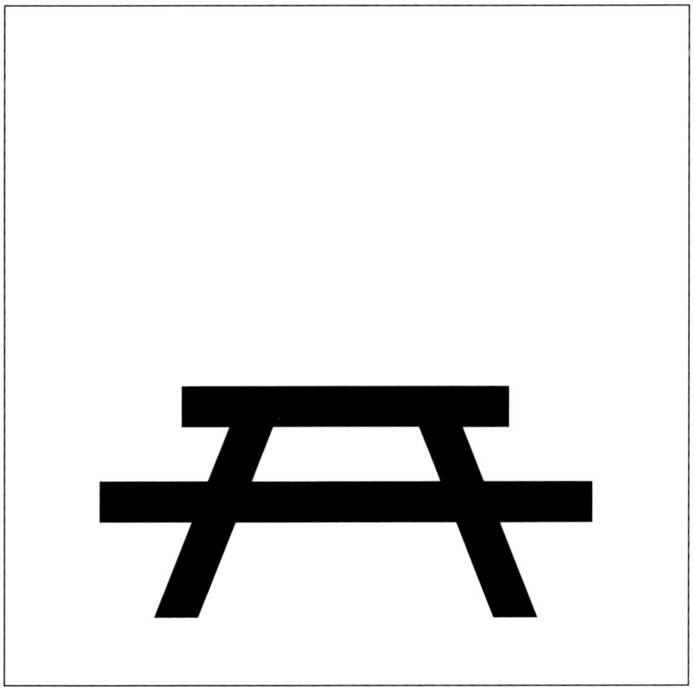

1.1

1.2

2.1

2.2

3.1

3.2

3096

PICNIC BENCH, UNDER ROOF

3.2 Picnic pavilion

1.1

1.2

2.1

2.2

3.1

3.2

3097

TENT, WITH FLAP OPEN

1.1 No camping

3.2 Camping

1.1

1.2

2.1

2.2

3.1

3.2

3098

BARN, FENCE

3.2 Farm

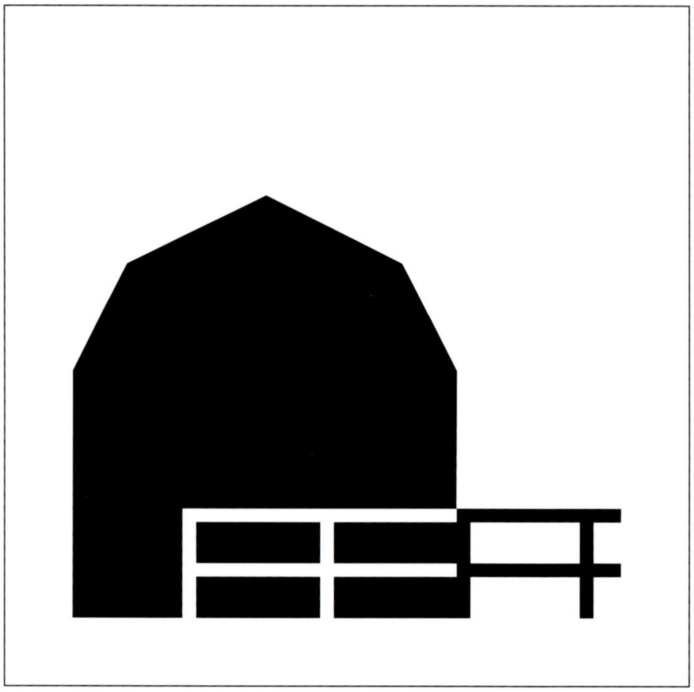

1.1

1.2

2.1

2.2

3.1

3.2

3099

CARROTS, TOMATO, PEPPERS

3.2 Vegetable patch

3100

FLOWERS

3.2 Flowers, flower garden, nursery

3101

DOG, LEASH (OPTIONAL)

1.1 No dogs allowed

1.2 Dogs must be on leash

3.2 Dogs, leash-free area

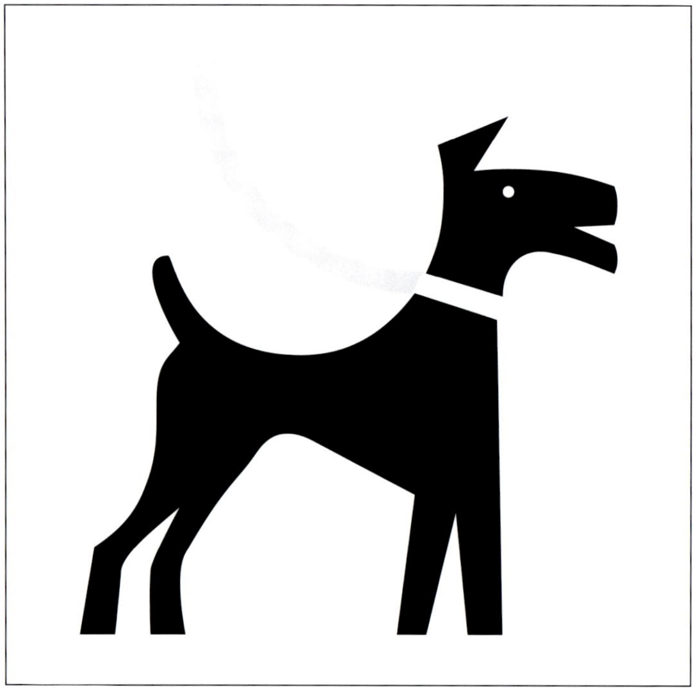

1.1

1.2

2.1

2.2

3.1

3.2

3102

FECES, DOG, ARROW, BASKET

1.2 Pick up after your pet

1.1

1.2

2.1

2.2

3.1

3.2

3103

DUCKS

2.1 Caution! Ducks crossing

3.2 Ducks

1.1

1.2

2.1

2.2

3.1

3.2

3104

ANIMAL, PEANUTS

1.1 No animal feeding

3.2 Animal feeding

1.1

1.2

2.1

2.2

3.1

3.2

0
1
2
3
4
5
6
7
8
Index

3105

MATCH, FLAMES ABOVE

1.1 No open flames, fires allowed

1.1

1.2

2.1

2.2

3.1

3.2

3106

LOGS, WITH FLAMES ABOVE

1.1 No fires allowed

3.2 Campfire, bonfire, outdoor cooking

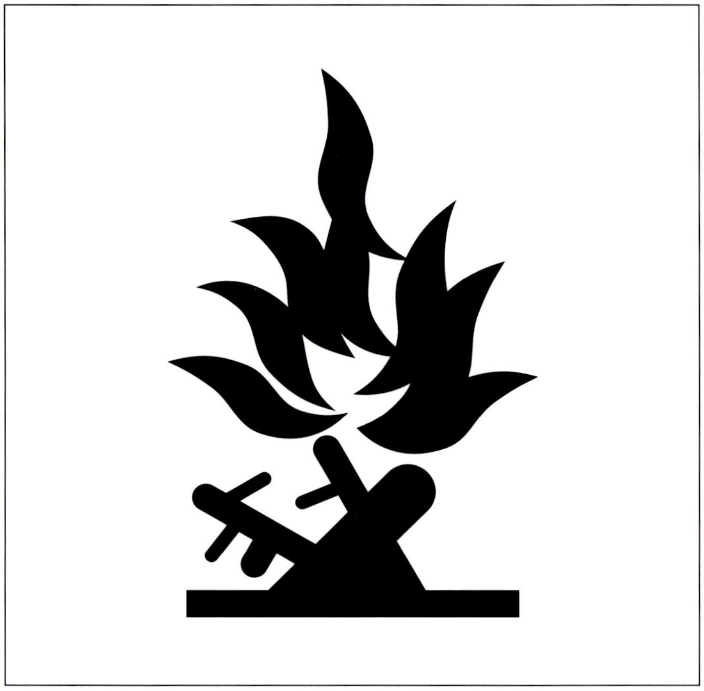

1.1

1.2

2.1

2.2

3.1

3.2

3107

EVERGREEN TREE

1.1 Do not cut trees

3.2 Christmas trees for cutting

3108

HUMAN HEAD, WITH CHEF'S HAT

3.2 Cook(ing), kitchen

3109

STEMWARE GLASS, SWIZZLE STICK

3.2 Bar

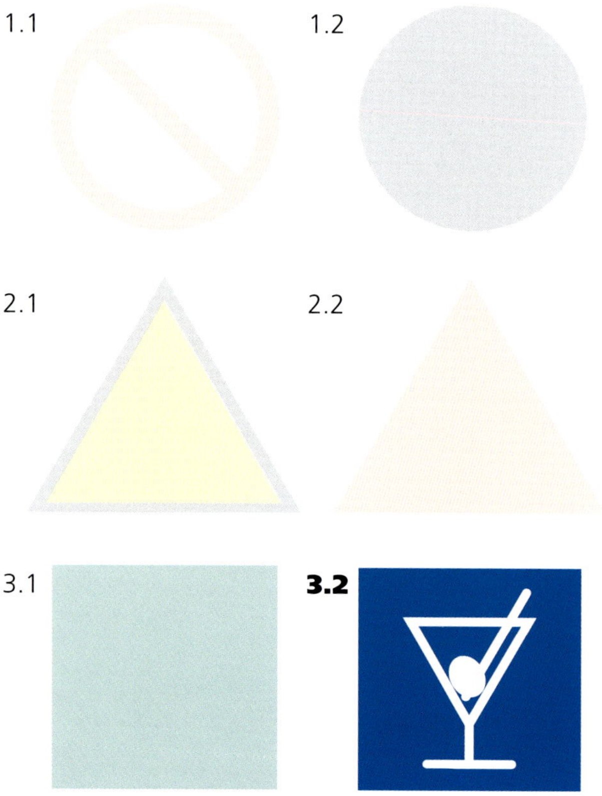

3110

BEER MUG, FOAM OVER THE EDGE

3.2 Pub, beer store

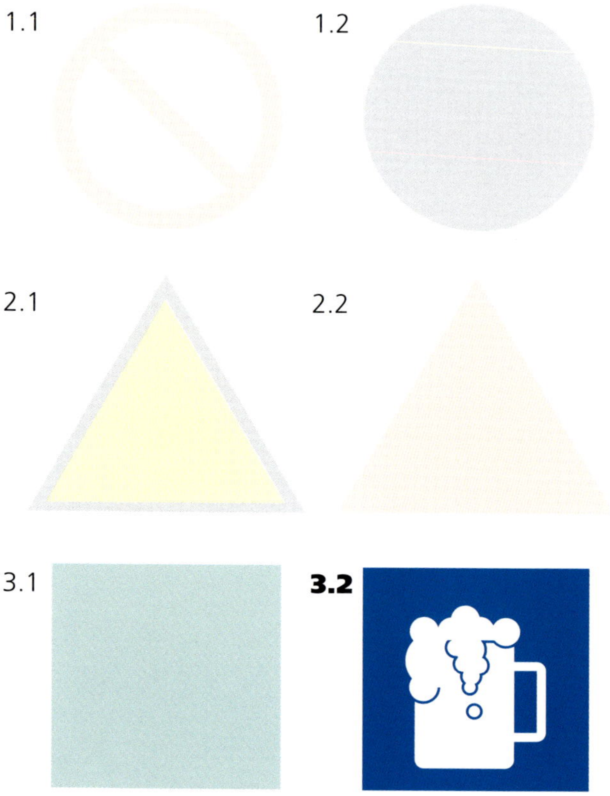

3111

MOON

3.2 Moon, night

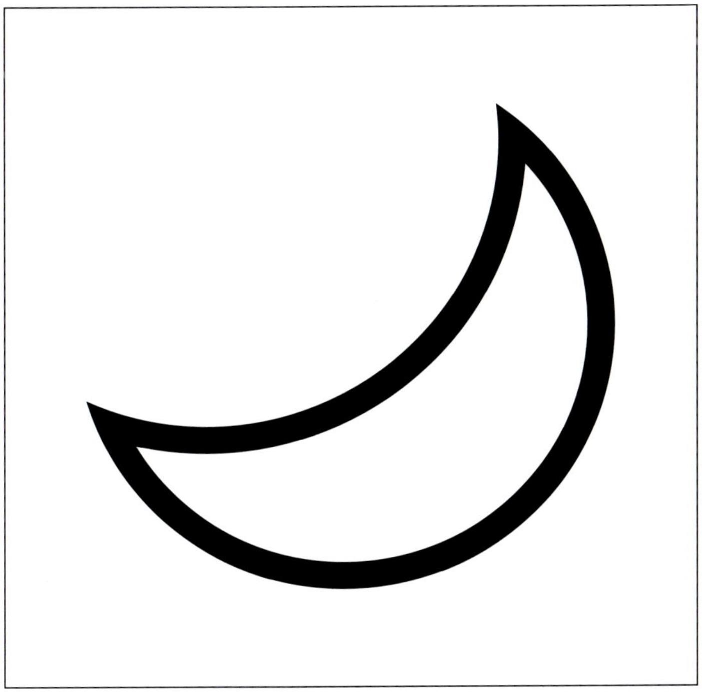

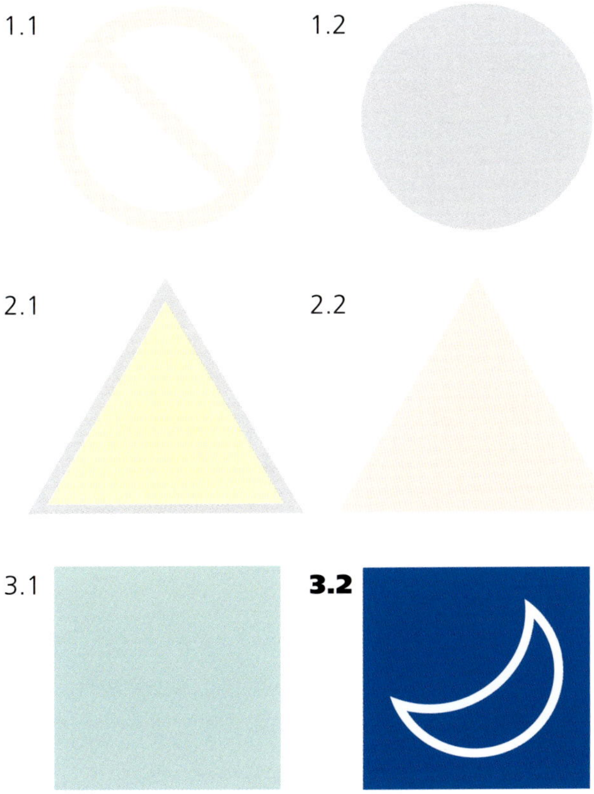

3112

CLOUD

3.2 Clouds

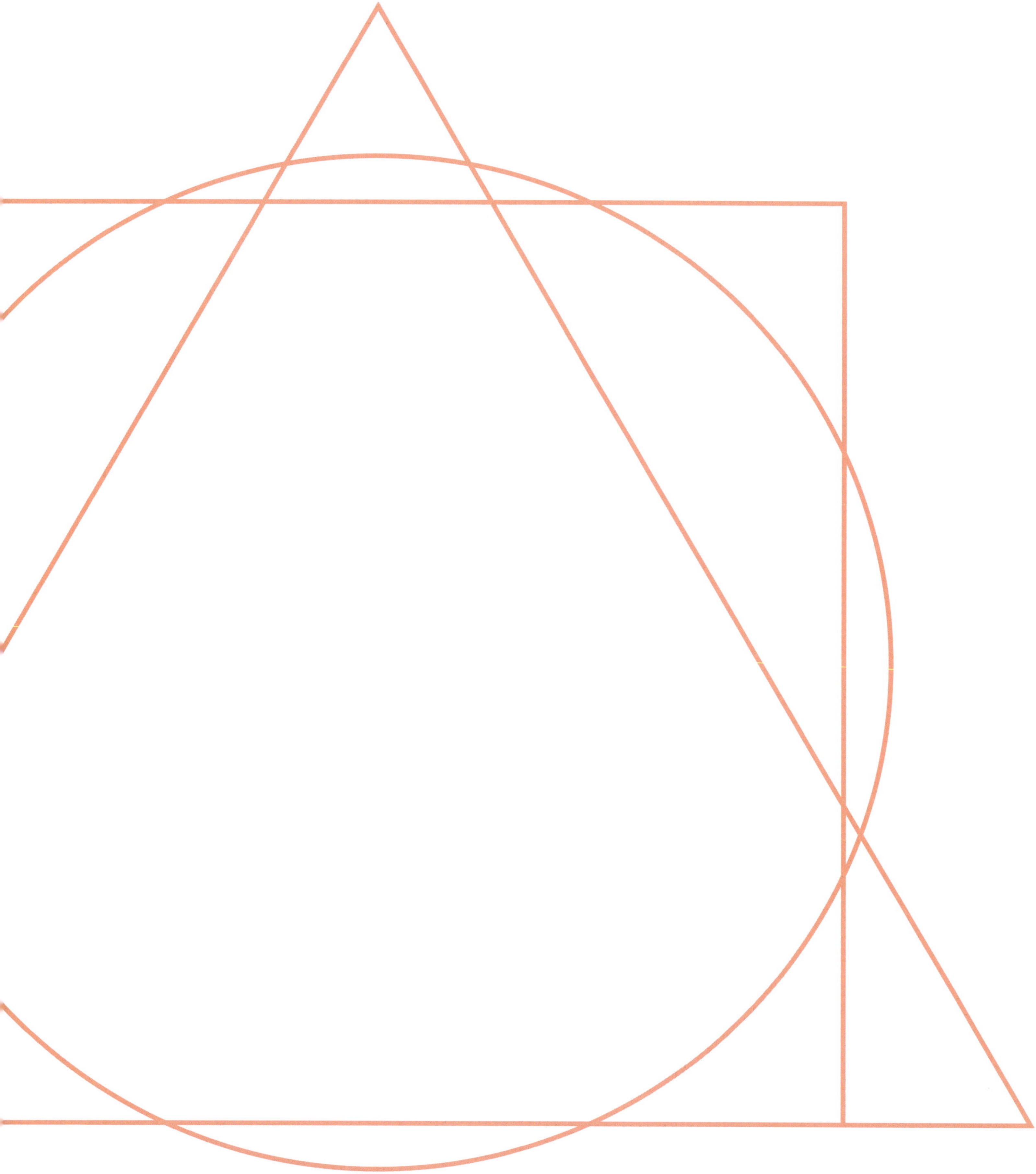

4001

H

3.2 Hospital

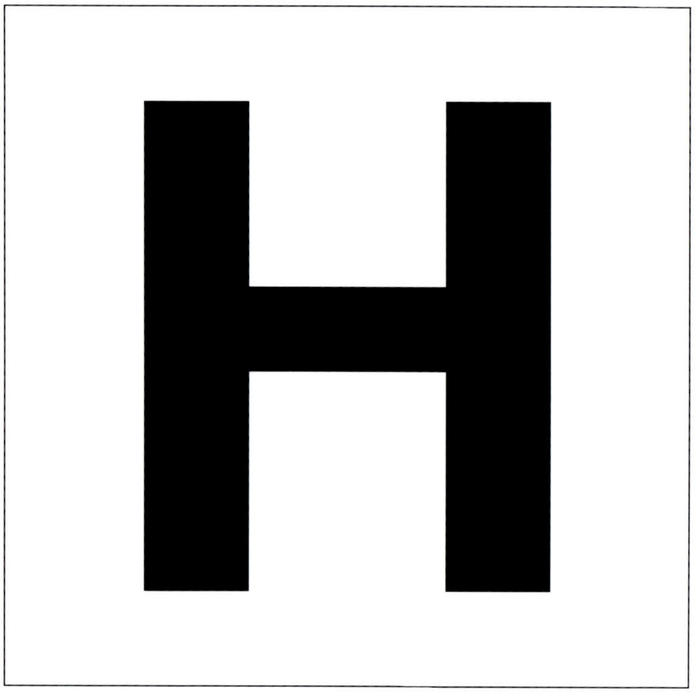

1.1

1.2

2.1

2.2

3.1

3.2

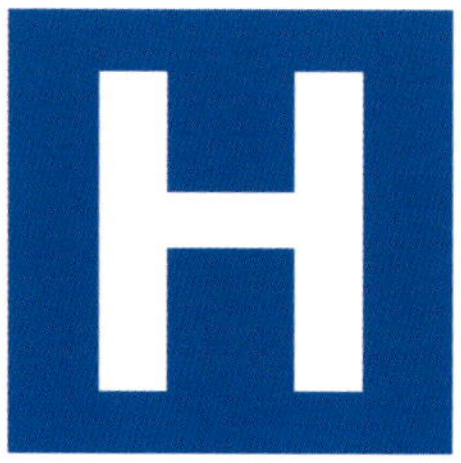

4002

HUMAN FIGURES, SEATED, (OPTIONAL CLOCK)

3.2 Waiting/holding room

1.1

1.2

2.1

2.2

3.1

3.2

4003

SEGMENT OF A CALENDAR

3.2 Appointments

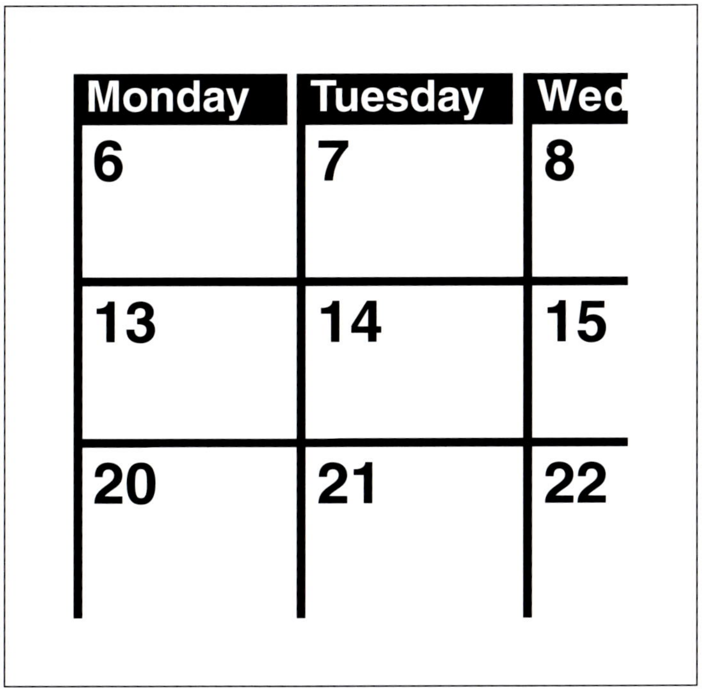

1.1

1.2

2.1

2.2

3.1

3.2

4004

STRETCHER, GREEK CROSS ABOVE

3.1 First aid, stretcher

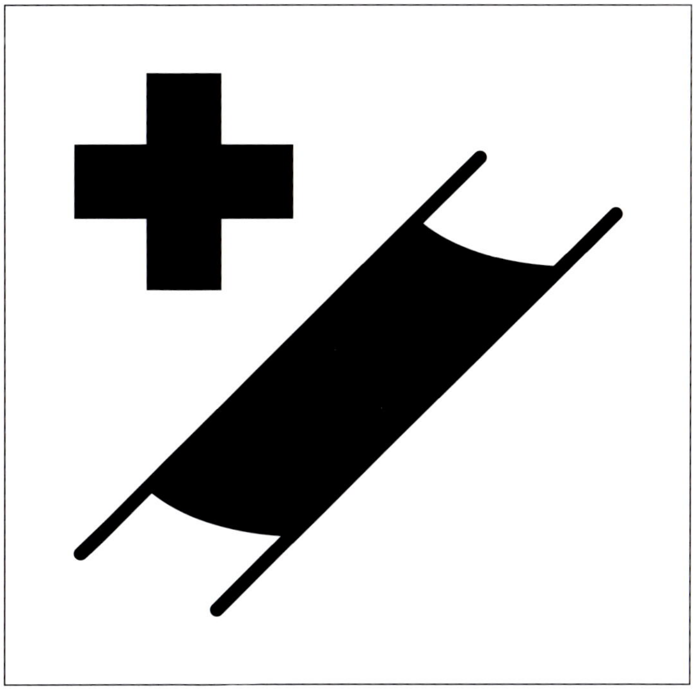

1.1

1.2

2.1

2.2

3.1

3.2

0
1
2
3
4
5
6
7
8
Index

4005

STRETCHER, WITH GREEK CROSS

3.2 Stretcher

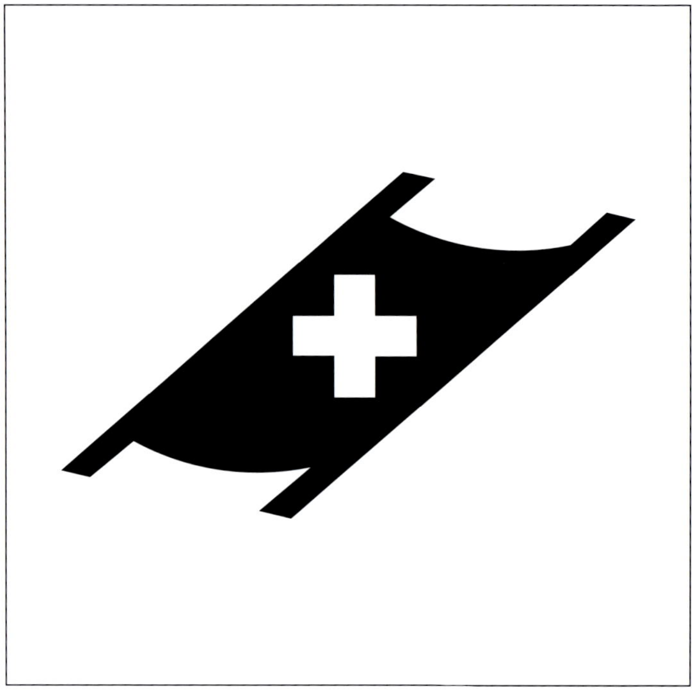

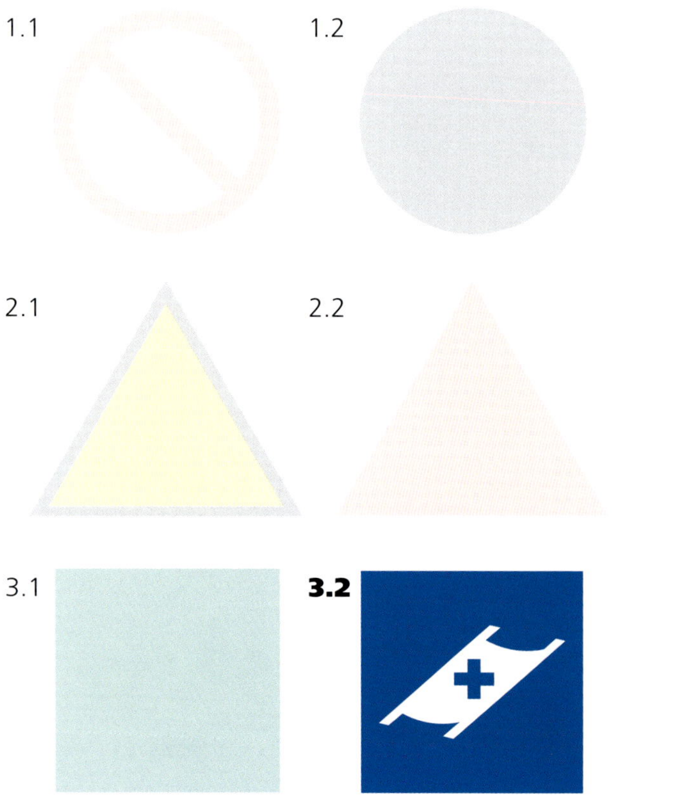

4006

WHEELCHAIR

3.2 Wheelchairs

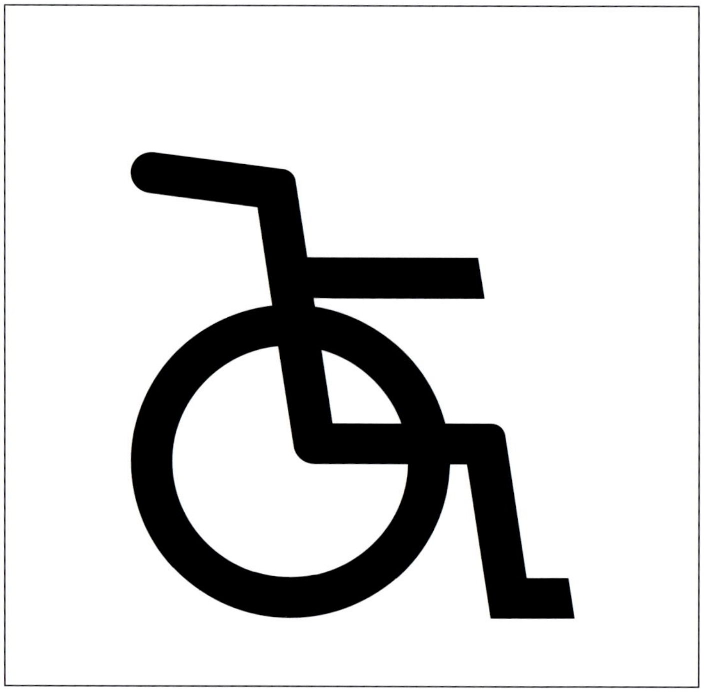

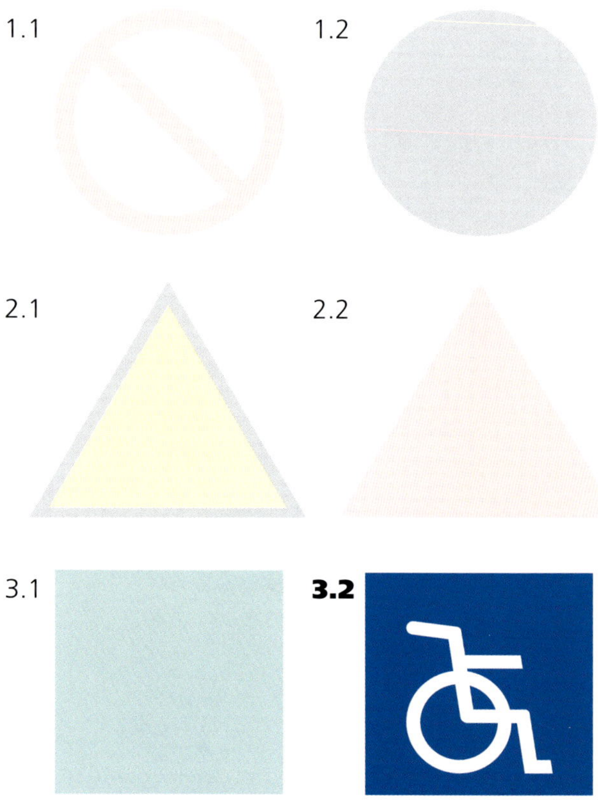

4007

SHORT-SLEEVED GOWN,
(OPTIONAL ALPHA-NUMERIC ON THE CHEST FOR ROOM IDENTIFICATION)
3.2 Examination room

1.1 1.2 2.1 2.2 3.1 **3.2**

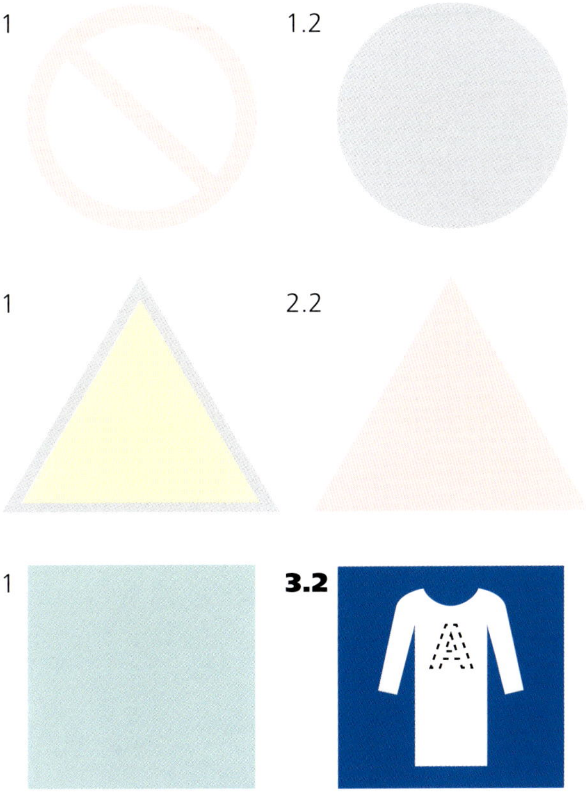

4008

EAR
3.2 Hearing, audiology

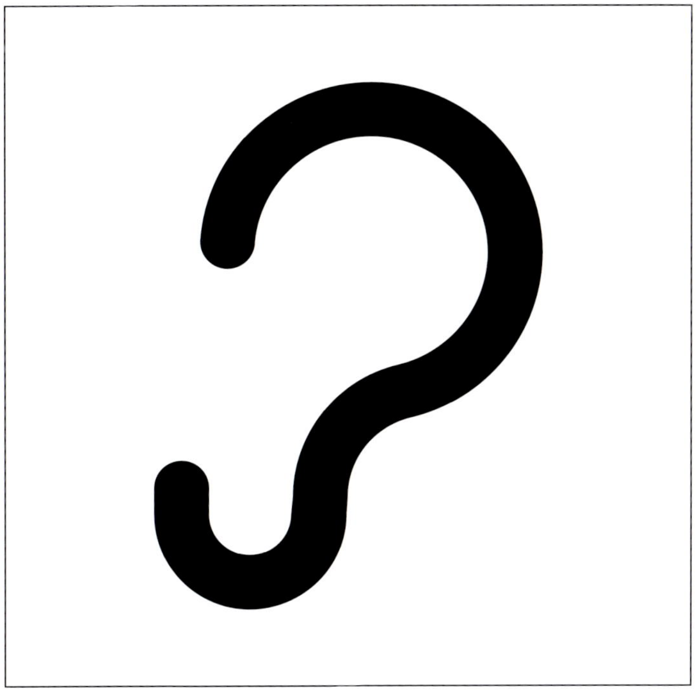

1.1 1.2 2.1 2.2 3.1 **3.2**

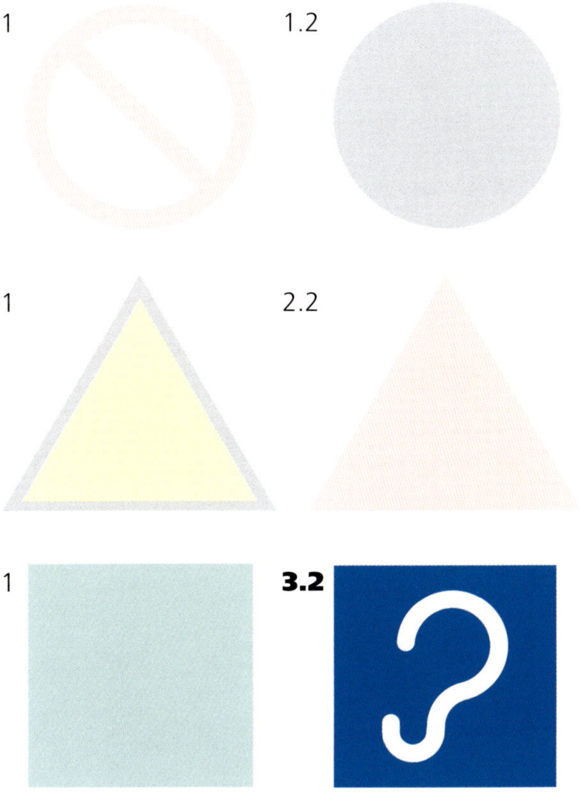

4009

EYE

3.2 Eye, ophthalmology

4010

HUMAN HEAD, DOTS AT EAR, NOSE AND THROAT

3.2 ENT (Ear, nose and throat), otolaryngology

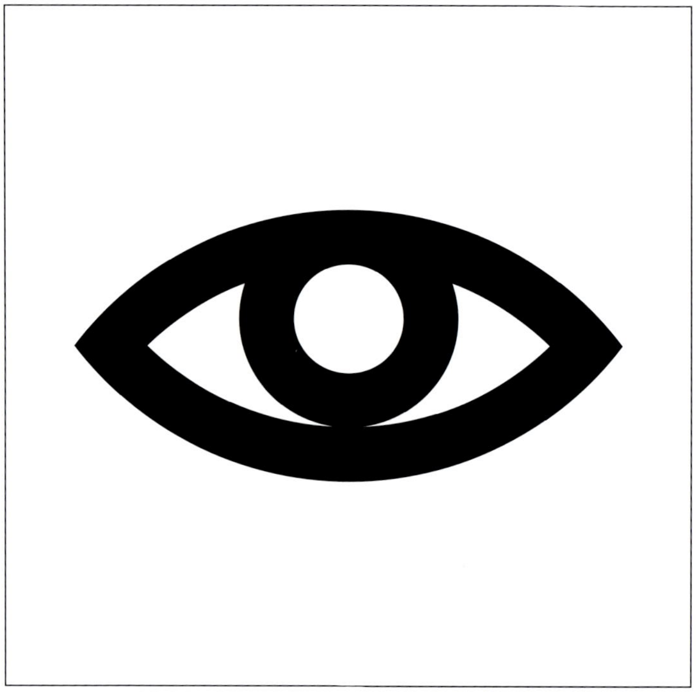

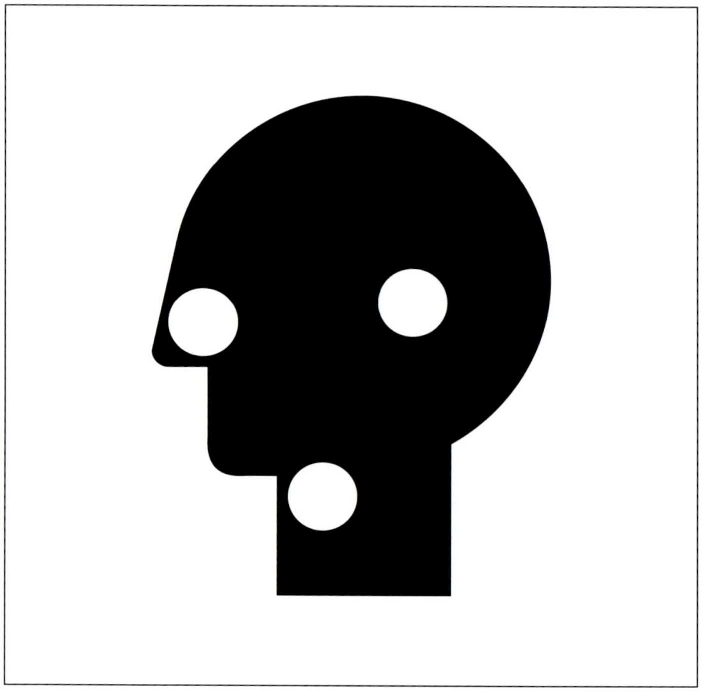

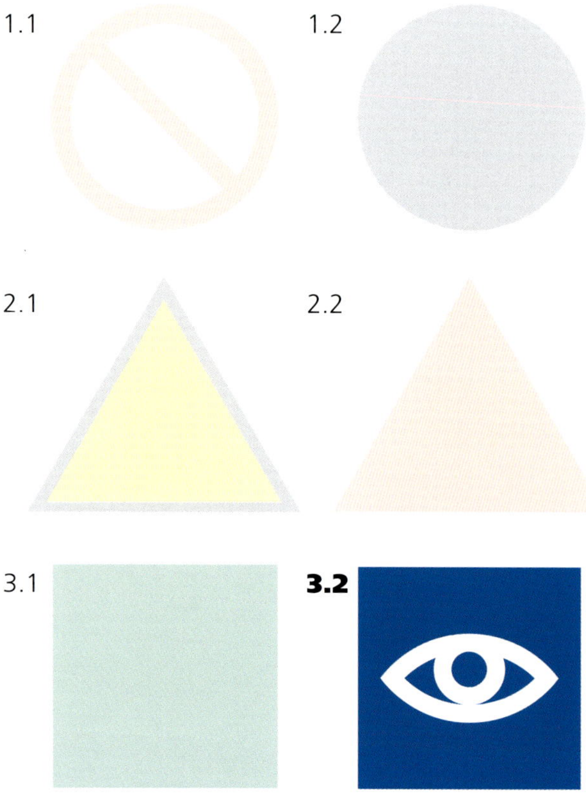

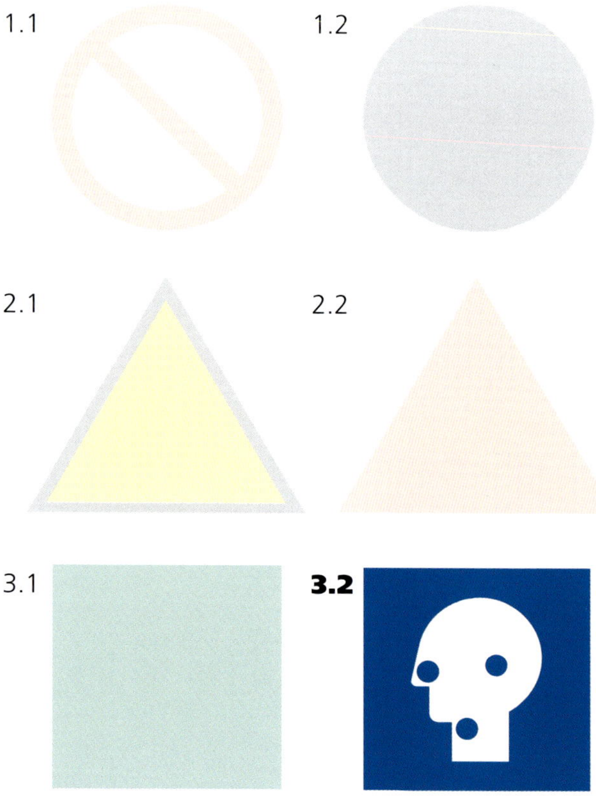

4011

MOUTH

3.2 Speech therapy

4012

HAND, PALM, WITH SPOTS

3.2 Skin therapy, dermatology

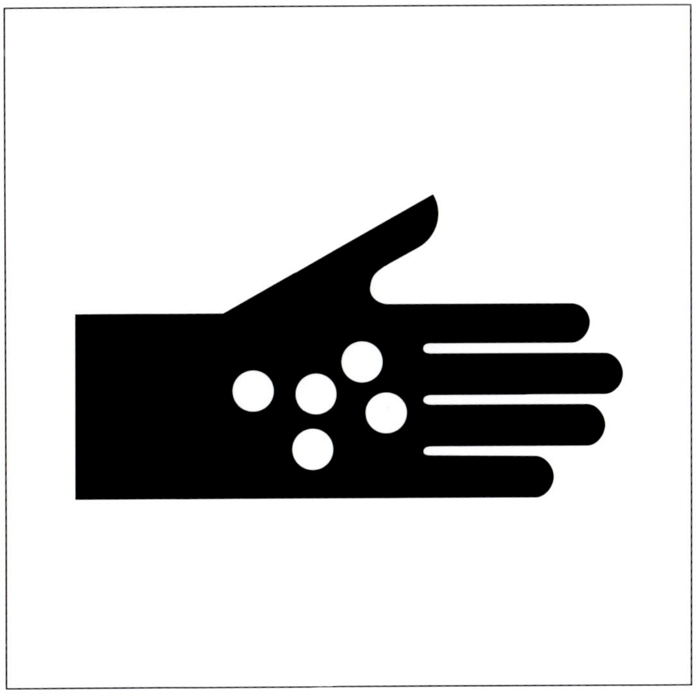

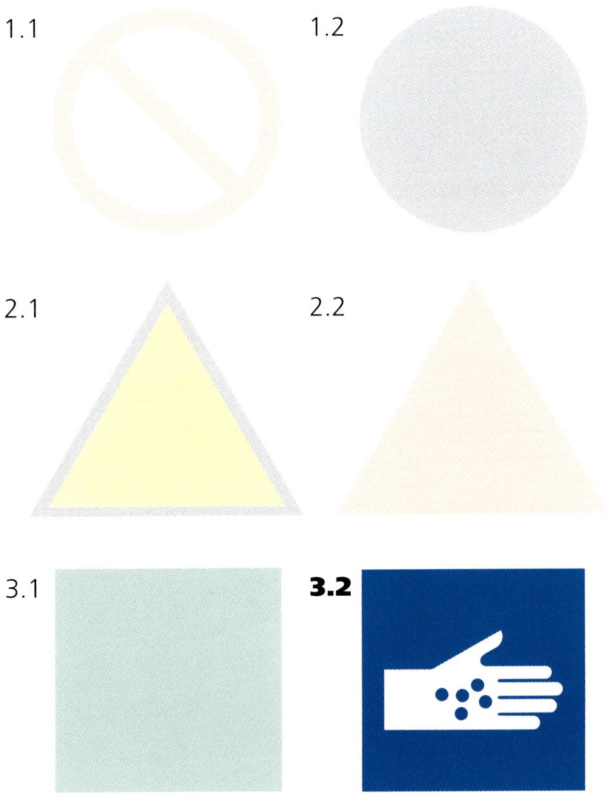

4013

FOOTPRINT

1.1 No bare feet

3.2 Podiatry

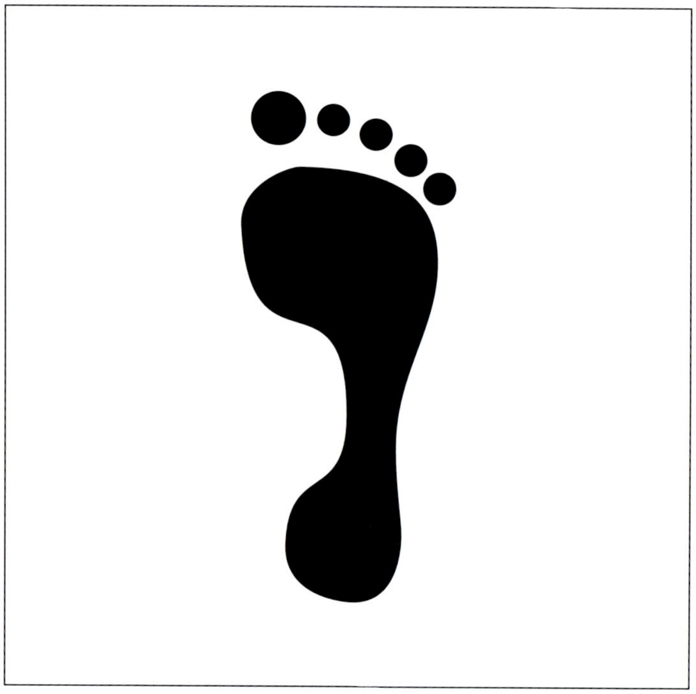

1.1

1.2

2.1

2.2

3.1

3.2

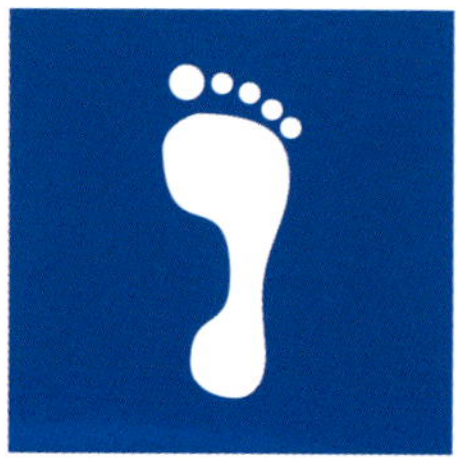

4014

PAIR OF KIDNEY SHAPES, FACING EACH OTHER

3.2 Kidney, renal

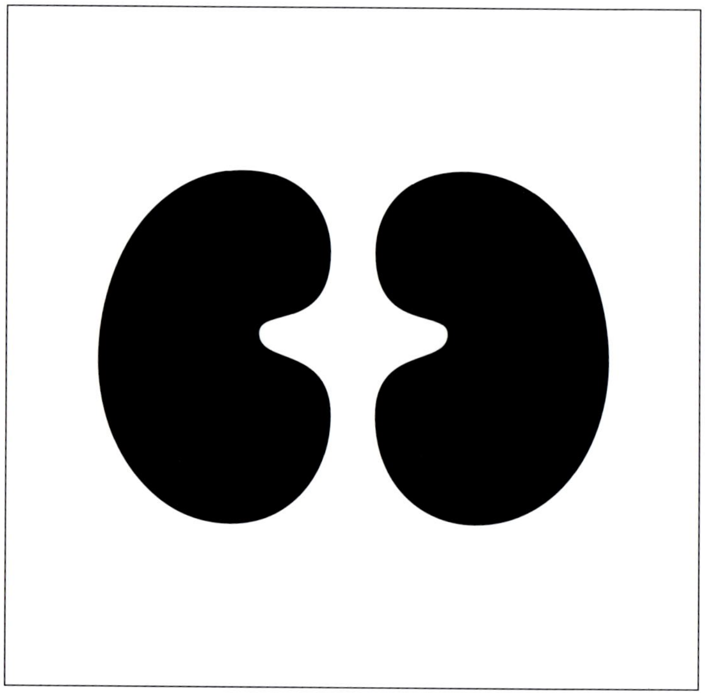

1.1

1.2

2.1

2.2

3.1

3.2

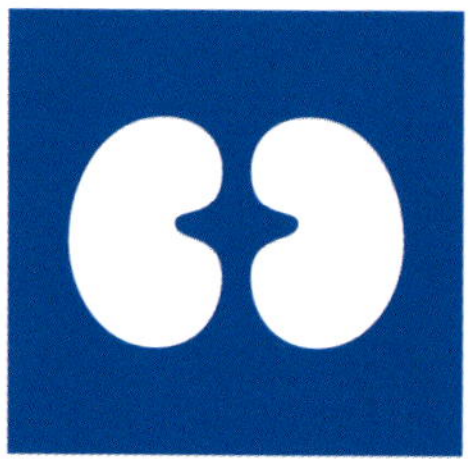

4015

WATER DROPS, HORIZONTAL BAR

3.2 Kidney dialysis, filter

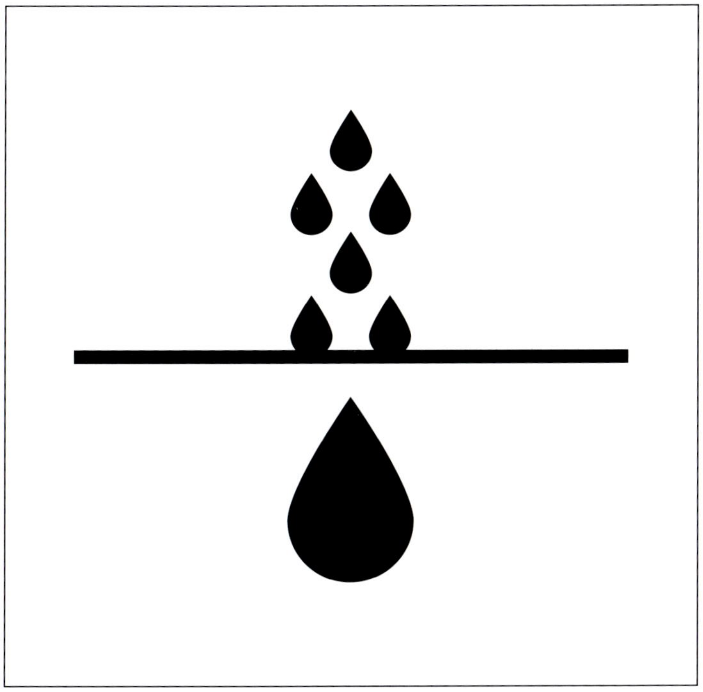

1.1

1.2

2.1

2.2

3.1

3.2

4016

BALLOONS

1.1 No balloons allowed

3.2 Gift shop

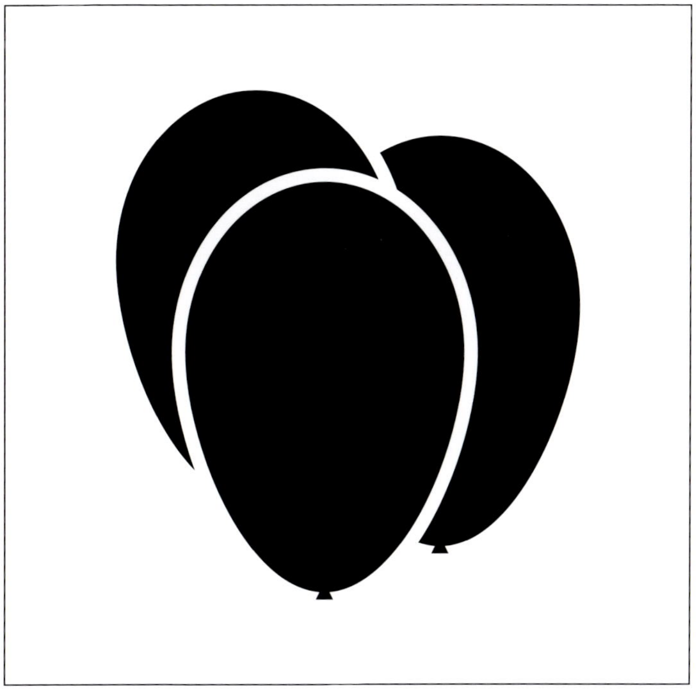

1.1

1.2

2.1

2.2

3.1

3.2

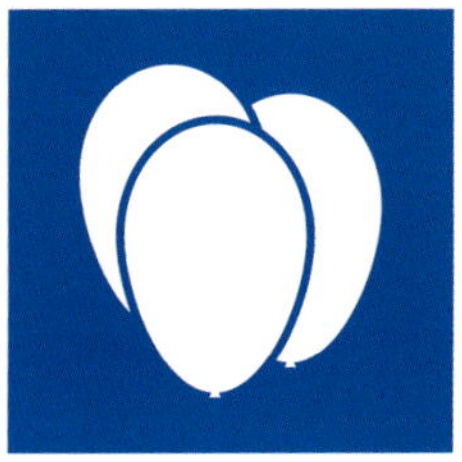

4017

PENIS, TESTICLES

3.2 Urology

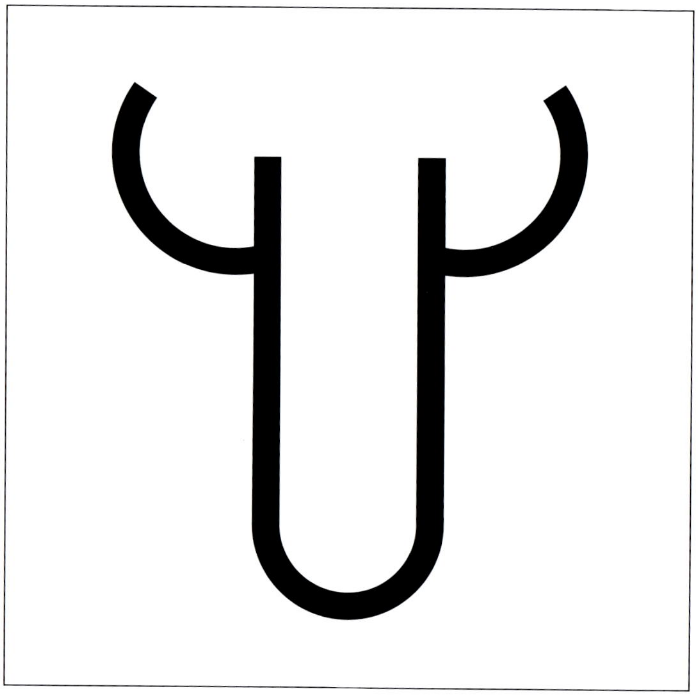

4018

SYMBOL FOR MALE IN BIOLOGY

3.2 Male medicine, male

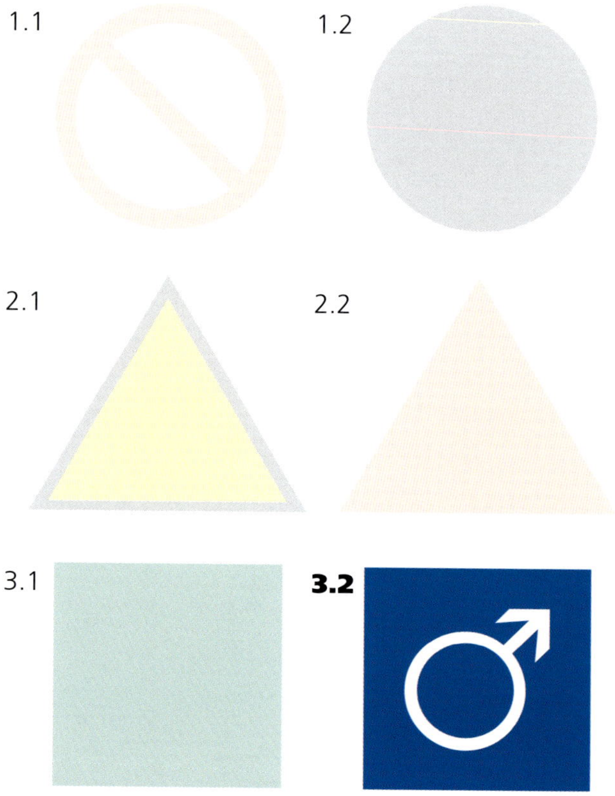

4019

SYMBOL FOR FEMALE IN BIOLOGY

3.2 Female medicine, gynecology

4020

VALENTINE-SHAPED HEART

3.2 Heart, cardiology

0
1
2
3
4
5
6
7
8
Index

4021

TOOTH WITH CROWN, NECK AND ROOT

3.2 Dental services

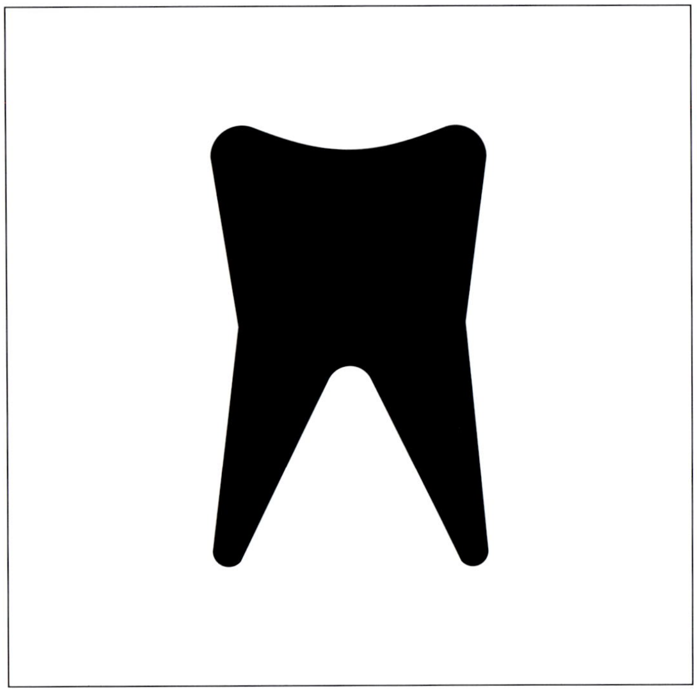

4022

SUNBURST

3.2 Mental health

4023

BABY, UNWRAPPED DIAPER

3.2 Babies (ward), nursery

4024

BABIES, LYING ON BACK

3.2 Maternity (ward)

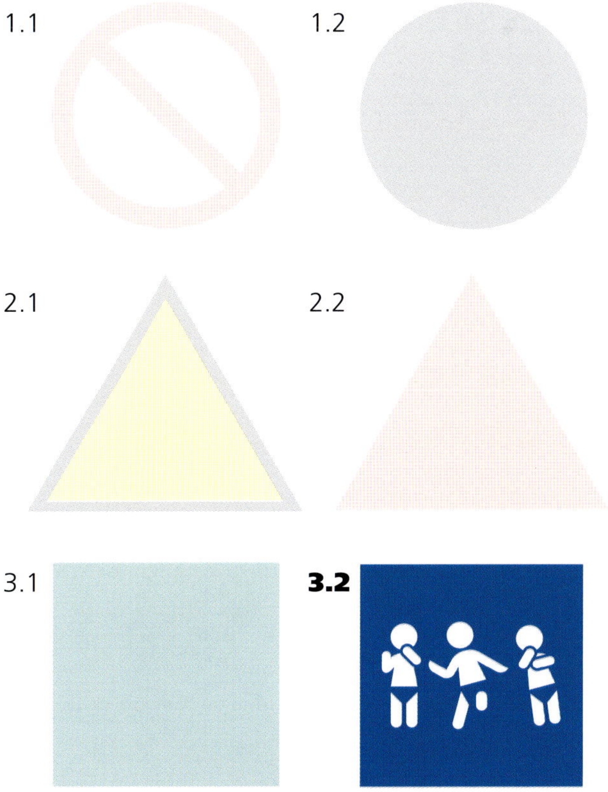

4025

BABY'S BOTTLE WITH NIPPLE

3.2 Nursery

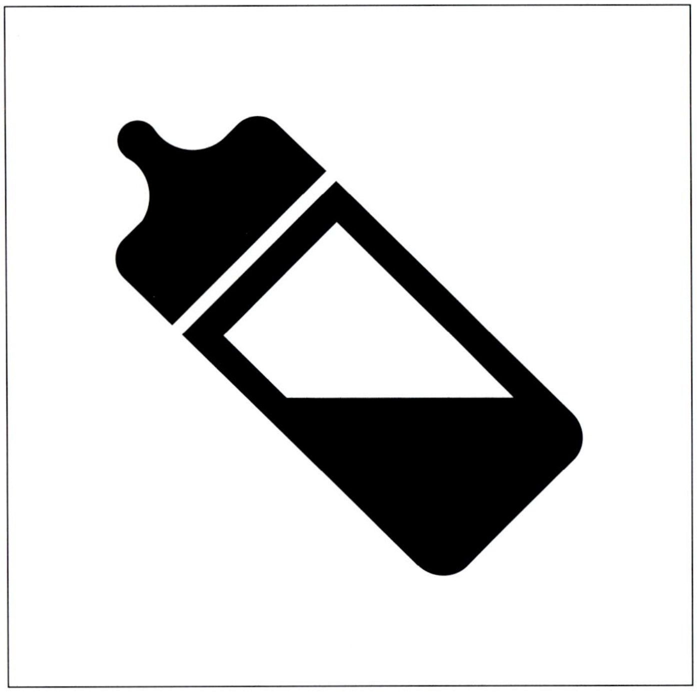

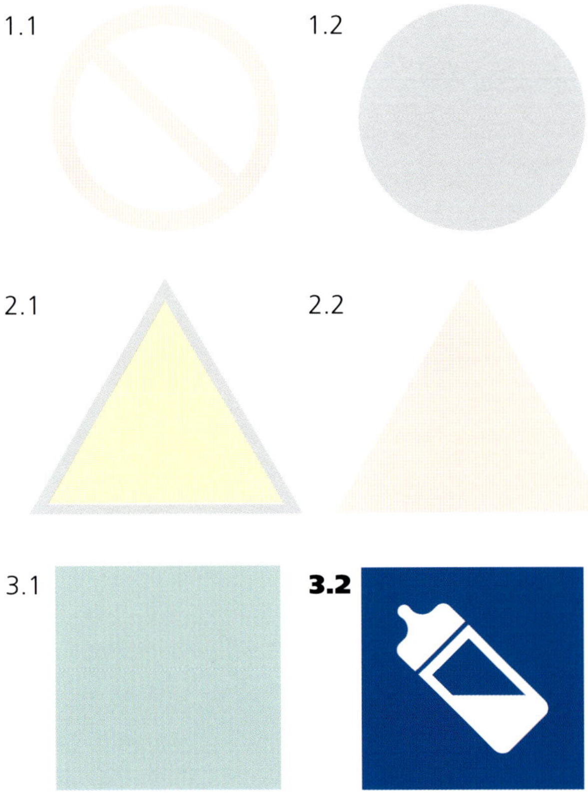

4026

BABY'S HEAD, AT BREAST

3.2 Breast-feeding (area)

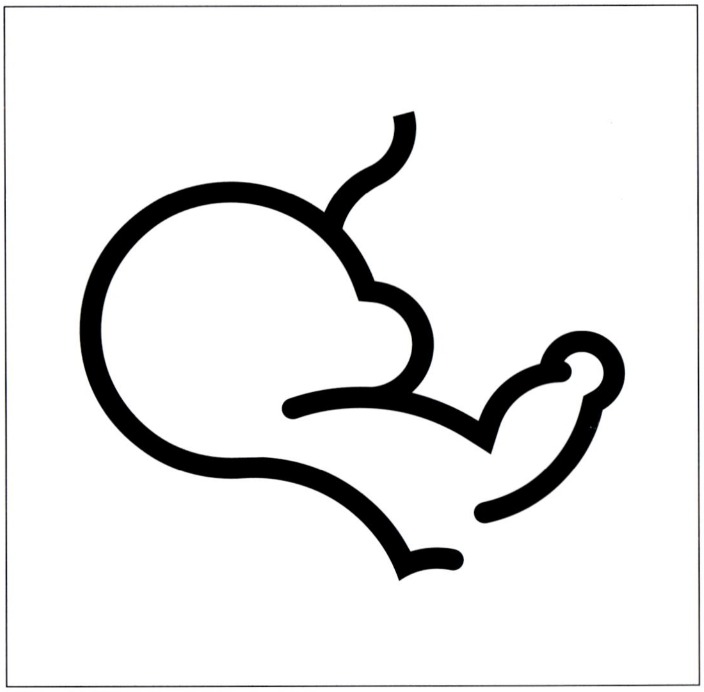

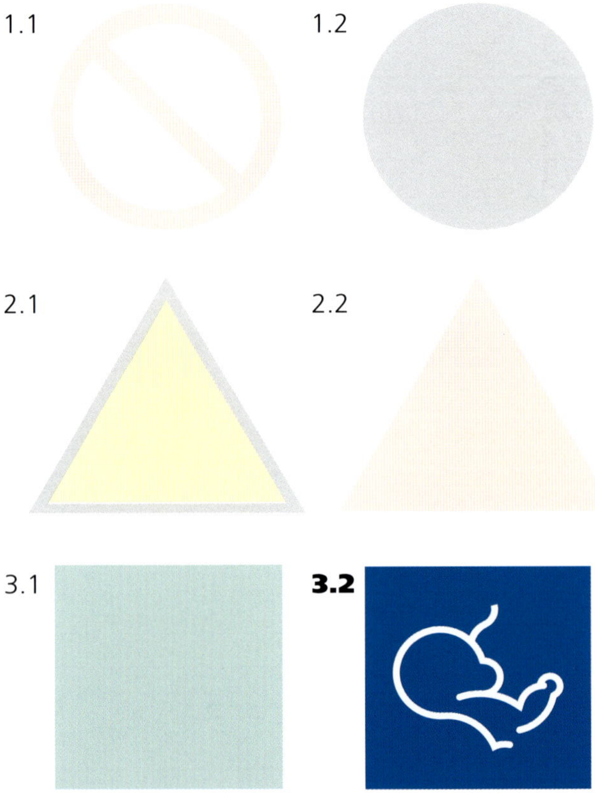

4027

CHILD

1.1 No children allowed

3.2 Children

1.1

1.2

2.1

2.2

3.1

3.2

4028

HUMAN FIGURES, ADULT, INFANT

3.2 Child care, day care

1.1

1.2

2.1

2.2

3.1

3.2

0
1
2
3
4
5
6
7
8
Index

4029

ROCKING HORSE

3.2 Toy room, play room

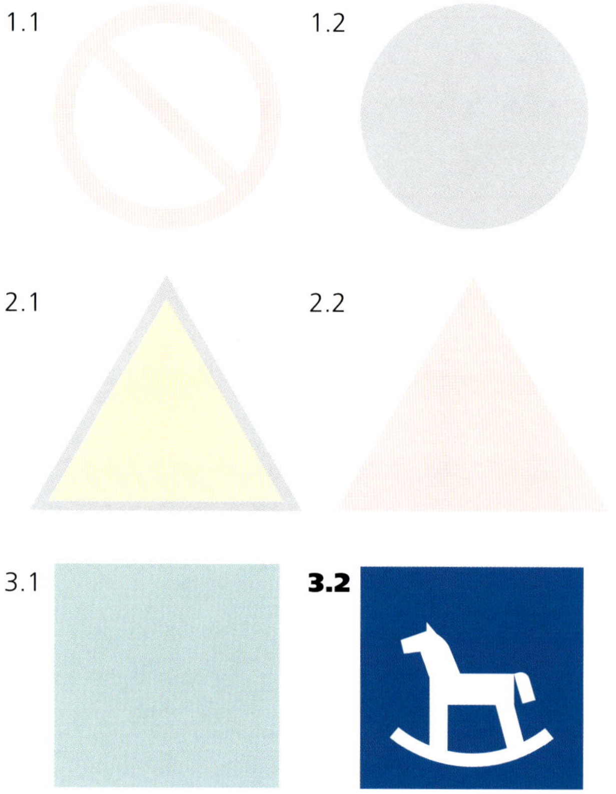

4030

LATEX GLOVE

1.2 Latex gloves must be worn

3.2 Latex gloves

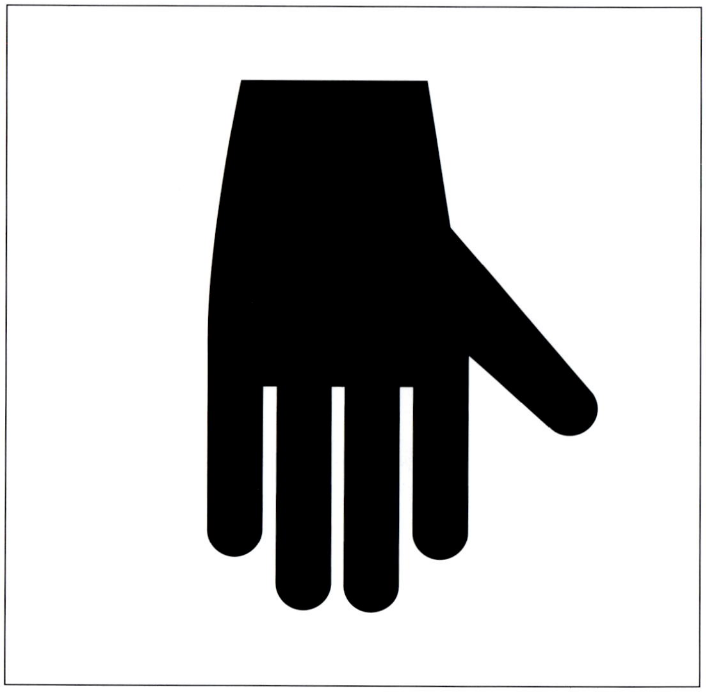

4031

HUMAN HEAD, WITH MEDICAL MASK

1.2 Medical mask must be worn

3.2 Medical mask(s)

1.1

1.2

2.1

2.2

3.1

3.2

4032

HUMAN HEAD, WITH HAIR NET

1.2 Hair net must be worn

3.2 Hair net(s)

1.1

1.2

2.1

2.2

3.1

3.2

0
1
2
3
4
5
6
7
8
Index

4033

RECTANGLES, SQUARES, CIRCLES, OVER HORIZONTAL BARS

3.2 Medical supplies, storage

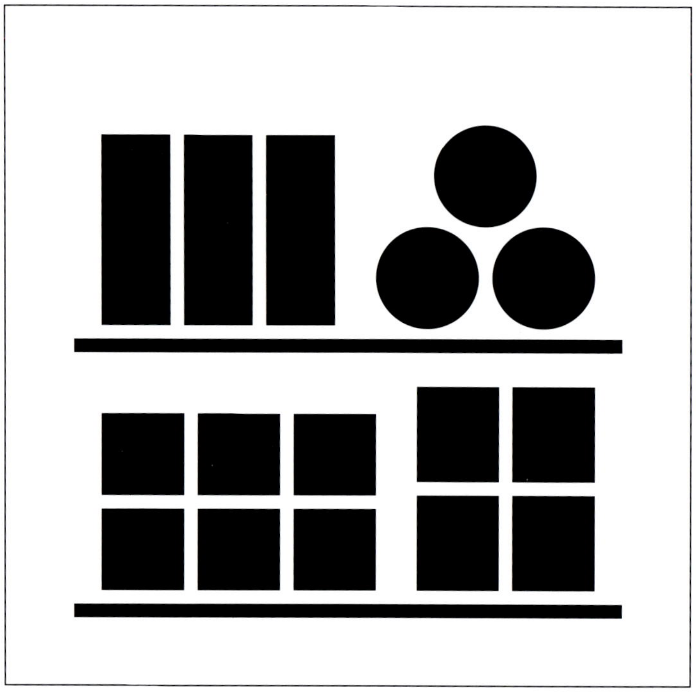

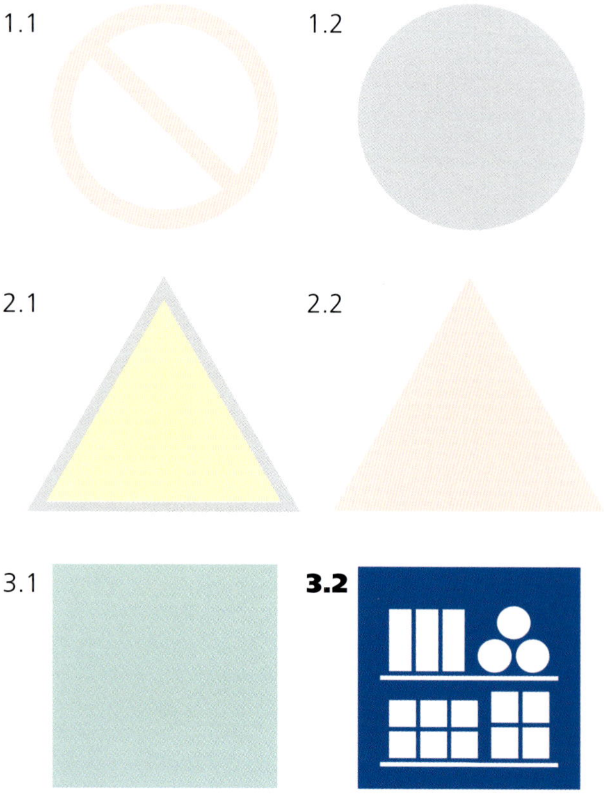

4034

WATER DROPS, OVER CLASPED HANDS

1.2 Wash your hands

3.2 Hand-washing station

4035

HUMAN FIGURE, REVEALING INTERIOR BONES

2.1 Caution! X ray

3.2 X ray

1.1

1.2

2.1

2.2

3.1

3.2

4036

IONIZING RADIATION

2.1 Caution! Ionizing radiation

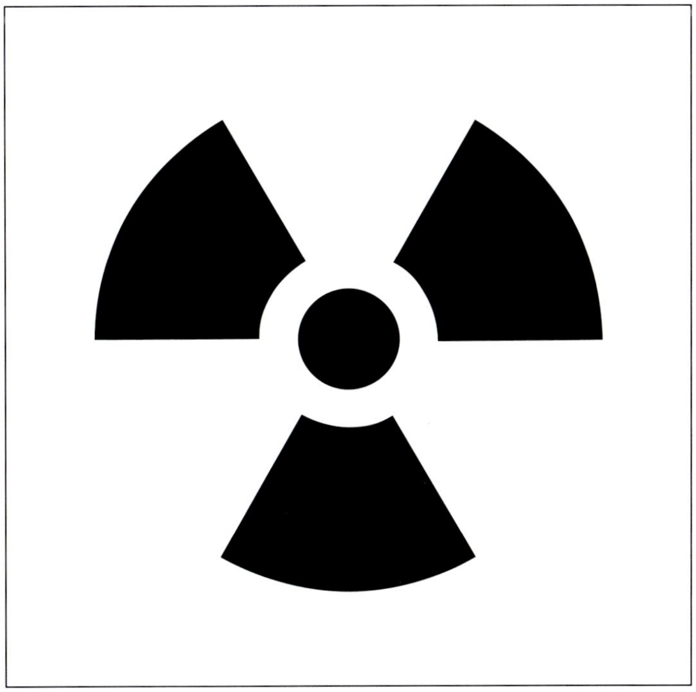

1.1

1.2

2.1

2.2

3.1

3.2

0
1
2
3
4
5
6
7
8
Index

4037

BIOHAZARD

2.2 Danger! Biohazard

1.1

1.2

2.1

2.2

3.1

3.2

4038

COMPRESSED GAS CYLINDER, WITH GAUGE

2.2 Danger! Compressed gas

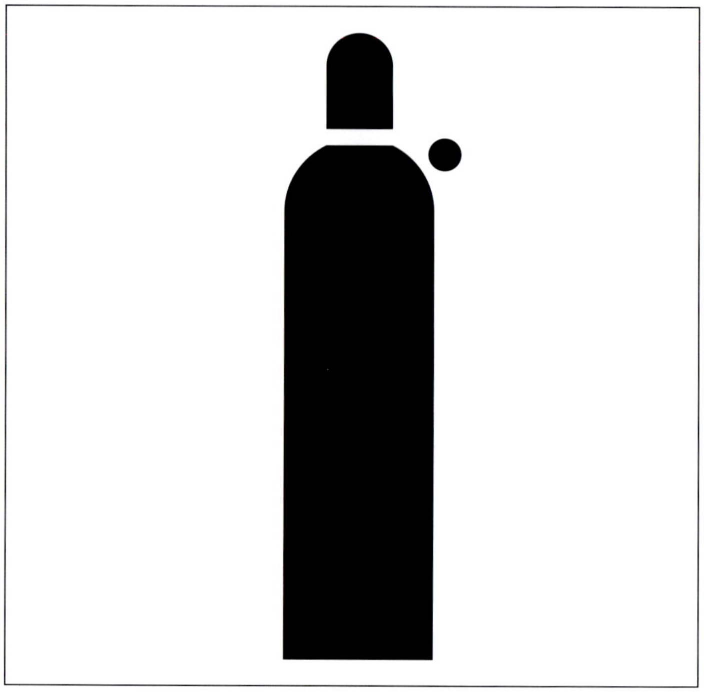

1.1

1.2

2.1

2.2

3.1

3.2

4039

MICROSCOPE

3.2 Laboratories

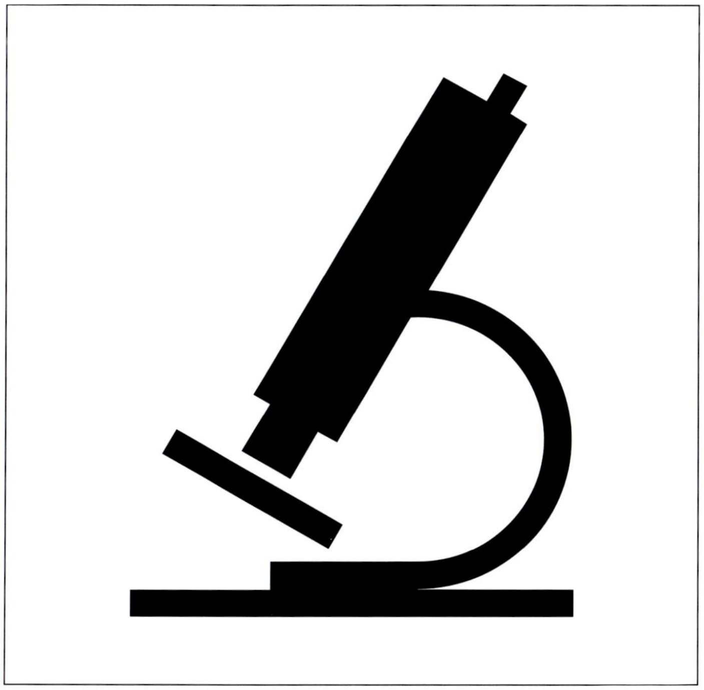

4040

TEARDROP SHAPE, WITH GREEK CROSS INSIDE

3.2 Bloodwork, hematology

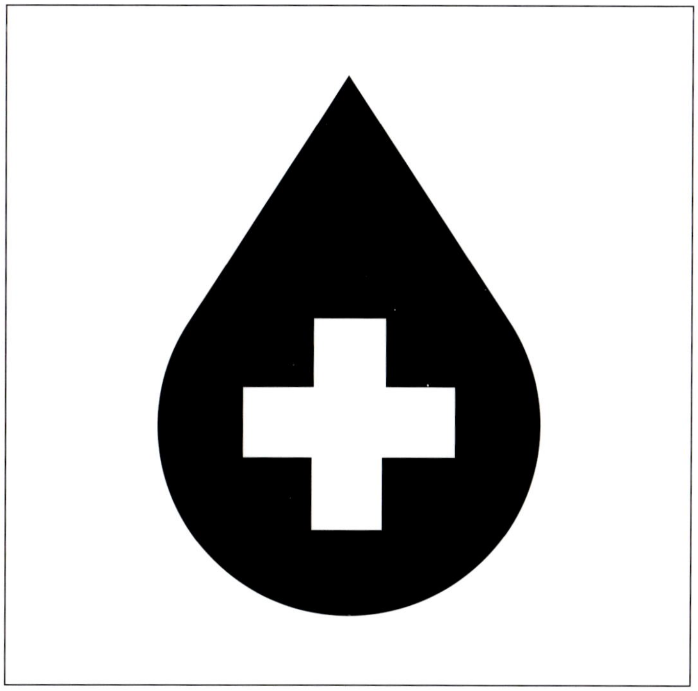

4041

HUMAN FIGURE, ON HORIZONTAL PLANE, RAYS RADIATING

2.1 Caution! Radiotherapy

3.2 Radiotherapy

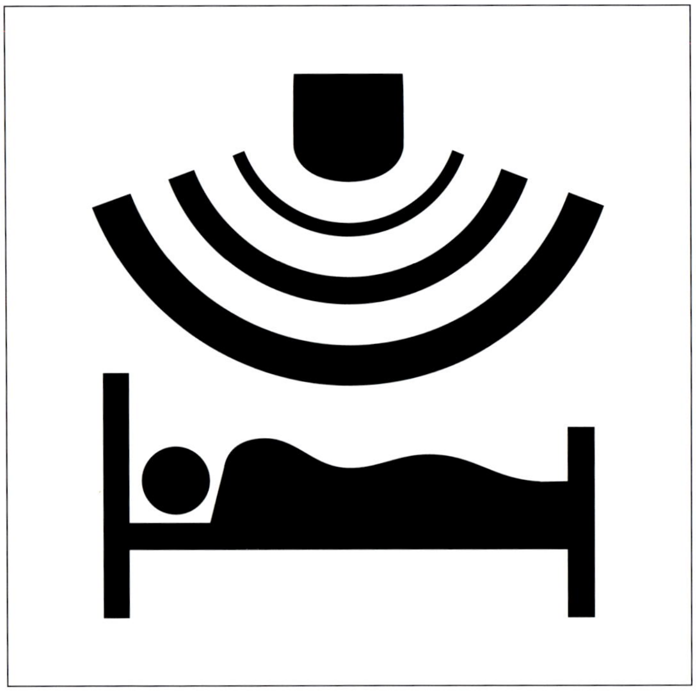

1.1

1.2

2.1

2.2

3.1

3.2

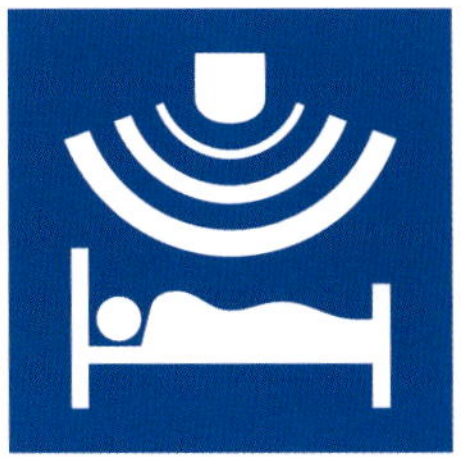

4042

OK

3.2 Clean, sterilized utility

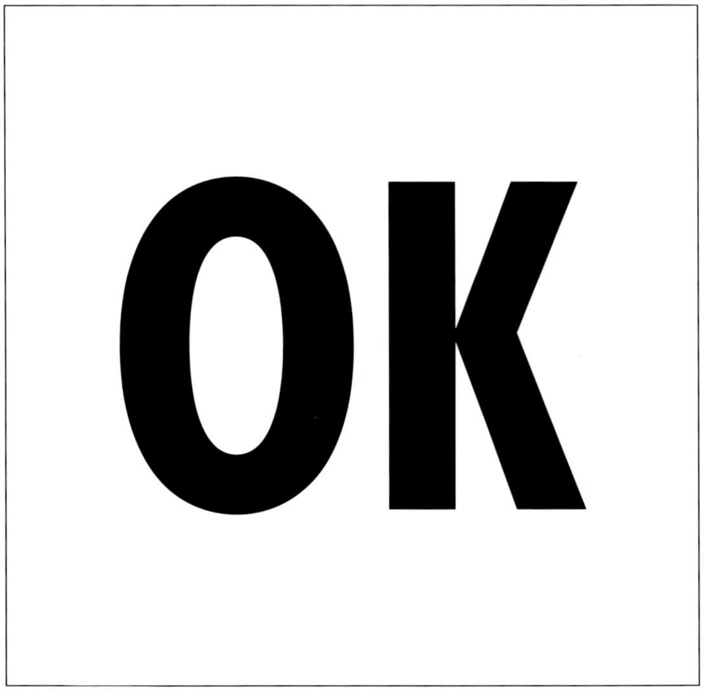

1.1

1.2

2.1

2.2

3.1

3.2

4043

OK, CROSSED OVER

3.2 Soiled, unsterilized utility

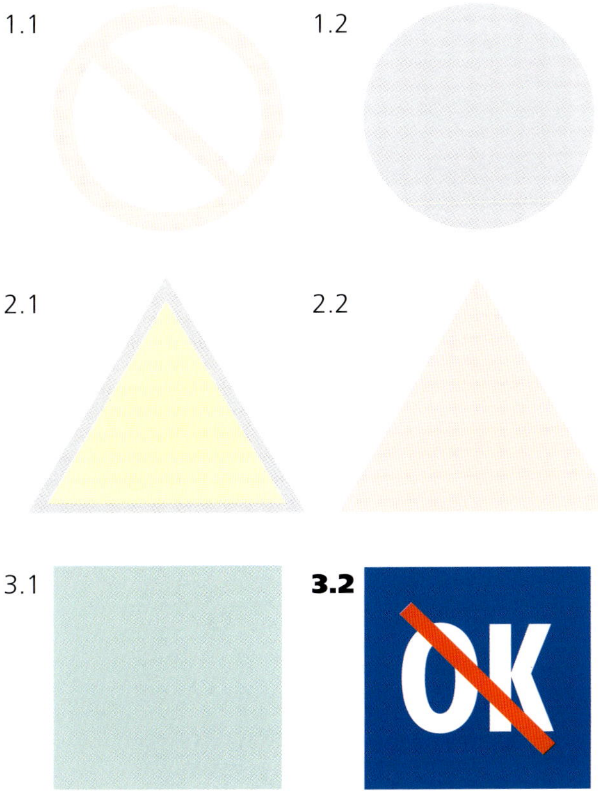

4044

OPEN BOOK, WITH GREEK CROSS INSIDE

3.2 Medical records

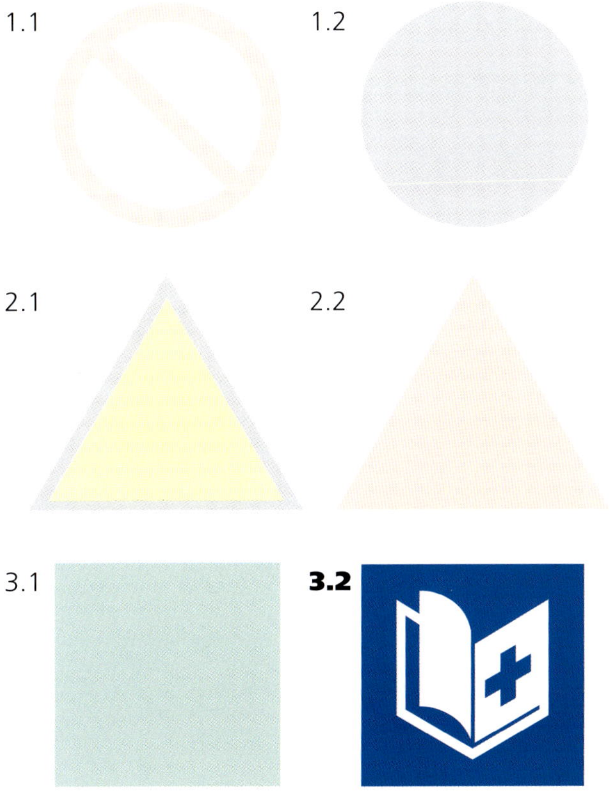

4045

ICU

3.2 ICU, intensive care unit

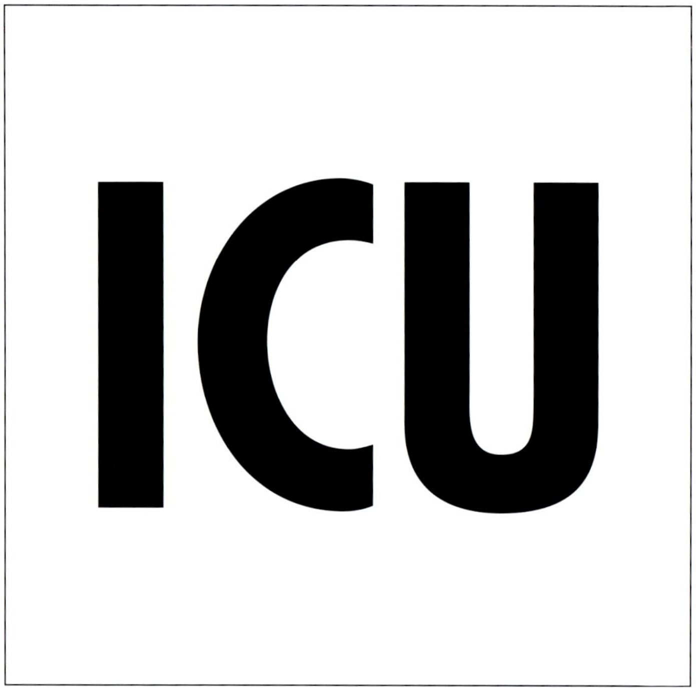

1.1 1.2 2.1 2.2 3.1

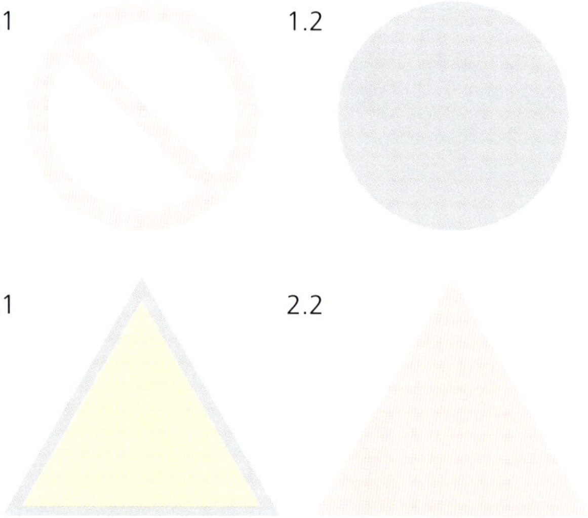

3.2

4046

ARMS, SUPPORTING CIRCLE

3.2 Supportive, palliative care

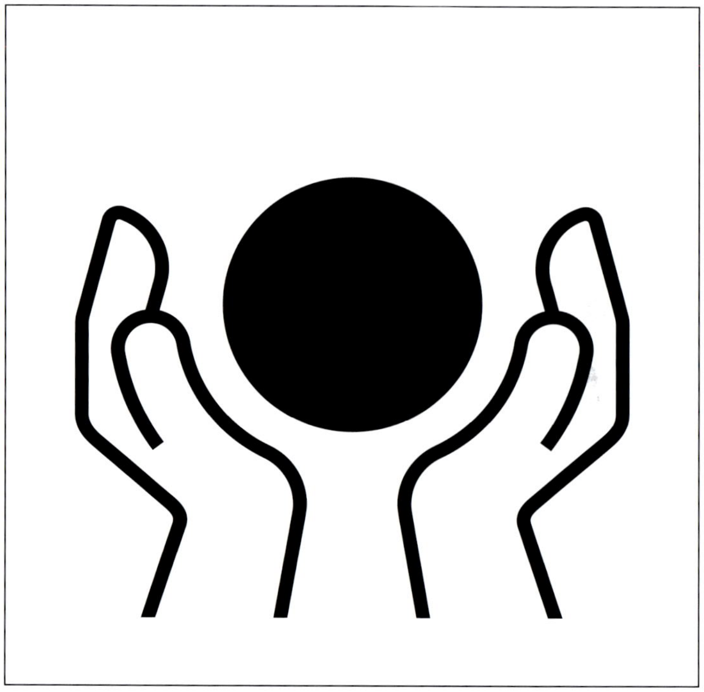

1.1 1.2 2.1 2.2 3.1

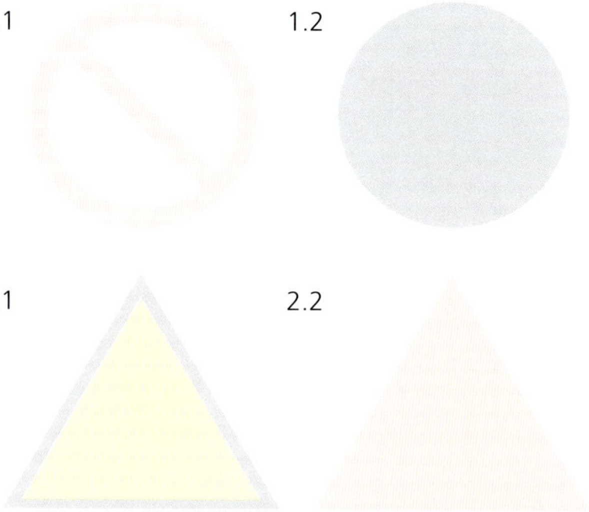

3.2

4047

DOT, INSIDE BOX, WITH MANY DOTS OUTSIDE

3.1 Isolation

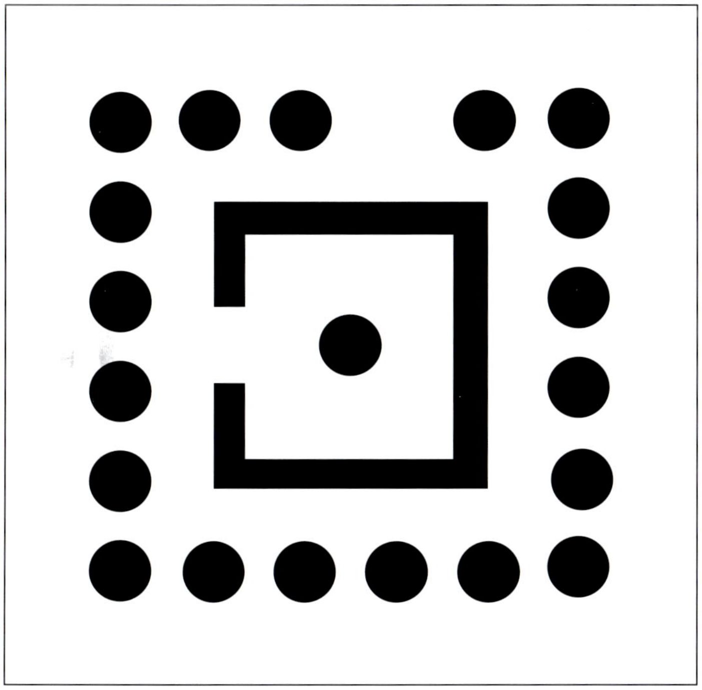

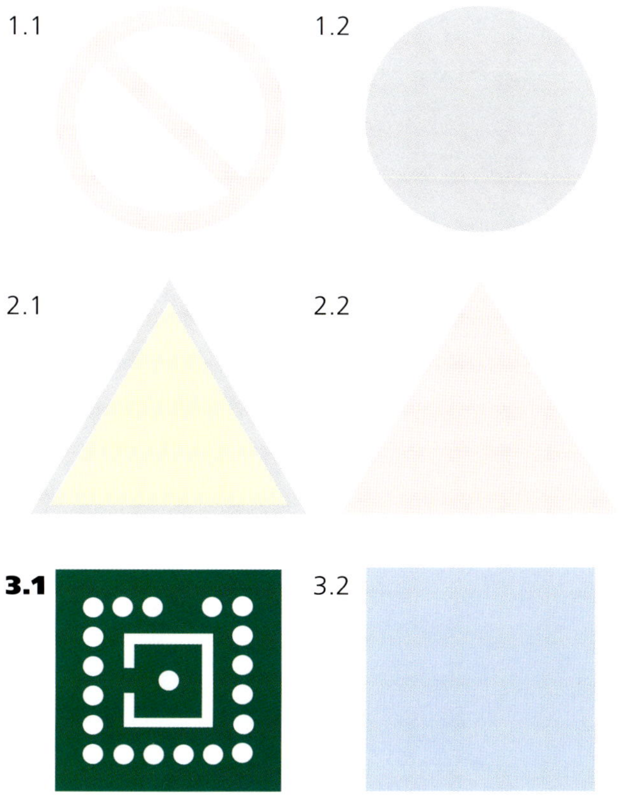

4048

HUMAN FIGURE, IN BED

3.2 Recovery room, bed rest

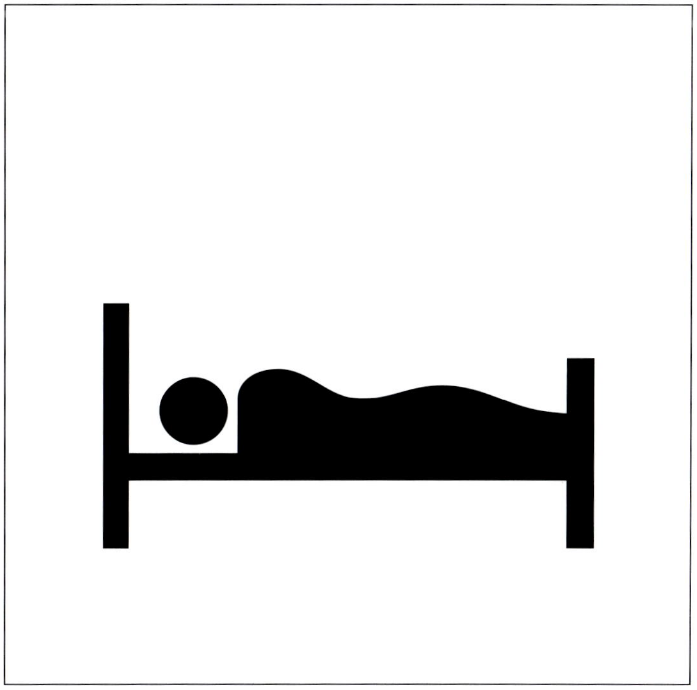

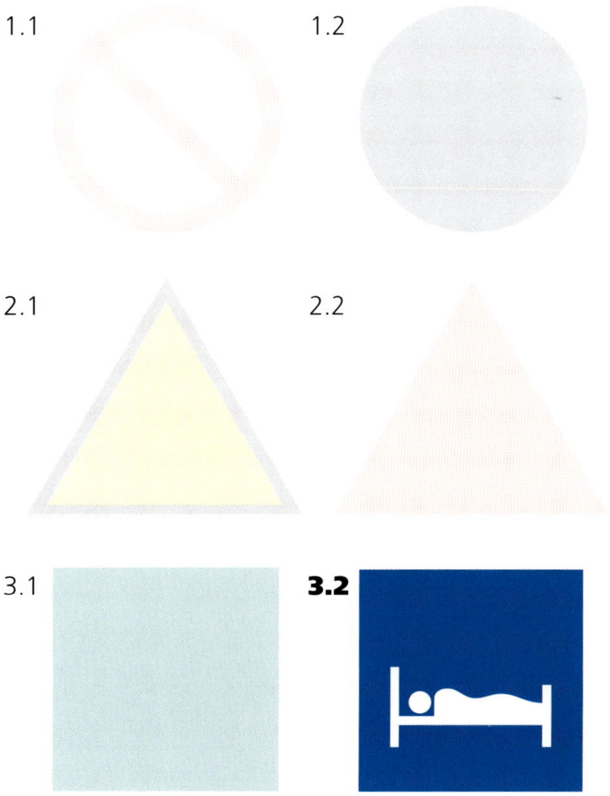

4049

BED AND PILLOW

3.2 Quiet room, resting room

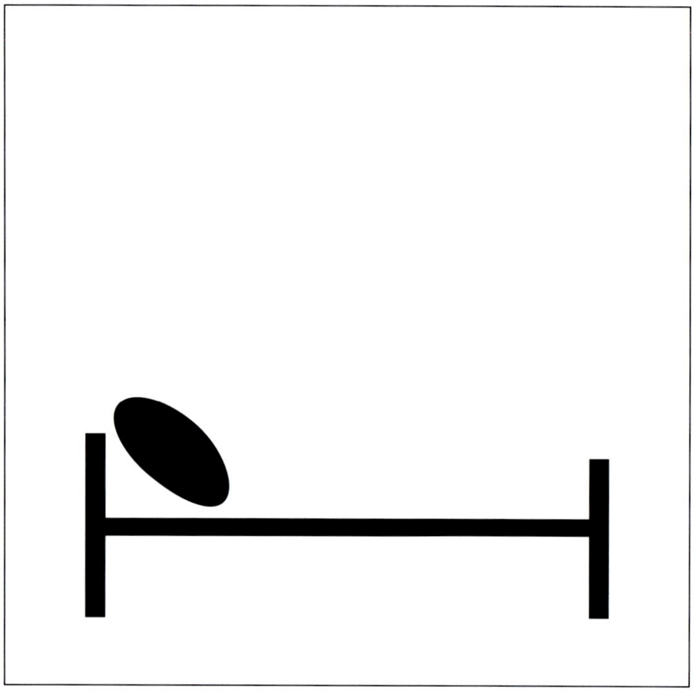

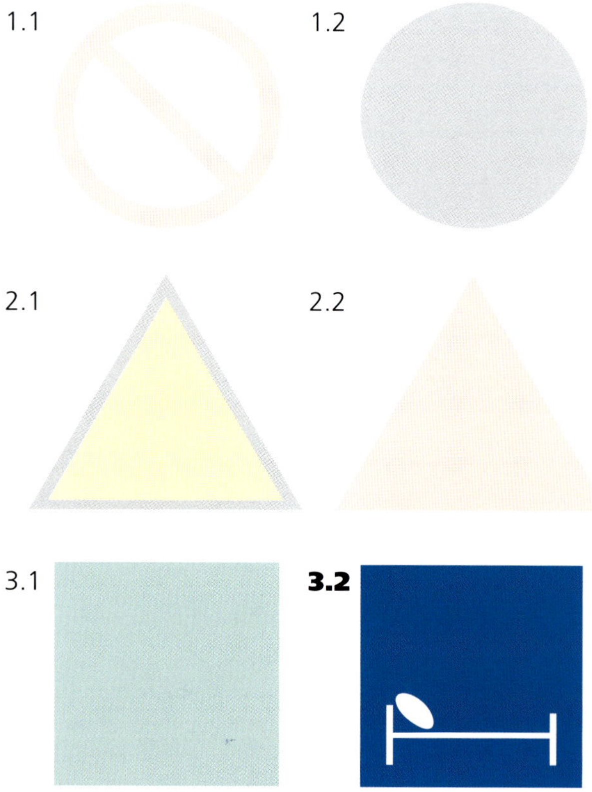

4050

BATHTUB

3.2 Bath, bathroom

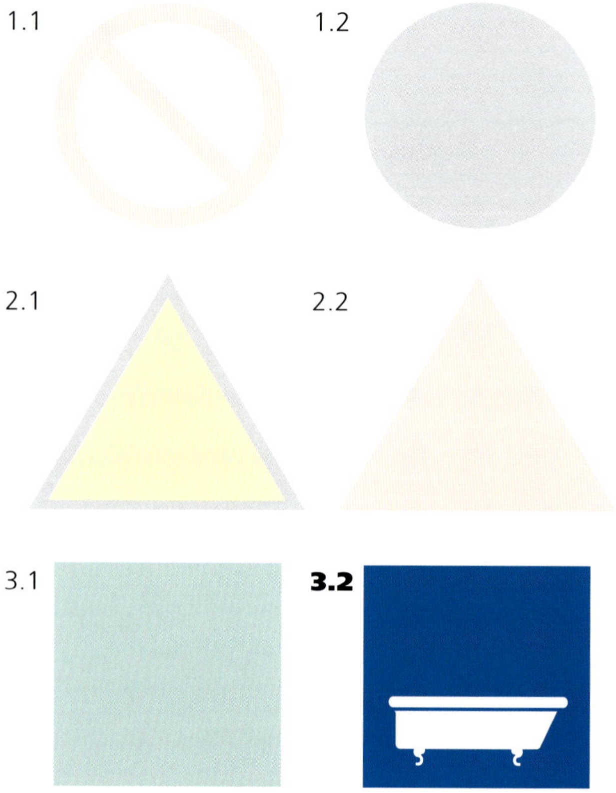

4051

SHOWER HEAD, WATER DROPS

3.2 Shower

4052

SHEETS, FOLDED AND STACKED

3.2 Linen, housekeeping

4053

HUMAN FIGURES, OVERHEAD PROJECTOR

3.2 Screening room

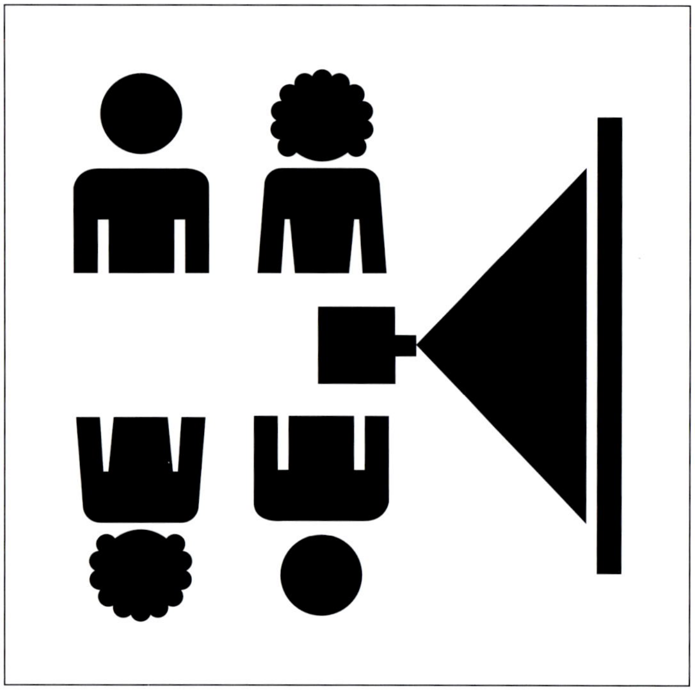

1.1

1.2

2.1

2.2

3.1

3.2

4054

HUMAN FIGURES, AROUND TABLE

3.2 Meeting room

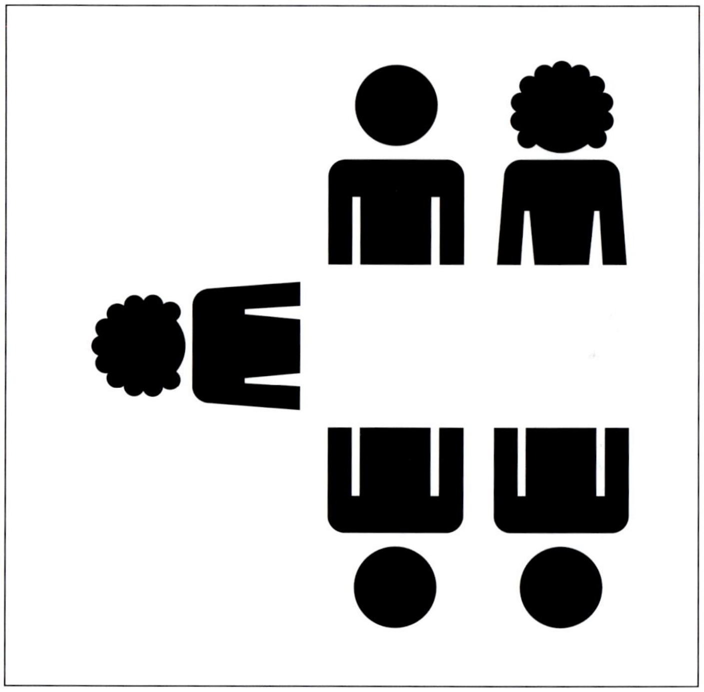

1.1

1.2

2.1

2.2

3.1

3.2

4055

MORTAR WITH GREEK CROSS, PESTLE

3.2 Pharmacy, drugstore

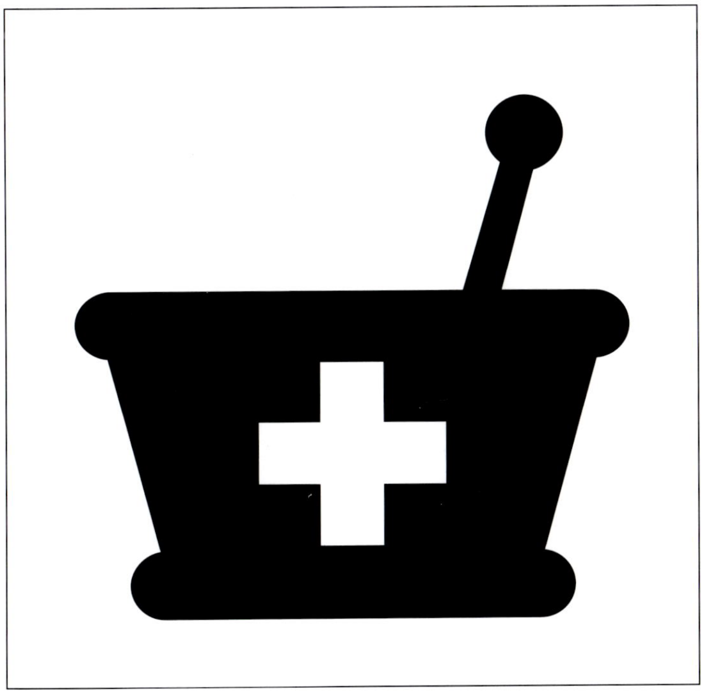

1.1

1.2 

2.1 

2.2 

3.1 

3.2 

4056

ELEVATOR, MORTAR AND PESTLE

3.2 Pharmacy elevator

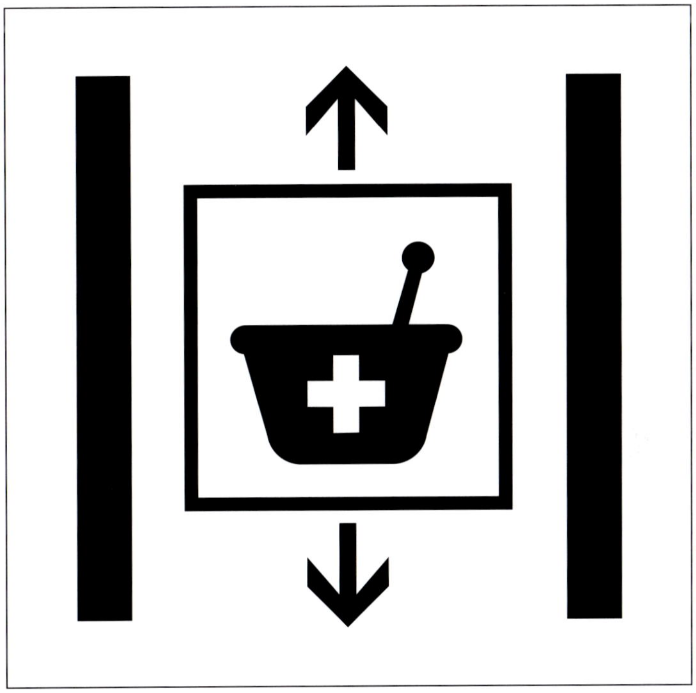

1.1

1.2 

2.1 

2.2 

3.1 

3.2 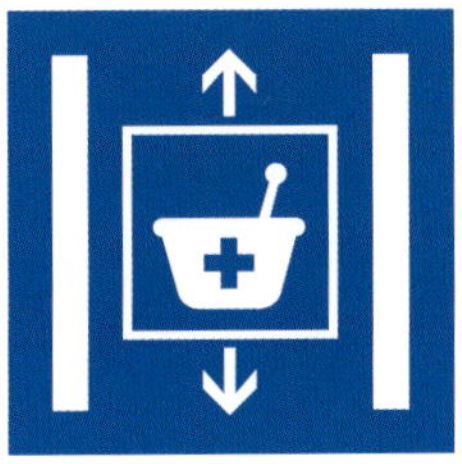

4057

EVERGREEN TREE, WITH BRANCH MISSING

3.2 Rehabilitation

1.1

1.2

2.1

2.2

3.1

3.2

4058

HUMAN FIGURES, AROUND TABLE

3.2 Activity room

1.1

1.2

2.1

2.2

3.1

3.2

4059

SIX LAYERS OF WATER SYMBOLS

3.2 Hydrotherapy

4060

HUMAN FIGURE, ARMS OUTSTRETCHED, HOLDING WEIGHTS

3.2 Physiotherapy

4061

HUMAN HEAD, WITH CHEF'S HAT

3.2 Cook(ing), kitchen

4062

CHURCH

3.2 Church

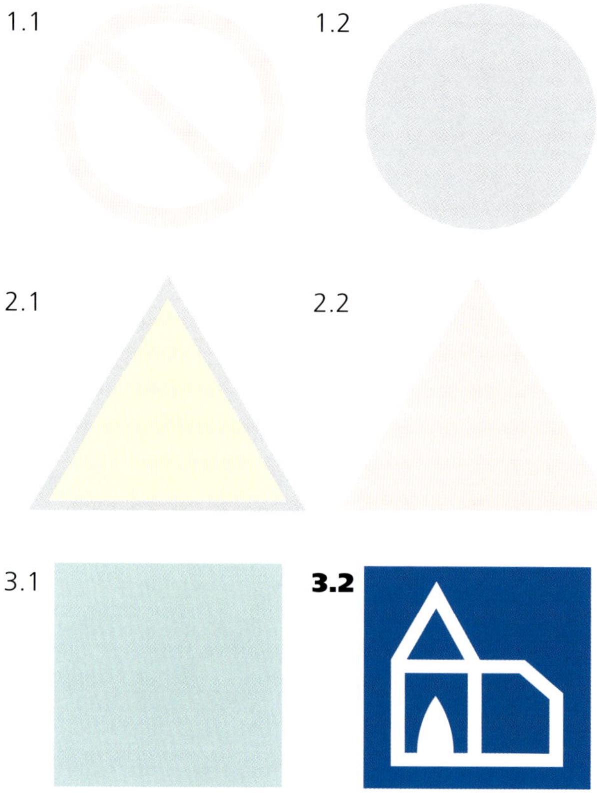

4063

PAIR OF HANDS, PRAYING

3.2 Worship, chapel

4064

SKULL AND CROSSBONES

2.2 Danger! Poison

3.2 Death, morgue

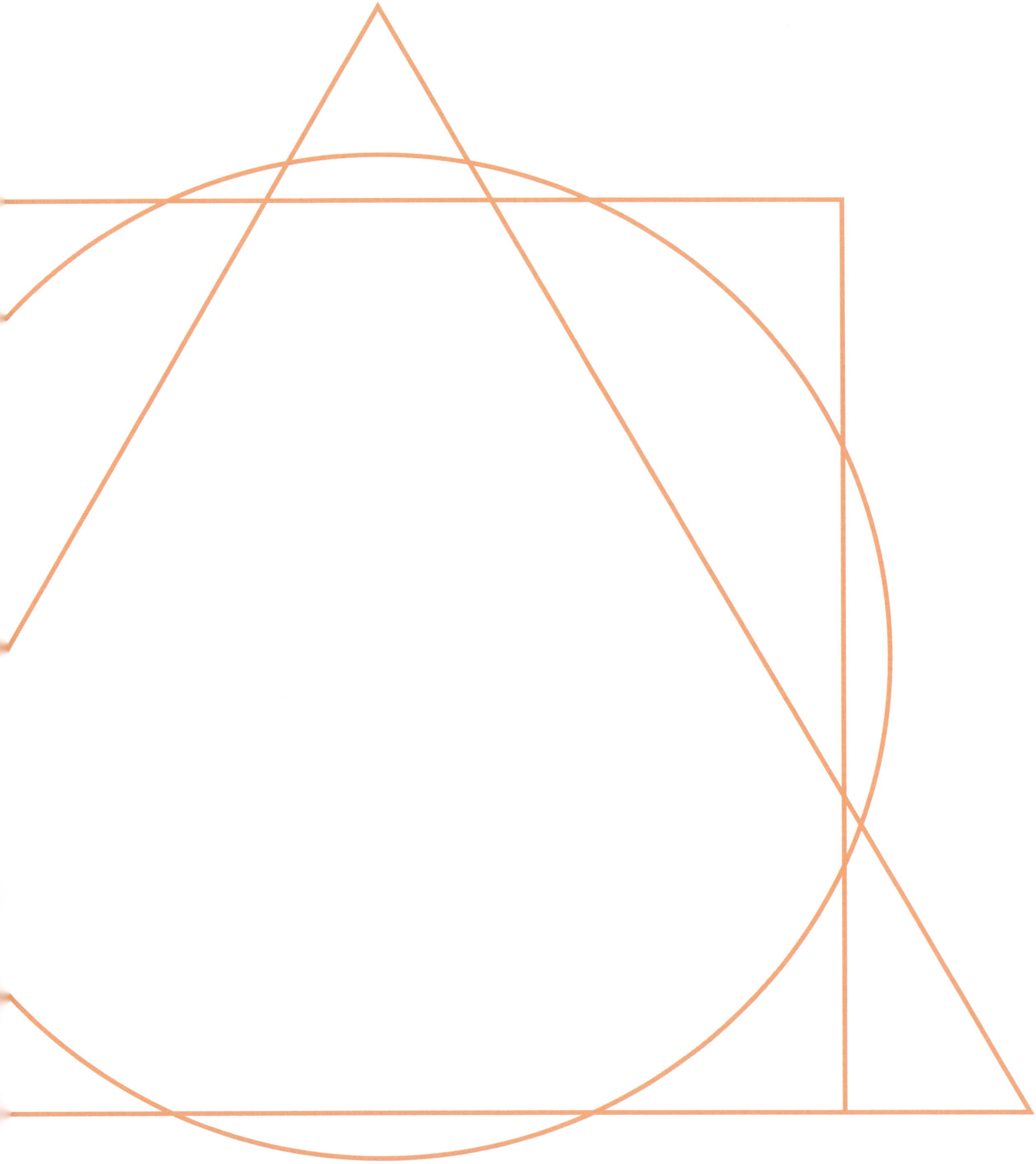

5001

DISC, WITH ARROW POINTING TO DIRECTION

1.2 One way (left, right, straight)

1.2

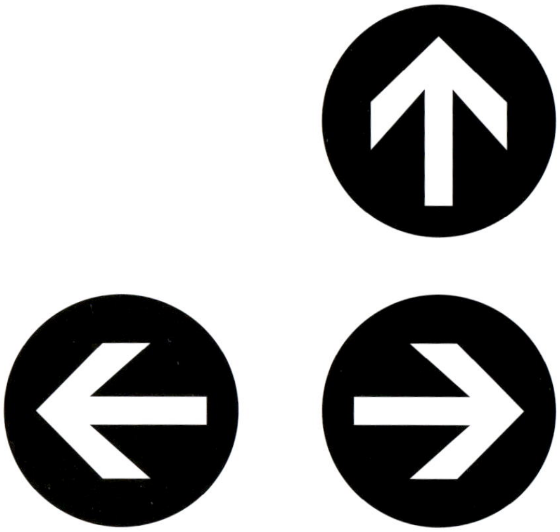

5002

BICYCLE

1.1 No bicycling

2.1 Caution! Bicycles

3.2 Bicycles

1.1

1.2

2.1

2.2

3.1

3.2

5003

BICYCLE, WITH RIDER

1.1 No bicycling

2.1 Caution! Bicyclers

3.2 Bicycling

5004

BICYCLE, IN THE RACK

1.1 No bicycle parking

3.2 Bicycle rack

0
1
2
3
4
5
6
7
8
Index

5005

MOTORCYCLE

1.1 No motorcycles allowed

2.1 Caution! Motorcycles

3.2 Motorcycles

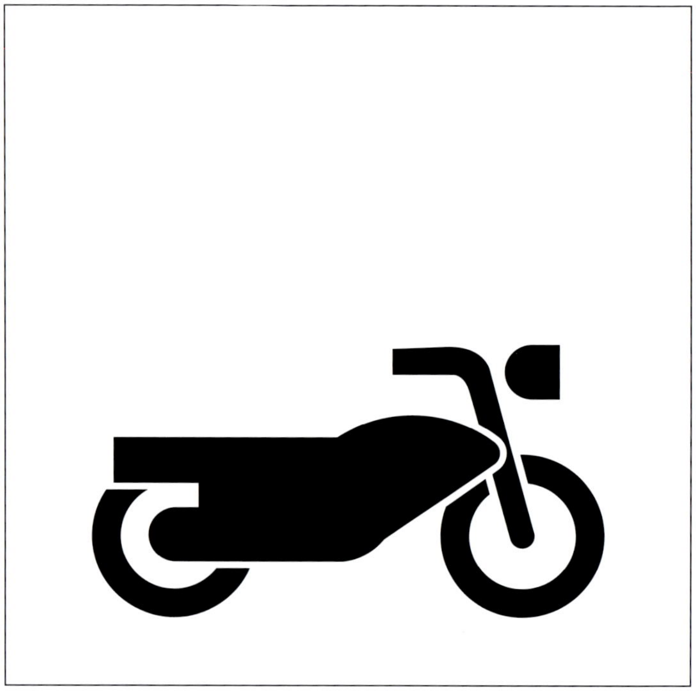

1.1

1.2

2.1

2.2

3.1

3.2

5006

MOTOR VEHICLE, BETWEEN TWO BARS

3.2 Garage

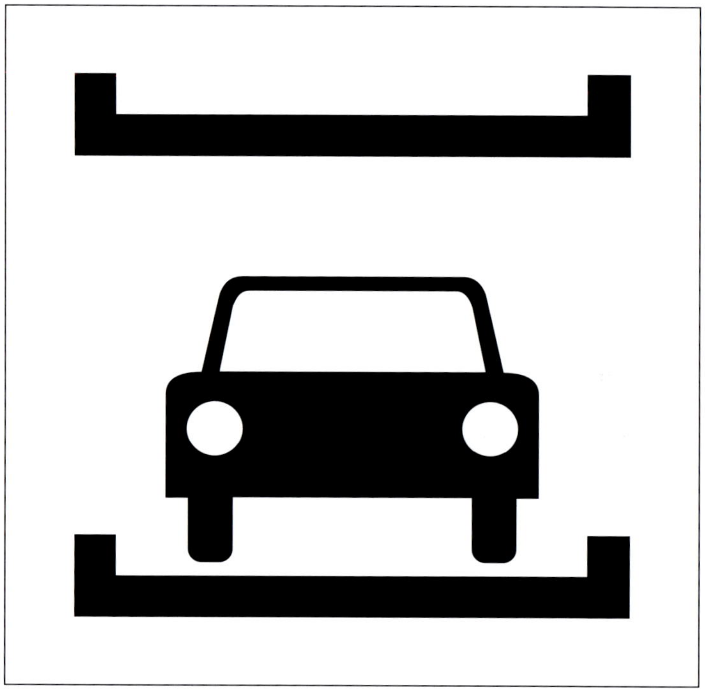

1.1

1.2

2.1

2.2

3.1

3.2

5007

KEY

1.1 Do not start

1.2 Lock up

3.2 Keys

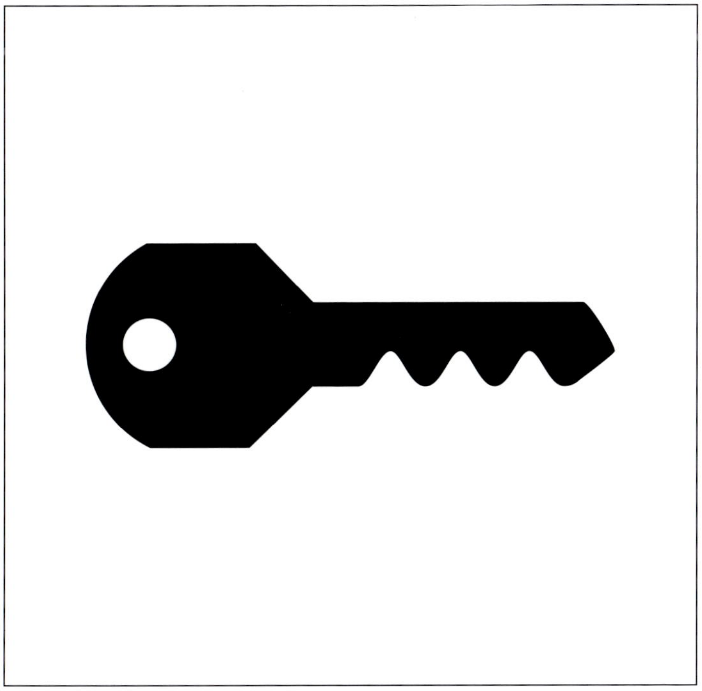

1.1

1.2

2.1

2.2

3.1

3.2

5008

HORN

1.1 Do not honk horn

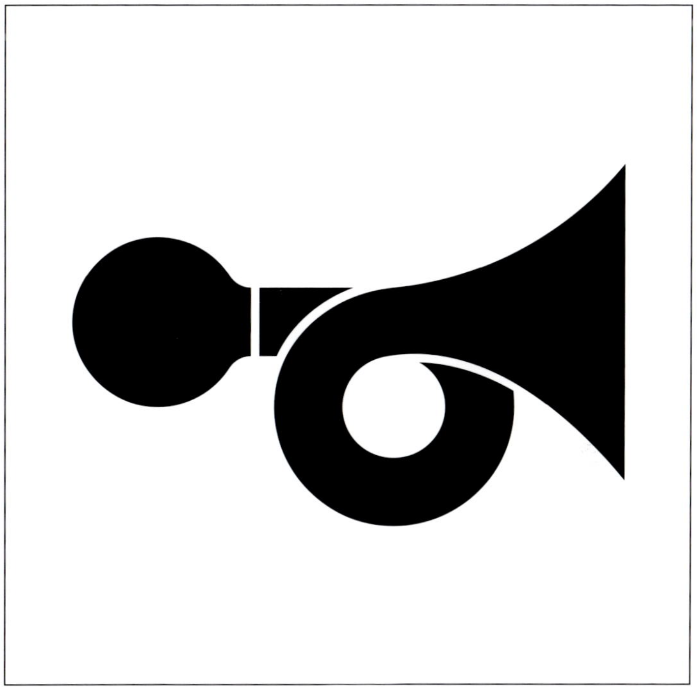

1.1

1.2

2.1

2.2

3.1

3.2

5009

SEAT BELT BUCKLES, WITH ARROWS INDICATING CONNECTION

1.2 Seatbelts must be worn

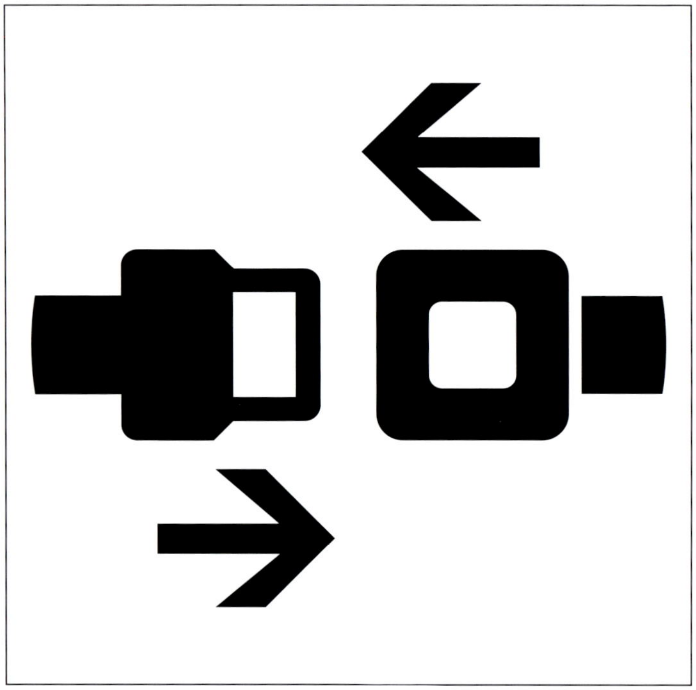

1.1

1.2

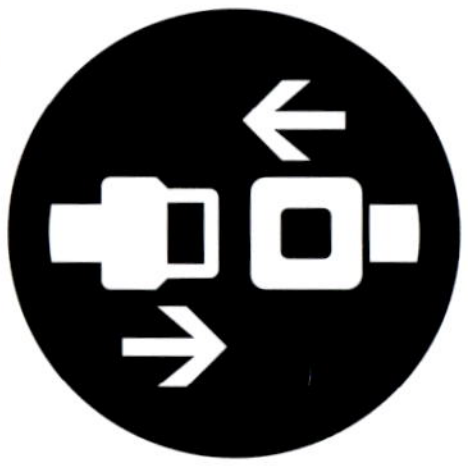

2.1

2.2

3.1

3.2

5010

TOW TRUCK, TOWING MOTOR VEHICLE

3.2 Tow truck, tow-away zone

1.1

1.2

2.1

2.2

3.1

3.2

5011

GAS PUMP, WITH HOSE

3.2 Gasoline, gas station

1.1

1.2

2.1

2.2

3.1

3.2

5012

GAS PUMP, WITH HOSE, D

3.2 Diesel fuel, gas station

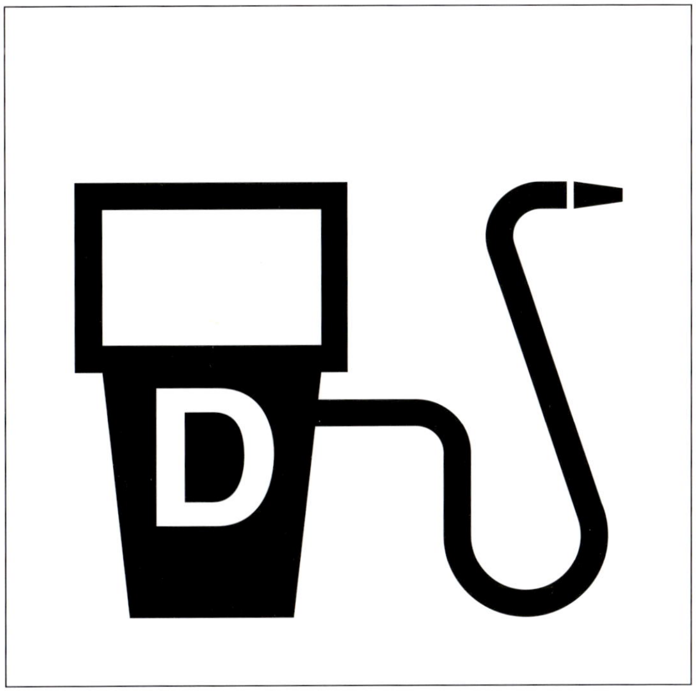

1.1

1.2

2.1

2.2

3.1

3.2

5013

PROPANE TANK

1.1 No propane tanks allowed

2.1 Caution! Propane gas

3.2 Propane gas

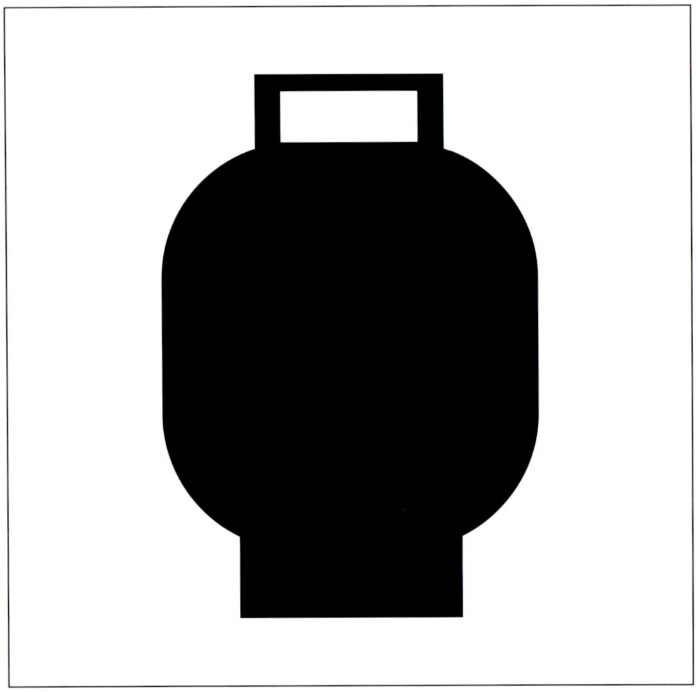

1.1

1.2

2.1

2.2

3.1

3.2

5014

MOTOR VEHICLE, FRONT VIEW

1.1 No motor vehicles allowed

2.1 Caution! Motor vehicles

3.2 Motor vehicles

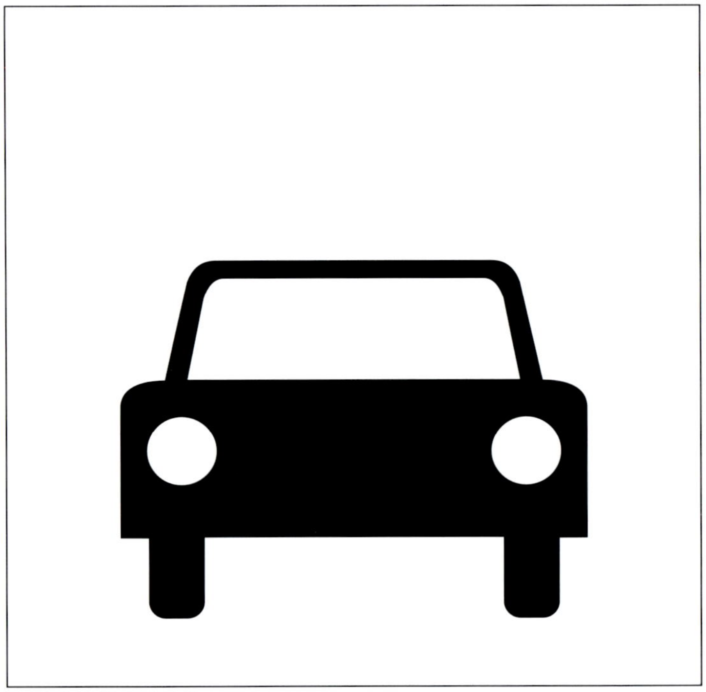

1.1

1.2

2.1

2.2

3.1

3.2

5015

MOTOR VEHICLE, SIDE VIEW

1.1 No motor vehicles allowed
2.1 Caution! Motor vehicles
3.2 Motor vehicles

1.1

1.2

2.1

2.2

3.1

3.2

5016

CAMPER TRAILER

1.1 No camping
3.2 Camper trailer

1.1

1.2

2.1

2.2

3.1

3.2

5017

CAMPER TRAILER, TUBE, GOING INTO HOLE

3.2 Sanitary station

1.1

1.2

2.1

2.2

3.1

3.2

5018

TENT, WITH FLAP OPEN

1.1 No camping

3.2 Camping

1.1

1.2

2.1

2.2

3.1

3.2

5019

PICNIC BENCH

1.1 No picnicking

3.2 Picnicking, picnic area

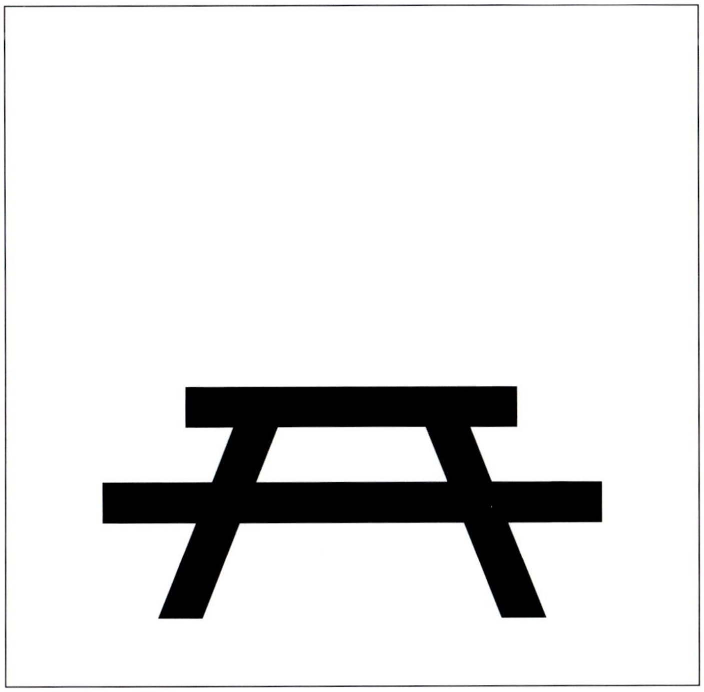

5020

MOTOR VEHICLE, WITH ROOF LIGHTS

3.2 Police car

5021

MOTOR VEHICLE, WITH TAXI ROOF SIGN

1.1 No taxis allowed

3.2 Taxis

1.1

1.2

2.1

2.2

3.1

3.2

5022

MOTOR VEHICLE, WITH IGNITION KEY ABOVE

3.2 Car rentals

1.1

1.2

2.1

2.2

3.1

3.2

5023

MOTOR VEHICLE, CLOUDED

2.1 Caution! Fog hazard

5024

BUS, PASSENGER ENTERING

3.2 Bus station

5025

BUS

1.1 No buses allowed

3.2 Bus stop

1.1

1.2

2.1

2.2

3.1

3.2

5026

BUS (JITNEY)

1.1 No buses allowed

3.2 Minibus

1.1

1.2

2.1

2.2

3.1

3.2

5027

BUS, TAXI

3.2 Ground transportation

1.1

1.2 

2.1 

2.2 

3.1 

3.2 

5028

STREETCAR, POWER BARS ON TOP, WITH TRACKS

3.2 Streetcar

1.1

1.2 

2.1 

2.2 

3.1 

3.2 

5029

SUBWAY CAR, ON TRACKS, WITHIN A TUNNEL SHAPE

3.2 Subway

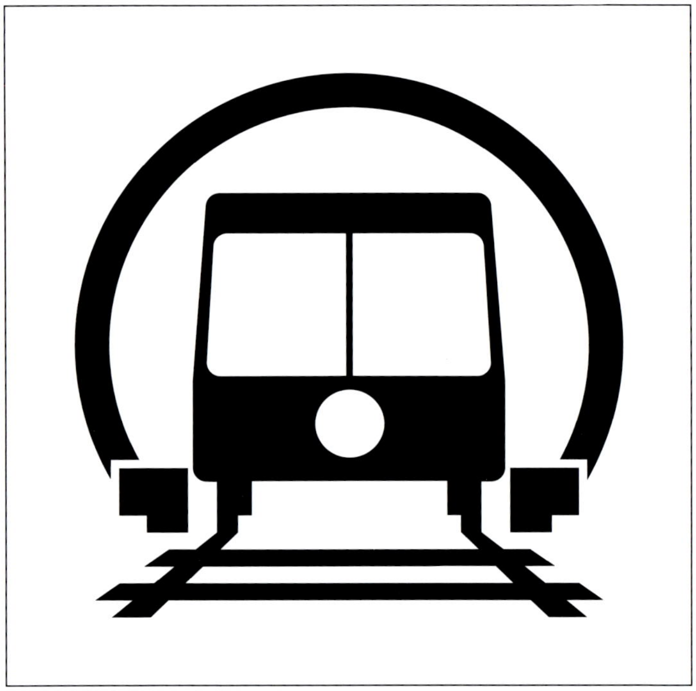

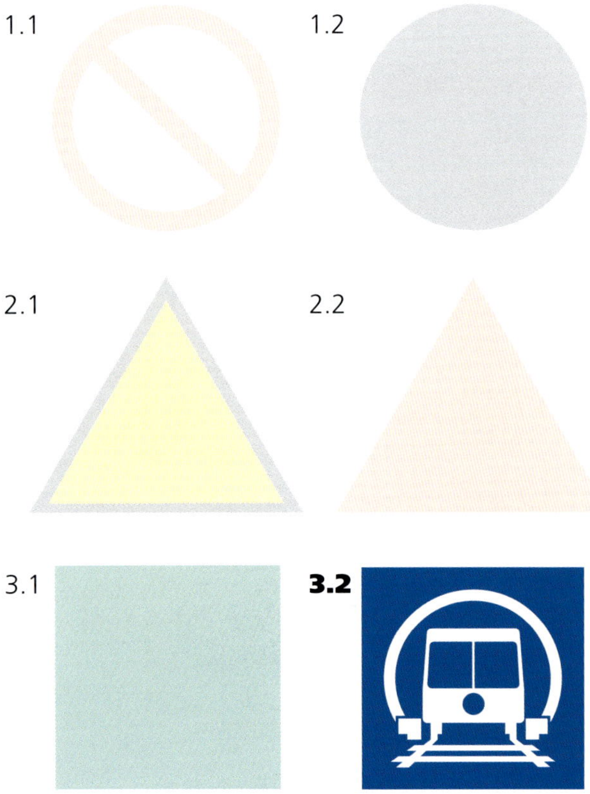

5030

MONORAIL CAB, ON RAIL

3.2 Monorail

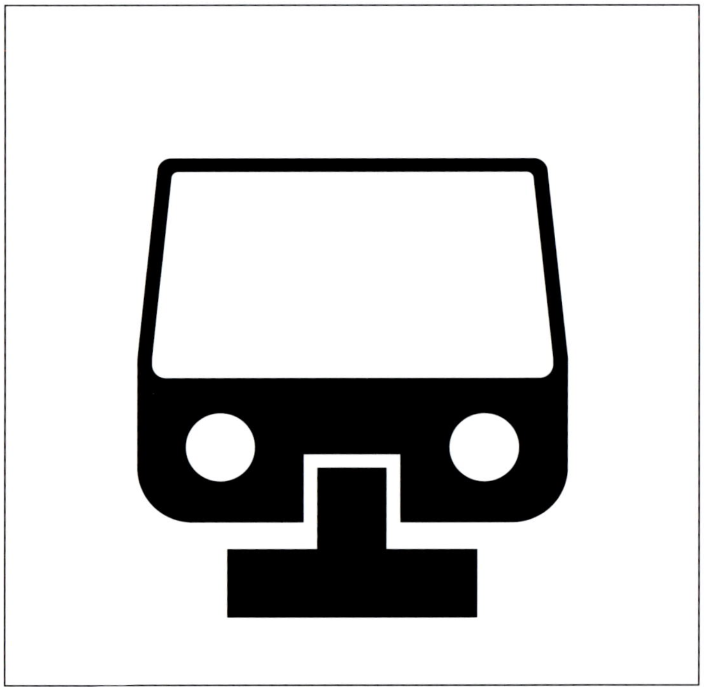

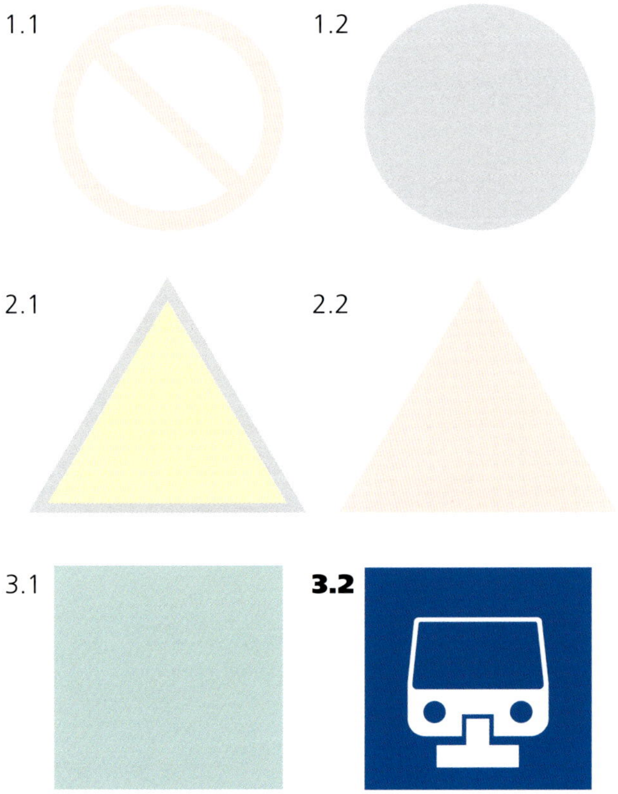

5031

CABLE CAR, WITH WIRE ABOVE

3.2 Cable car

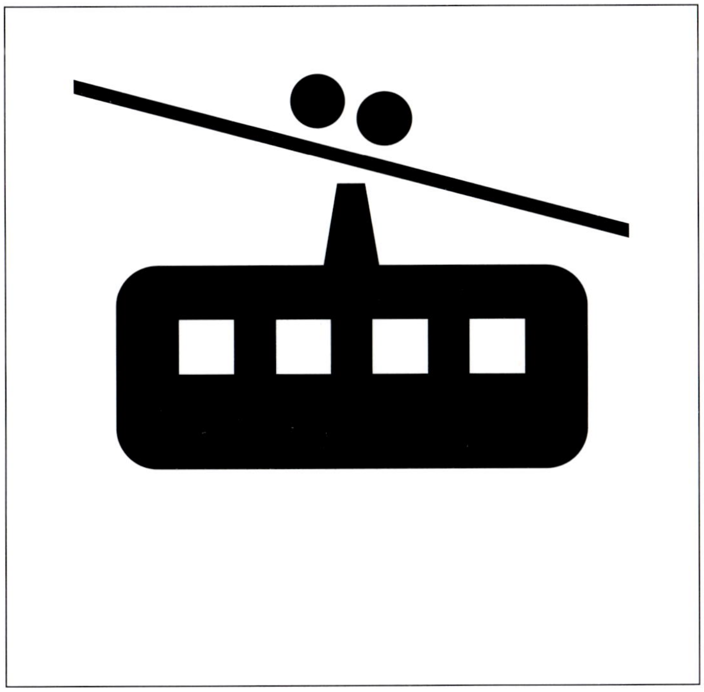

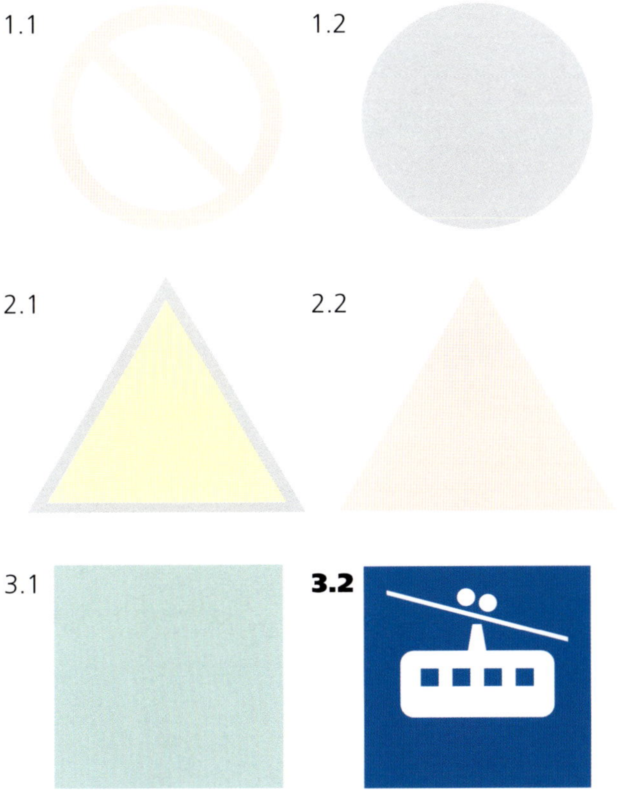

5032

AIRPLANE TICKET

3.2 Travel agency

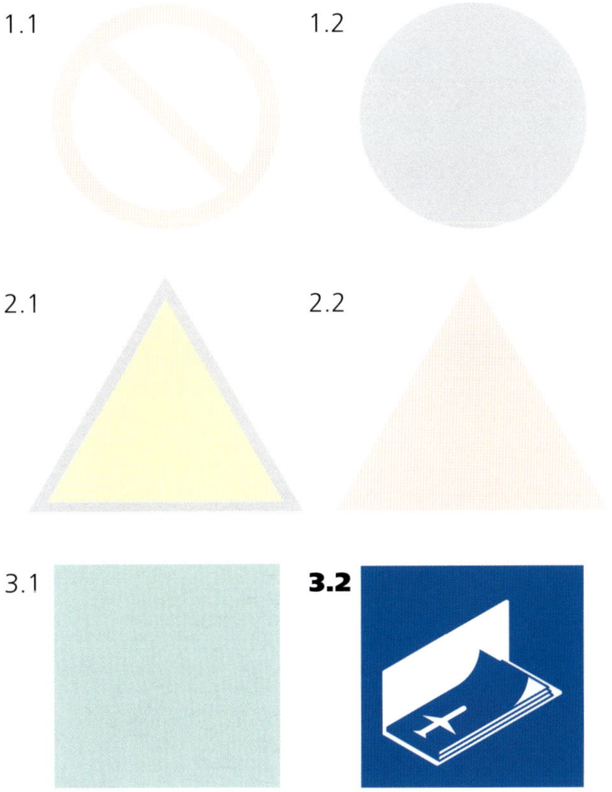

5033

HUMAN FIGURE, ON MOVING SIDEWALK

2.1 Caution! Moving sidewalk

3.2 Moving sidewalk

1.1

1.2

2.1

2.2

3.1

3.2

5034

HUMAN FIGURE, WEARING OFFICIAL CAP, INSPECTING BOOK

3.2 Immigration

1.1

1.2

2.1

2.2

3.1

3.2

5035

RUBBER STAMP

3.2 Immigration

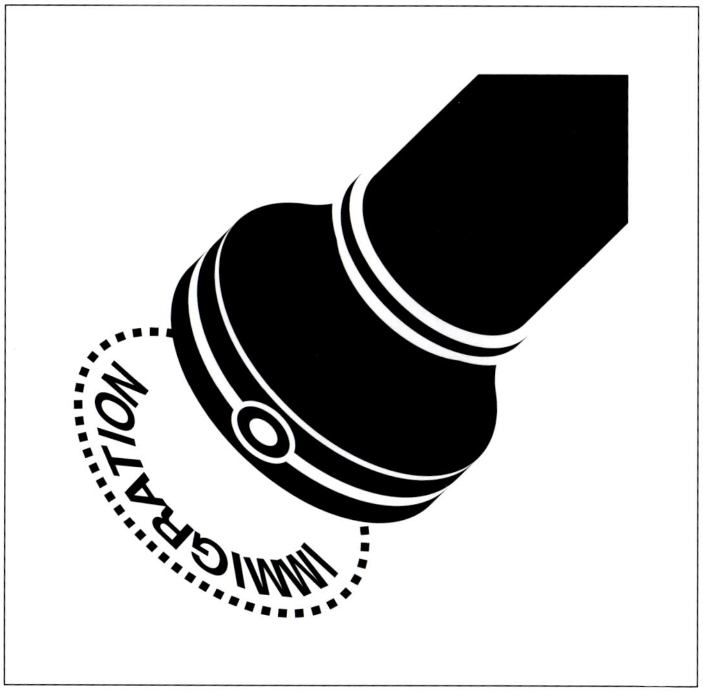

1.1

1.2

2.1

2.2

3.1

3.2
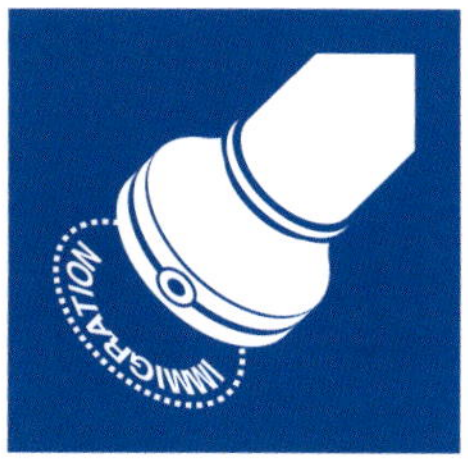

5036

SUITCASE WITH STRAPS

3.2 Baggage claim

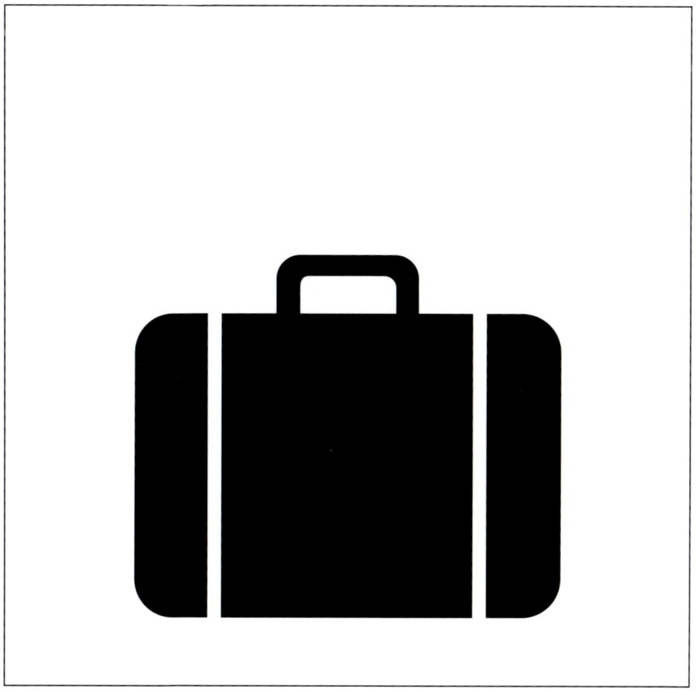

1.1

1.2

2.1

2.2

3.1

3.2

5037

HUMAN FIGURE, WEARING OFFICIAL CAP, OPEN SUITCASE

3.2 Customs

1.1

1.2

2.1

2.2

3.1

3.2

5038

SUITCASE WITH STRAPS, IN BOX, KEY ABOVE

3.2 Baggage locker(s)

1.1

1.2

2.1

2.2

3.1

3.2

5039

SUITCASE WITH STRAPS, ON DOLLY

3.2 Baggage carts

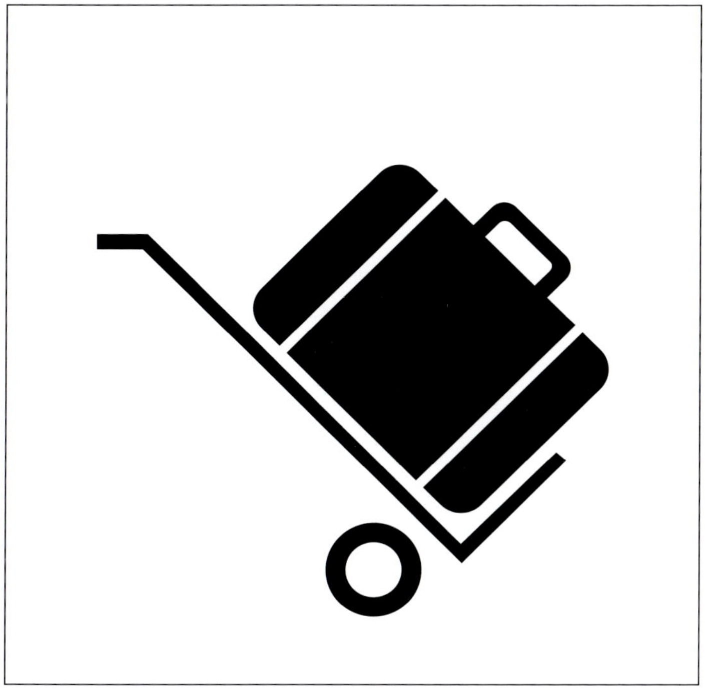

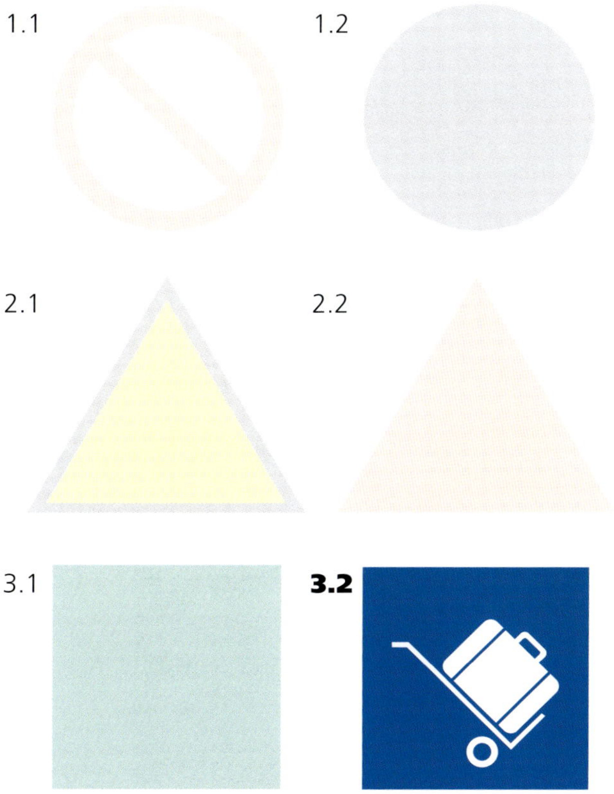

5040

SUITCASE WITH STRAPS, QUESTION MARK INSIDE

3.2 Lost baggage

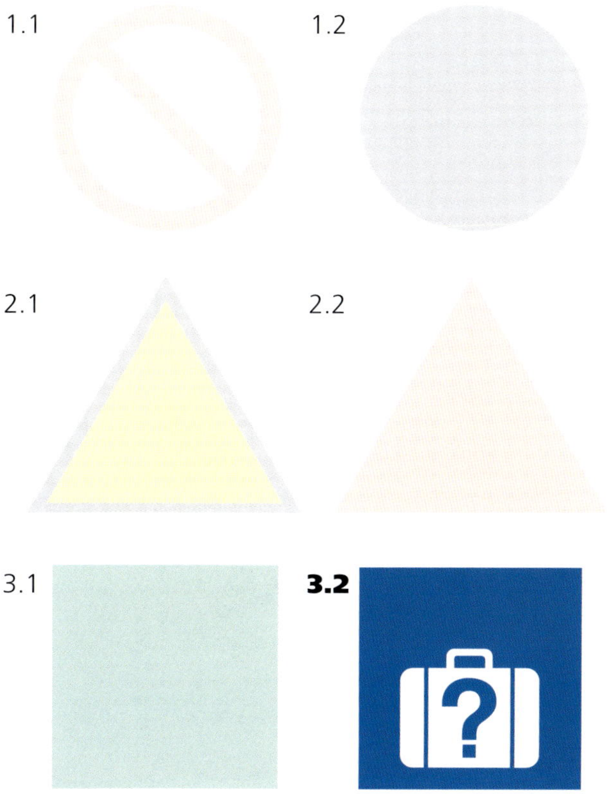

5041

UMBRELLA, CLOSED, QUESTION MARK ABOVE, GLOVE BELOW

3.2 Lost and found

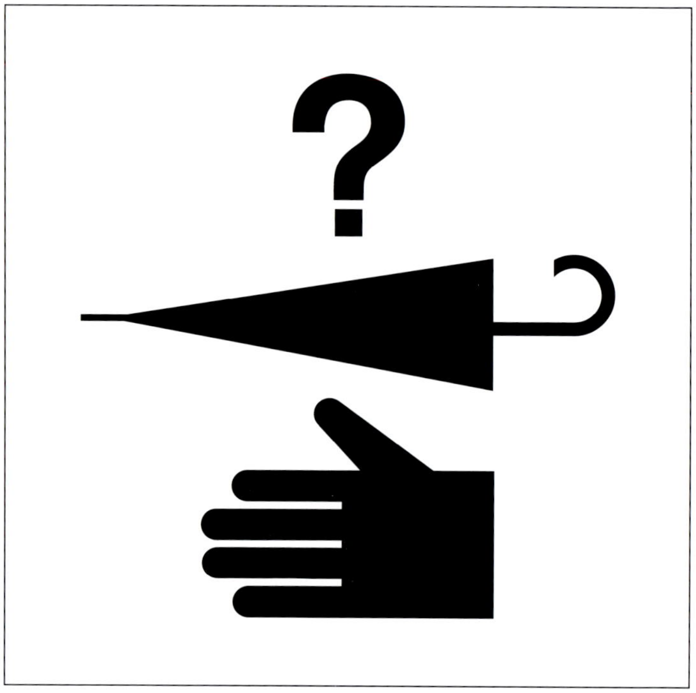

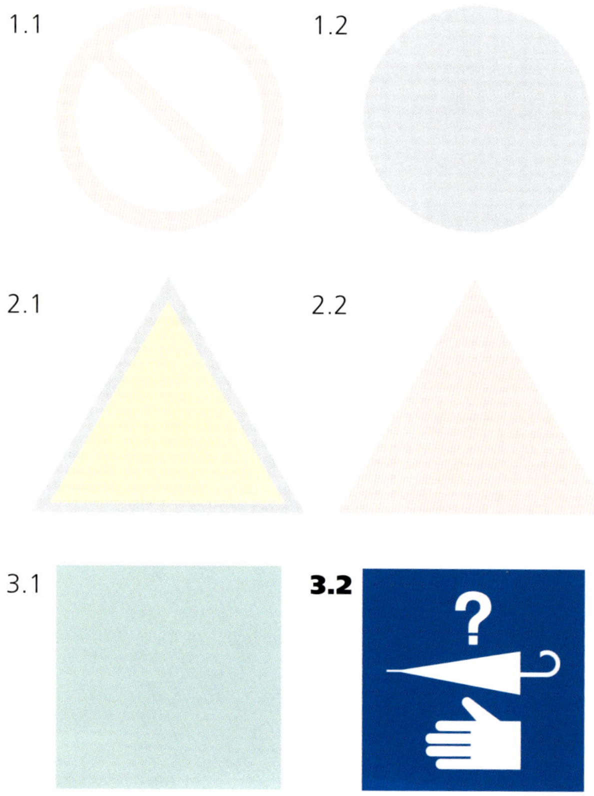

5042

HAND, HOLDING KEY, INSERTED IN THE SLOT

3.2 Locker(s)

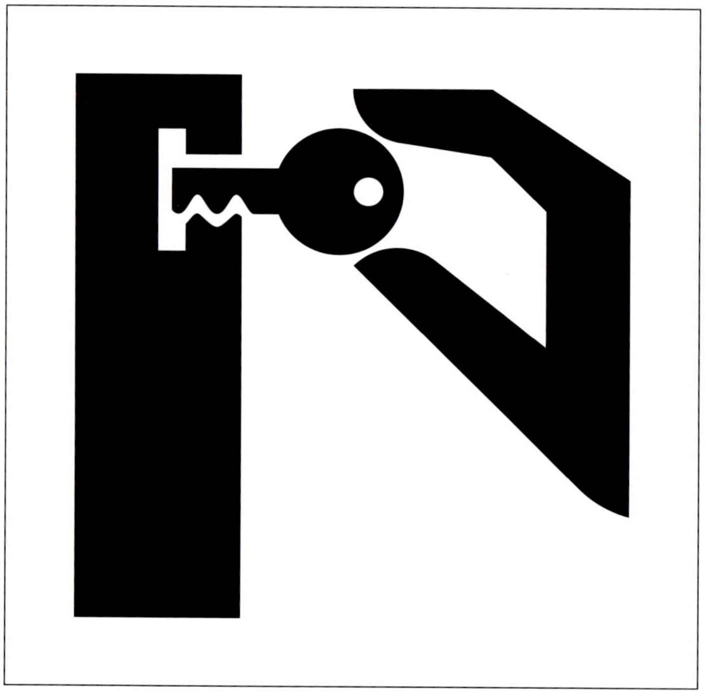

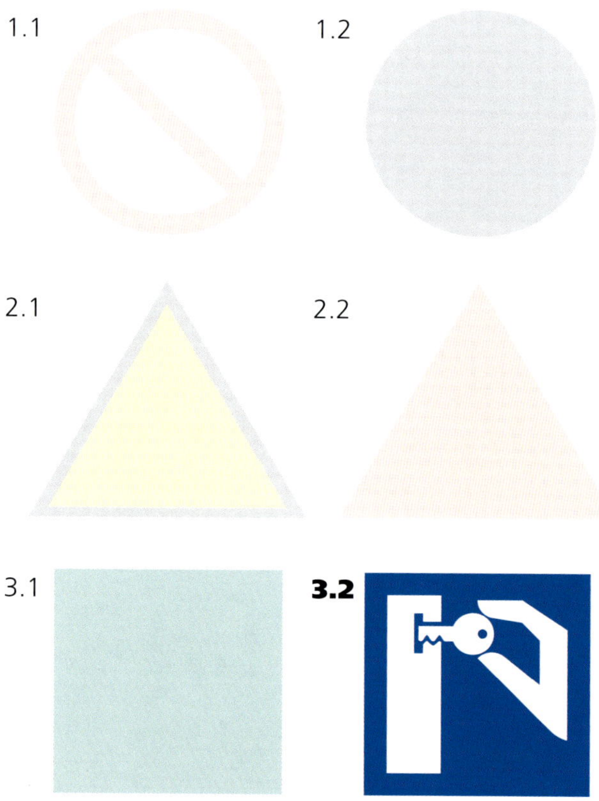

5043

HUMAN FIGURES, SEATED (OPTIONAL CLOCK)

3.2 Waiting/holding room

1.1

1.2

2.1

2.2

3.1

3.2

5044

WATER DROPS, OVER CLASPED HANDS

3.2 Hand-washing station

1.1

1.2

2.1

2.2

3.1

3.2

5045

BABY, UNWRAPPED DIAPER

3.2 Diaper change station

1.1

1.2

2.1

2.2

3.1

3.2

5046

BABY'S HEAD, AT BREAST

3.2 Breast-feeding (area)

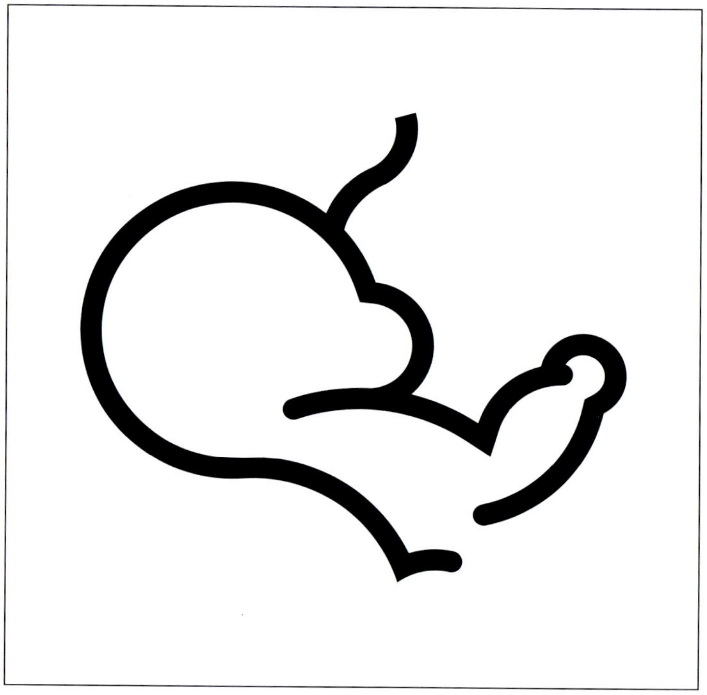

1.1

1.2

2.1

2.2

3.1

3.2

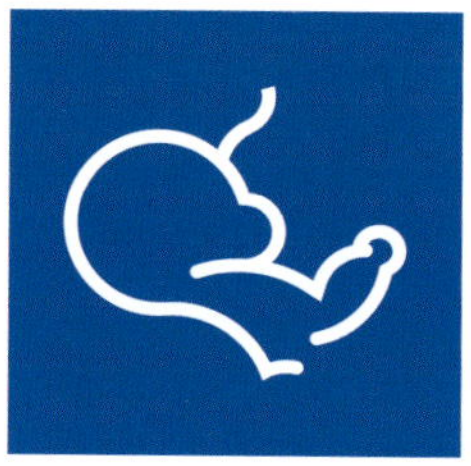

5047

DIESEL ENGINE, PASSENGER ENTERING

3.2 Train, train station

1.1

1.2

2.1

2.2

3.1

3.2

5048

DIESEL ENGINE, WITH RAILS

2.1 Caution! Train

3.2 Train

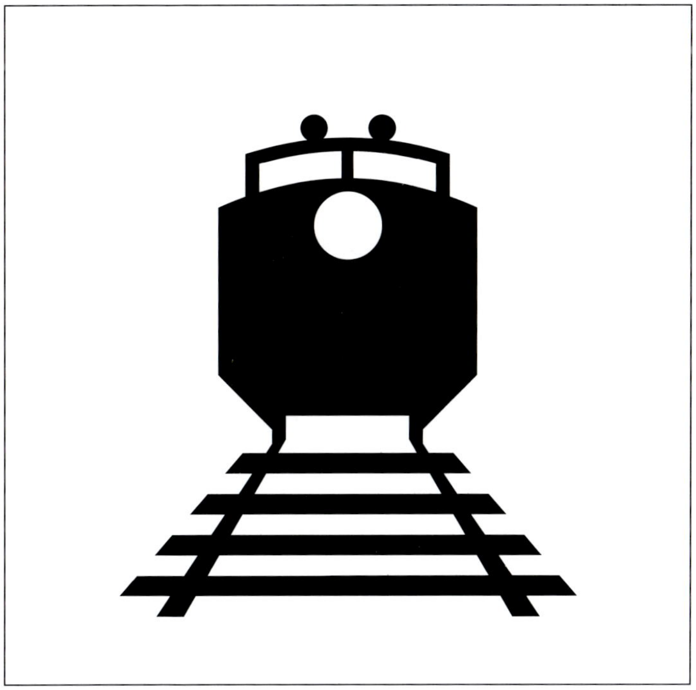

1.1

1.2

2.1

2.2

3.1

3.2

0
1
2
3
4
5
6
7
8
Index

5049

JET AIRPLANE, TOP VIEW

3.2 Major airport

1.1

1.2

2.1

2.2

3.1

3.2

5050

JET AIRPLANE, SIDE VIEW, WHEELS DOWN, LANDING, OVER HORIZONTAL BAR

3.2 Arrivals

1.1

1.2

2.1

2.2

3.1

3.2

5051

JET AIRPLANE, SIDE VIEW, WHEELS UP, TAKING OFF, OVER HORIZONTAL BAR

3.2 Departures

1.1

1.2

2.1

2.2

3.1

3.2

5052

PROP AIRPLANE, TOP VIEW

3.2 Commercial airplanes

1.1

1.2

2.1

2.2

3.1

3.2

5053

SEAPLANE, WITH FLOATS, OVER WATER

1.1 No landing

3.2 Seaplane(s)

1.1

1.2

2.1

2.2

3.1

3.2

5054

HELICOPTER, WITH FLOAT

3.2 Helicopter(s), heliport

1.1

1.2

2.1

2.2

3.1

3.2

5055

HELICOPTER, WITH LANDING SKID

3.2 Helicopter(s), heliport

1.1

1.2

2.1

2.2

3.1

3.2

5056

HOVECRAFT, OVER WATER/LAND

3.2 Hovercraft(s) (passengers)

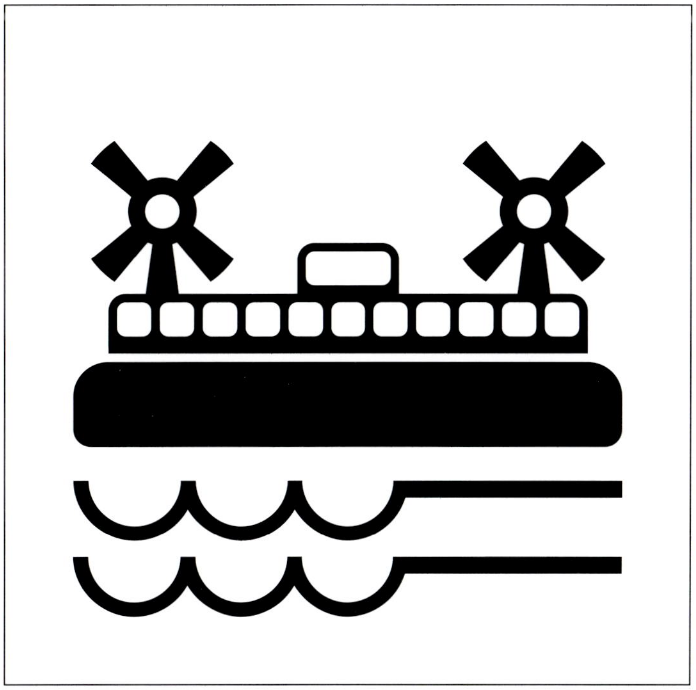

1.1

1.2

2.1

2.2

3.1

3.2

5057

HUMAN FIGURE, IN SMALL HOVERCRAFT, OVER WATER/LAND

3.2 Hovercraft(s)

1.1

1.2

2.1

2.2

3.1

3.2

5058

FERRYBOAT, OPEN PROW, MOTOR VEHICLE, OVER WATER

3.2 Ferry

1.1

1.2

2.1

2.2

3.1

3.2

5059

FERRYBOAT, TWO MOTOR VEHICLES, OVER WATER

3.2 Ferry

1.1

1.2

2.1

2.2

3.1

3.2

5060

OCEAN LINER, OVER WATER

3.2 Ocean travel

1.1

1.2

2.1

2.2

3.1

3.2

5061

MOTORBOAT, OVER WATER

1.1 No motorboats allowed

3.2 Boat (marina)

1.1

1.2

2.1

2.2

3.1

3.2

5062

MOTORBOAT, ON TRAILER, ASCENDING RAMP, OVER WATER

1.1 No boat launching

3.2 Boat launching ramp

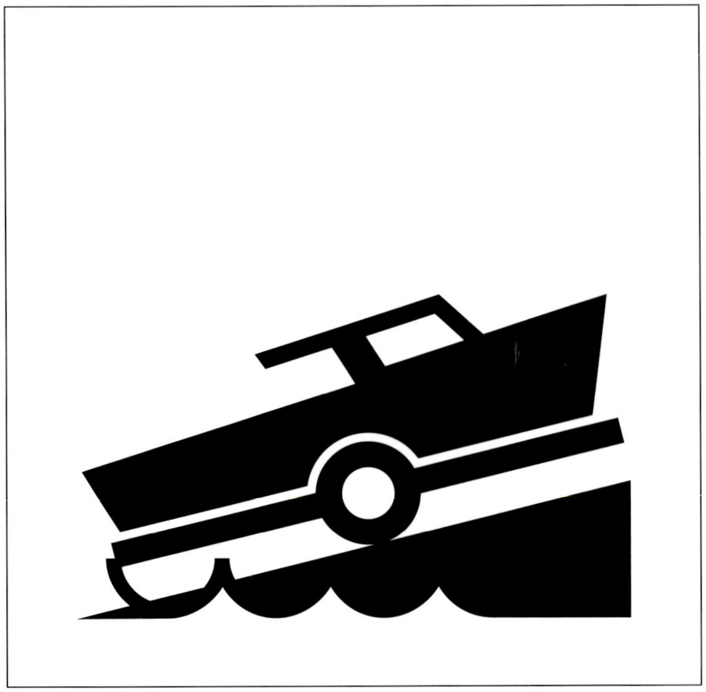

1.1

1.2

2.1

2.2

3.1

3.2

5063

HUMAN HEAD, WITH CHEF'S HAT

3.2 Cook(ing), kitchen

5064

HUMAN FIGURE IN BED, MOTOR VEHICLE, ROOF OVER BOTH

3.2 Motel

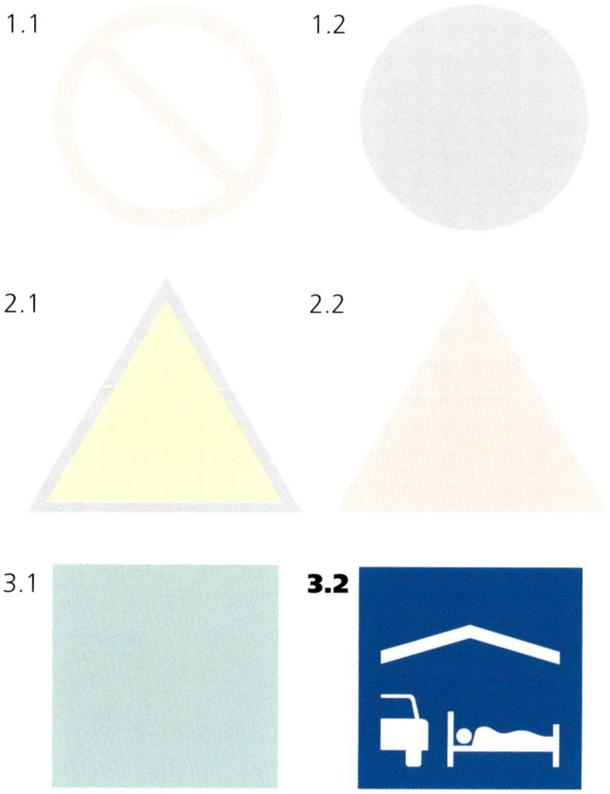

5065

HUMAN FIGURE, IN BED, ROOF ABOVE

3.2 Hotel, accommodations

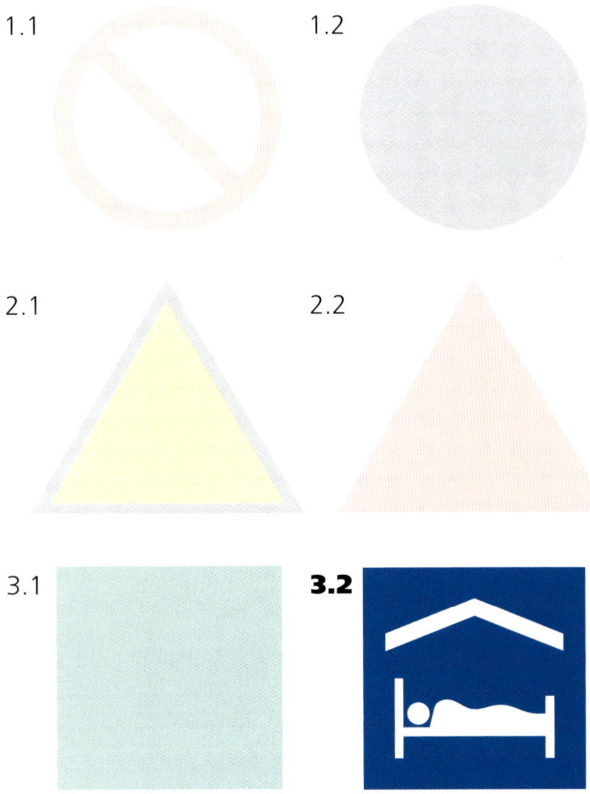

5066

BOX, WRAPPED WITH RIBBON, BOW ON TOP

3.2 Gift shop, gift wrapping

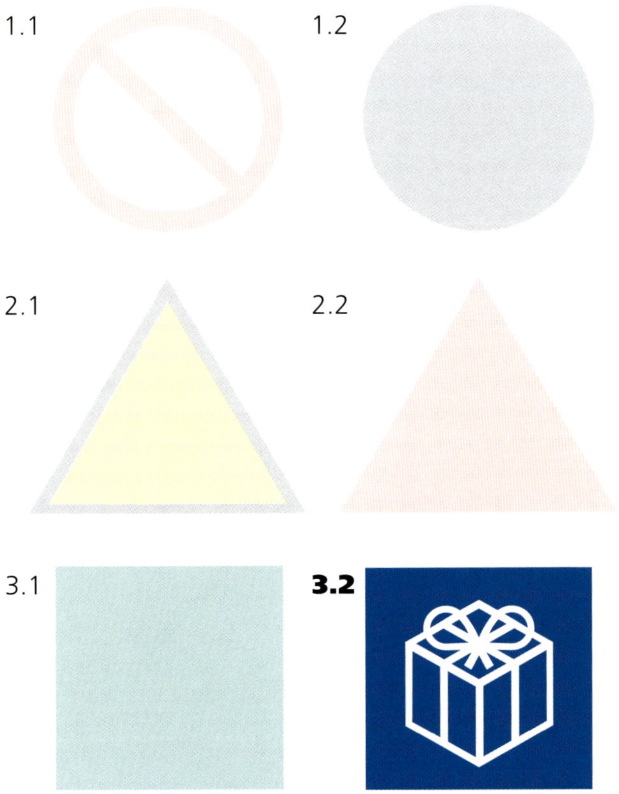

5067

BARN, FENCE

3.2 Farm

1.1

1.2

2.1

2.2

3.1

3.2

5068

TRACTOR

1.1 No farm machinery allowed

2.1 Caution! Farm machinery

3.2 Farm machinery

1.1

1.2

2.1

2.2

3.1

3.2

0
1
2
3
4
5
6
7
8
Index

5069

VAN

1.1 No deliveries allowed
2.1 Caution! Vans
3.2 Van(s)

1.1

1.2

2.1

2.2

3.1

3.2

5070

PICKUP TRUCK

1.1 No trucks allowed
2.1 Caution! Trucks
3.2 Pickup truck(s)

1.1

1.2

2.1

2.2

3.1

3.2

5071

CUBE VAN

1.1 No deliveries allowed
2.1 Caution! Trucks
3.2 Cube van(s)

1.1

1.2

2.1

2.2

3.1

3.2

5072

TRUCK, BOX TYPE

1.1 No trucks allowed
2.1 Caution! Trucks
3.2 Truck(s)

1.1

1.2

2.1

2.2

3.1

3.2

0
1
2
3
4
5
6
7
8
Index

5073

FLATBED TRUCK

1.1 No trucks allowed

2.1 Caution! Trucks

3.2 Flatbed truck(s)

1.1

1.2

2.1

2.2

3.1

3.2

5074

DUMP TRUCK, HYDRAULIC CYLINDER, BODY ANGLED

1.1 No dumping

2.1 Caution! Dump trucks

3.2 Dump truck(s)

1.1

1.2

2.1

2.2

3.1

3.2

5075

CONCRETE MIXER TRUCK

1.1 No dumping of cement

2.1 Caution! Cement trucks

3.2 Concrete mixer truck(s)

1.1

1.2

2.1

2.2

3.1

3.2

5076

HEAVY TRUCK

1.1 No heavy trucks allowed

2.1 Caution! Heavy trucks

3.2 Heavy truck(s)

1.1

1.2

2.1

2.2

3.1

3.2

5077

HEAVY TRUCK, ON WEIGH SCALE

3.2 Weigh station

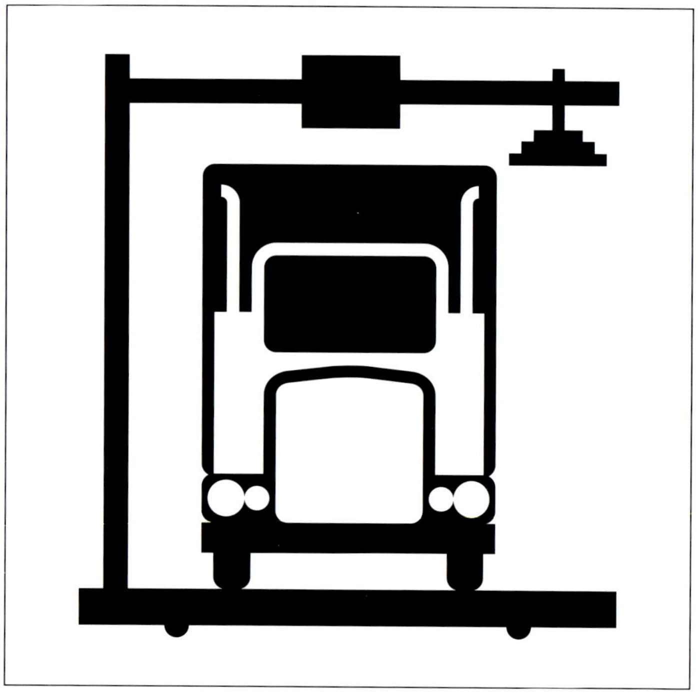

1.1

1.2

2.1

2.2

3.1

3.2

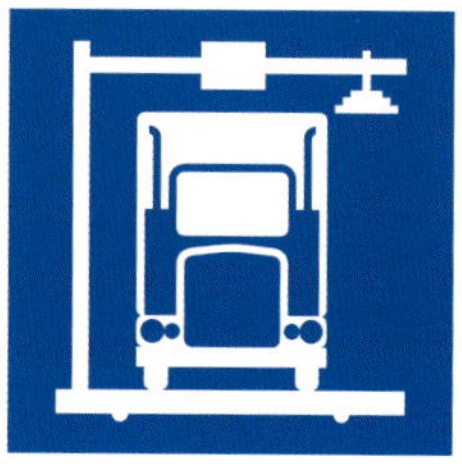

5078

TRUCK, WITH LOGGING TRAILER

1.1 No trucks allowed

2.1 Caution! Logging trucks

3.2 Logging truck(s)

1.1

1.2

2.1

2.2

3.1

3.2

5079

TRUCK, WITH LOGGING TRAILER, ON WEIGH SCALE

3.2 Weigh station

1.1

1.2

2.1

2.2

3.1

3.2

5080

TRUCK, CLOUDED

2.1 Caution! Fog hazard

1.1

1.2

2.1

2.2

3.1

3.2

0
1
2
3
4
5
6
7
8
Index

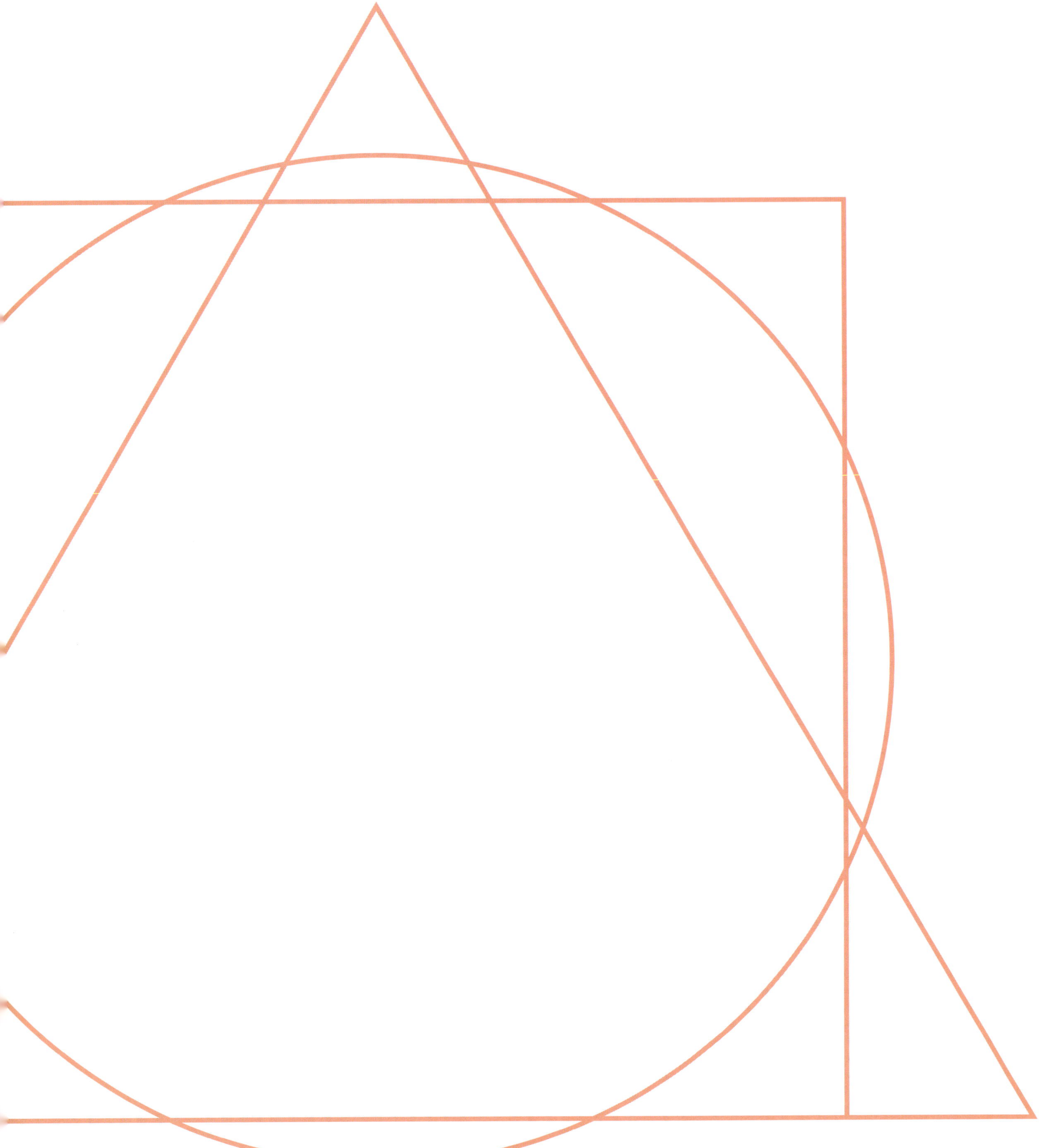

6001

EXCLAMATION POINT

2.1 Caution! Be alert, watch out

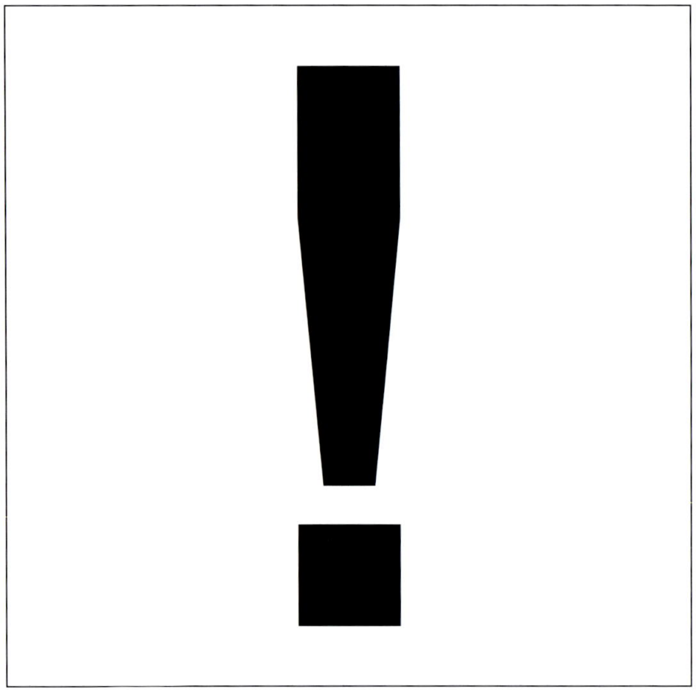

6002

DOOR, WITH WINDOW AND DOORKNOB

1.2 Close the door

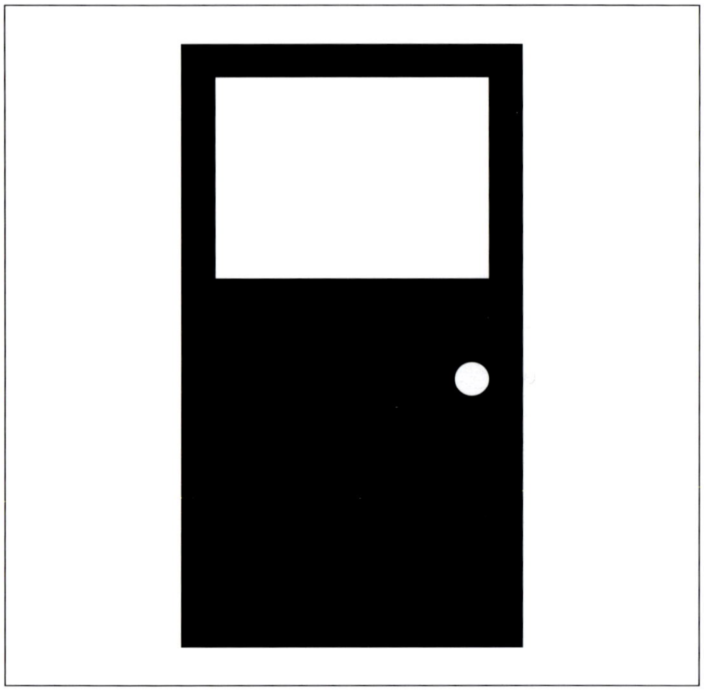

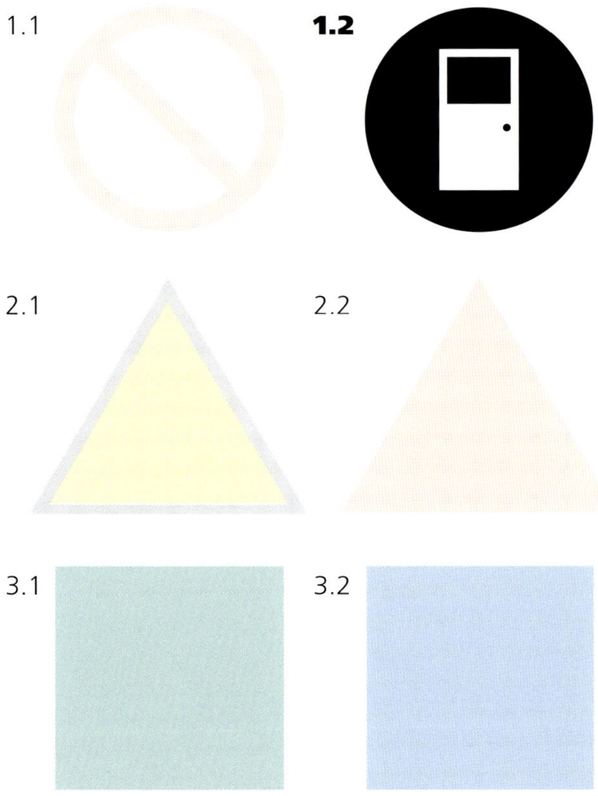

6003

DOOR, WITH SMALL WINDOW AND DOORKNOB

1.2 Close the door

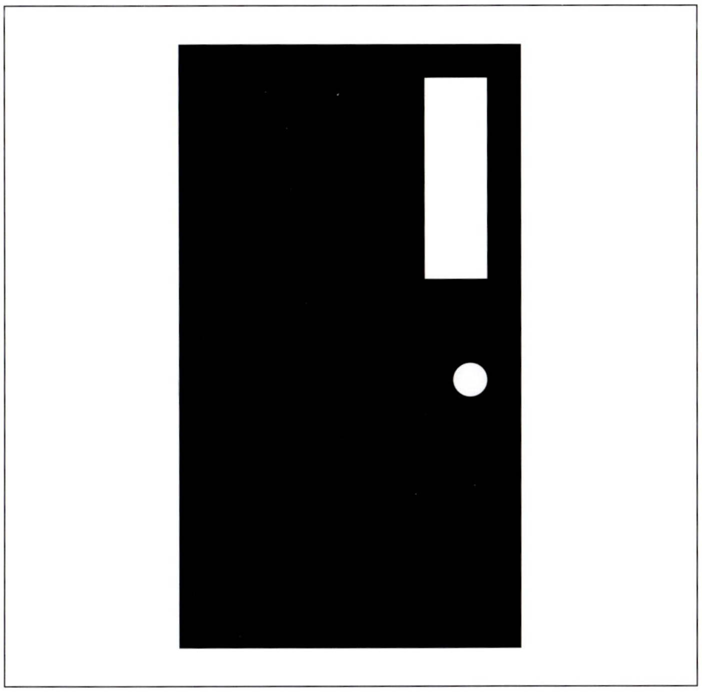

6004

BIOHAZARD SYMBOL

2.2 Danger! Biohazard

6005

IONIZING RADIATION

2.1 Caution! Ionizing radiation

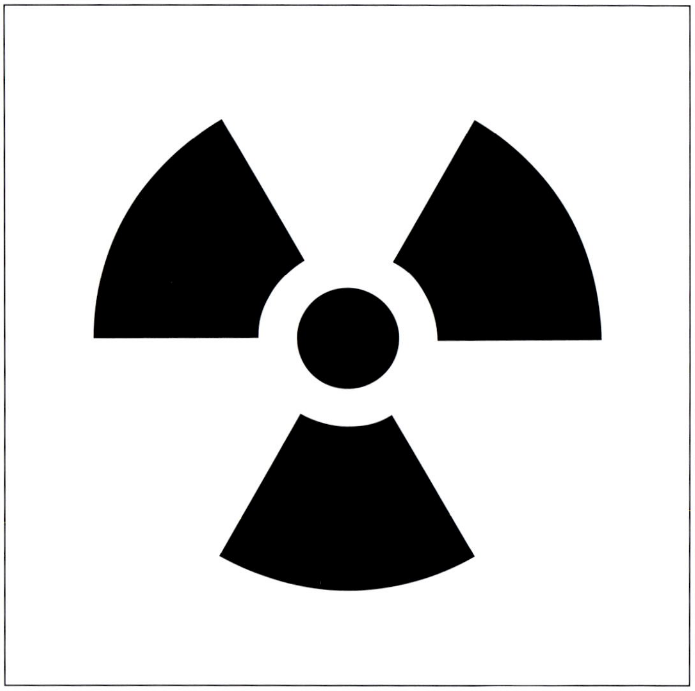

1.1

1.2

2.1

2.2

3.1

3.2

6006

CRANE HOOK, WITH SAFETY CATCH

2.1 Caution! Overhead crane

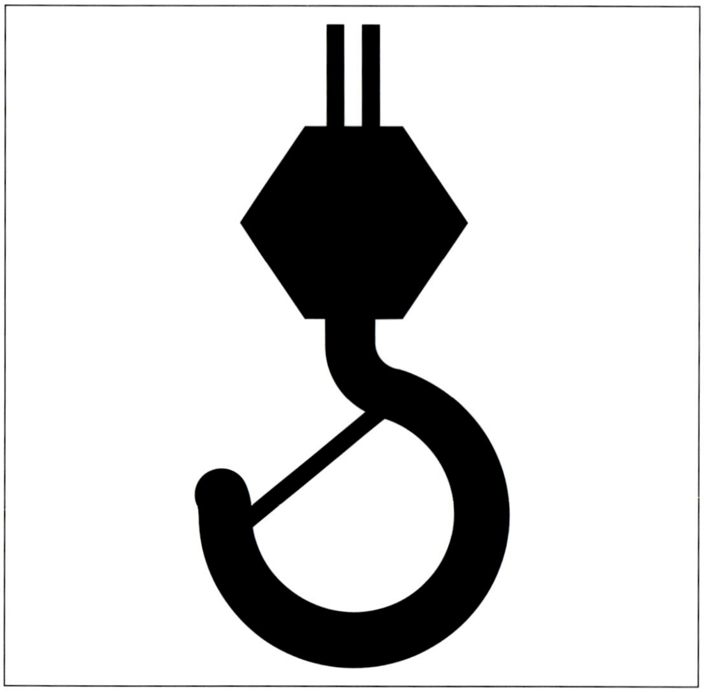

1.1

1.2

2.1

2.2

3.1

3.2

6007

CRANE HOOK

2.1 Caution! Overhead crane

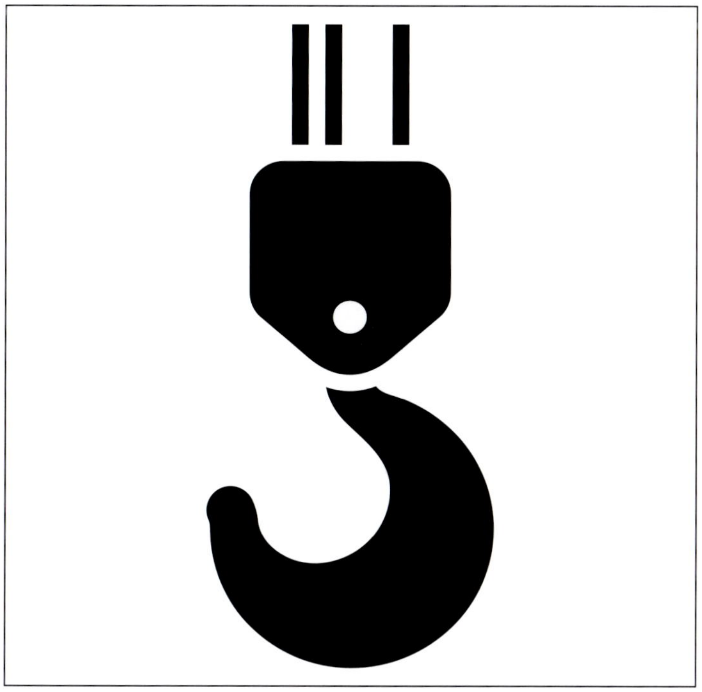

1.1

1.2

2.1

2.2

3.1

3.2

6008

MATCH, WITH FLAME

1.1 No open flames allowed

1.1

1.2

2.1

2.2

3.1

3.2

0
1
2
3
4
5
6
7
8
Index

6009

FLAMES, OVER HORIZONTAL LINE

2.2 Danger! Flammable

6010

FLAMES, OVER HORIZONTAL LINE

2.2 Danger! Flammable

6011

SMOKE RINGS, CONCENTRIC, RISING

2.1 Caution! Smoke

2.2 Danger! Smoke

3.2 Smoke

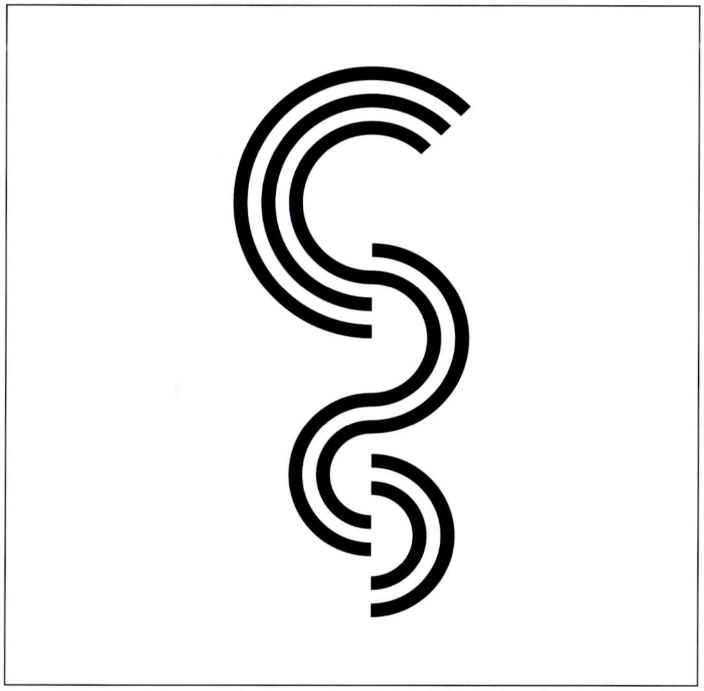

1.1

1.2

2.1

2.2

3.1

3.2

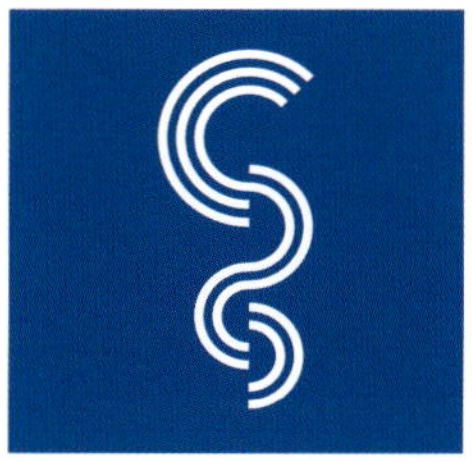

6012

VALVE

3.2 Valve, international engineering sign

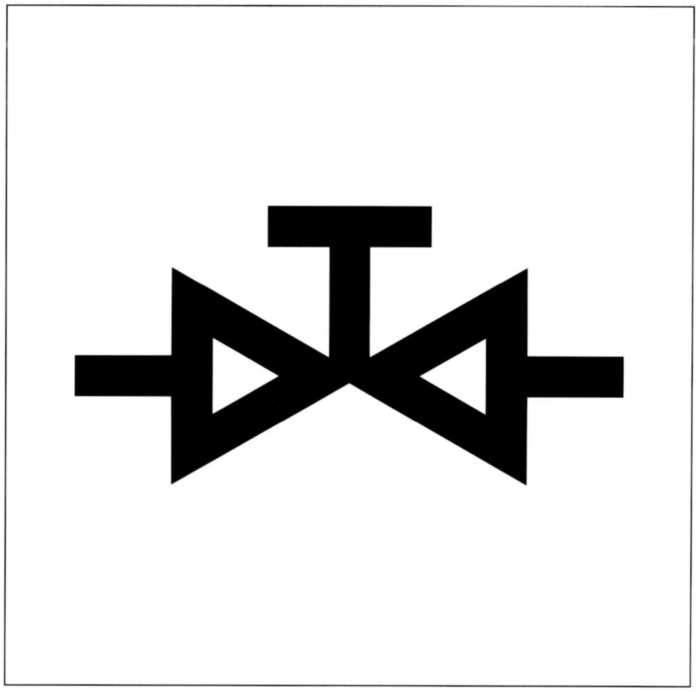

1.1

1.2

2.1

2.2

3.1

3.2

6013

VERTICAL BAR, HAND HOLDING WELDING TORCH, SPARKS

1.1 No welding

3.2 Welding

1.1

1.2

2.1

2.2

3.1

3.2

6014

VERTICAL BAR, WITH SWITCH, INDEX FINGER

1.1 Do not switch

3.2 Switch

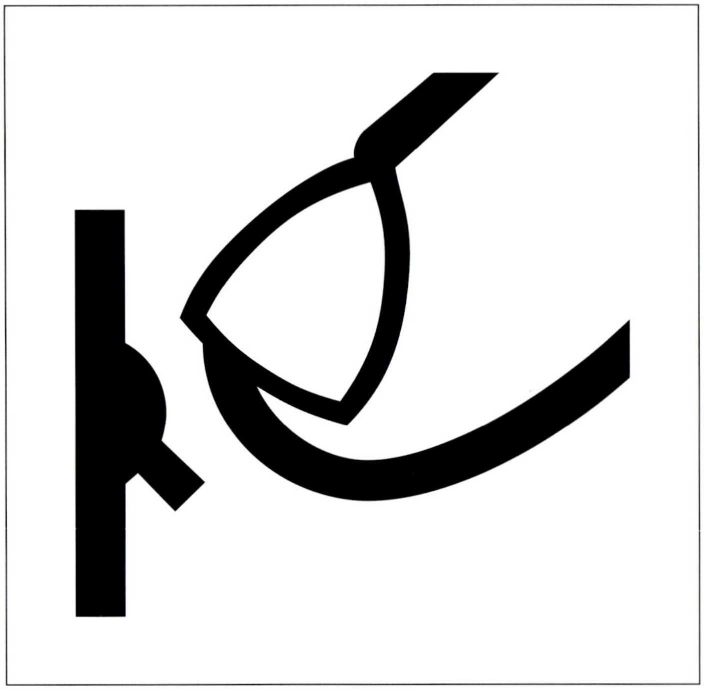

1.1

1.2

2.1

2.2

3.1

3.2

6015

INDEX FINGER, HORIZONTAL BAR

1.1 Do not touch

3.2 Touch

1.1

1.2

2.1

2.2

3.1

3.2

6016

COMPRESSED GAS CYLINDER, WITH GAUGE

2.2 Danger! Compressed gas

1.1

1.2

2.1

2.2

3.1

3.2

6017

TRIANGULAR FORMS, CLUSTERED, RADIATING FROM A CENTRAL POINT

2.2 Danger! Explosives

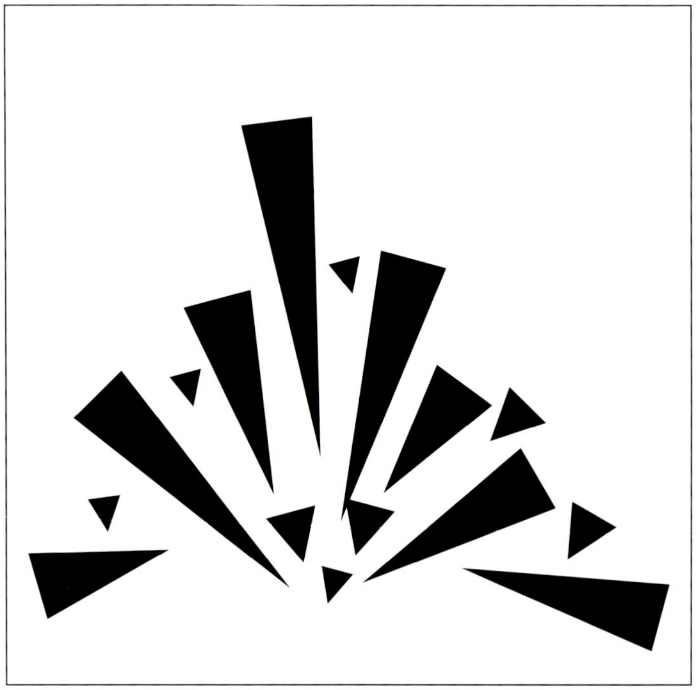

6018

PIN SHAPE, OVER DOT

2.2 Danger! Toxic

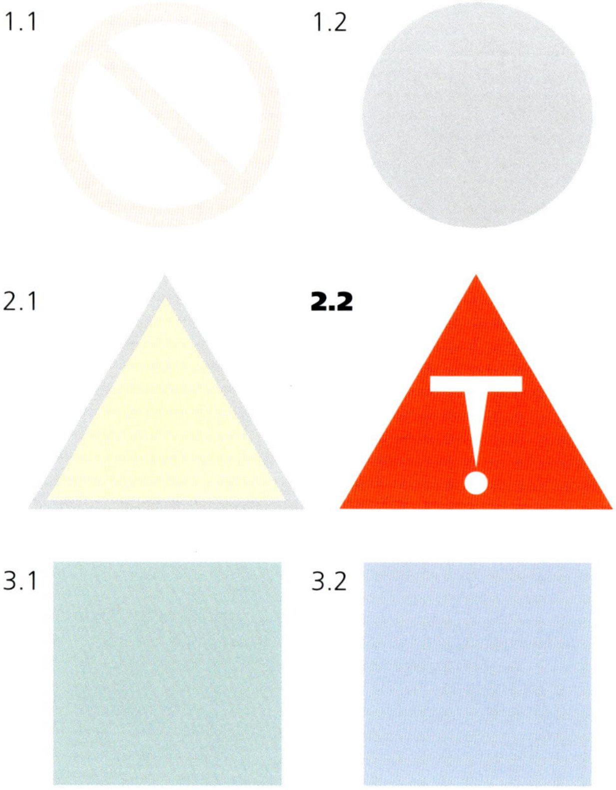

6019

HAND, PALM, DROPS, CORRODING FINGERS

2.2 Danger! Chemical burn (corrosive)

1.1

1.2

2.1

2.2

3.1

3.2

6020

HAND, EXTENDED PALM, WEDGE CUTTING FINGERS

2.2 Danger! Sharp object(s)

1.1

1.2

2.1

2.2

3.1

3.2

0
1
2
3
4
5
6
7
8
Index

6021

HAND, EXTENDED PALM, VERTICAL BAR, CRUSHING FINGERS

2.2 Danger! Heavy object(s)

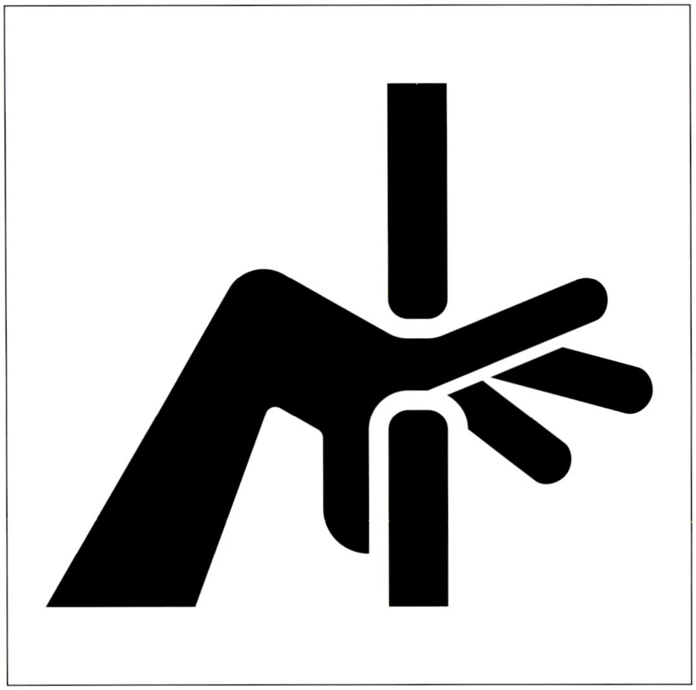

1.1

1.2

2.1

2.2

3.1

3.2

6022

FOOTPRINT

1.1 No bare feet allowed

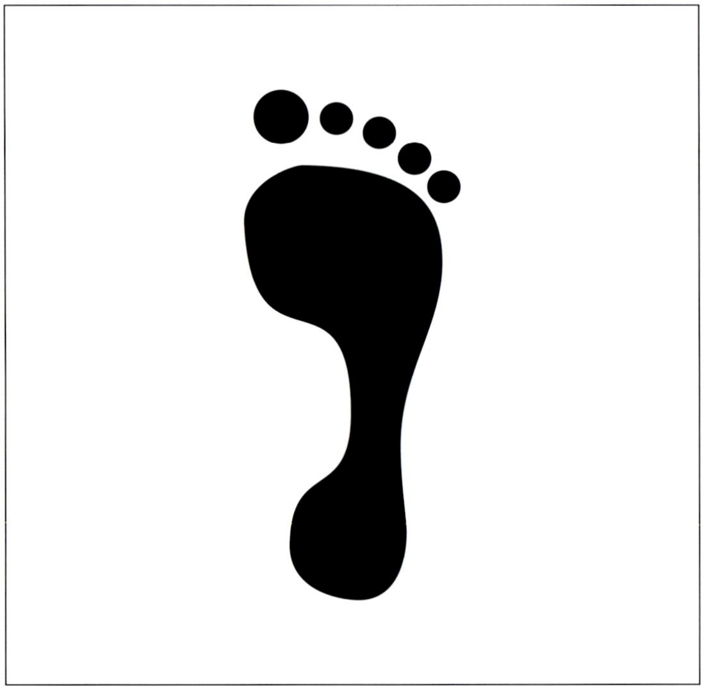

1.1

1.2

2.1

2.2

3.1

3.2

6023

SKULL AND CROSSBONES

2.1 Caution! Poison

2.2 Danger! Poison

1.1

1.2

2.1

2.2

3.1

3.2

6024

FAUCET, CLEAR RECEPTACLE, WITH WATER

1.1 Do not drink the water

3.2 Drinkable water

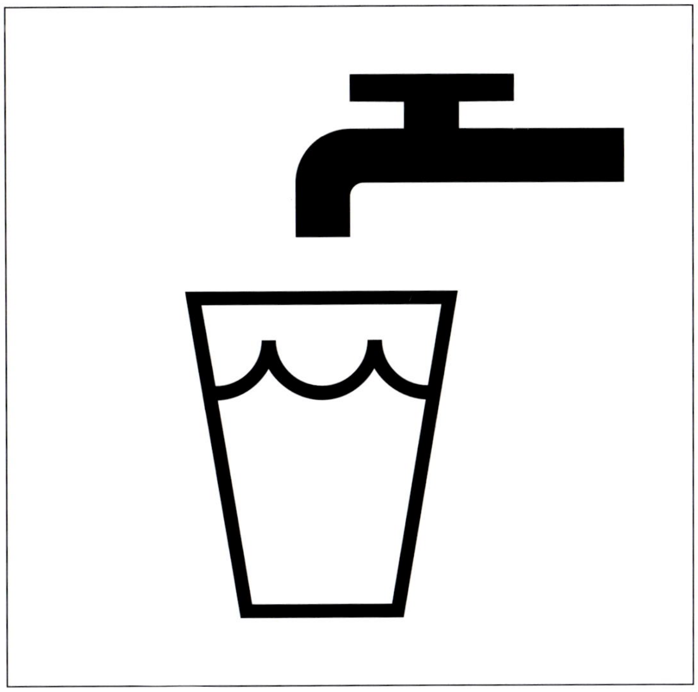

1.1

1.2

2.1

2.2

3.1

3.2

6025

HUMAN HEAD, SPRAYING DROPS

3.2 Drinking fountain

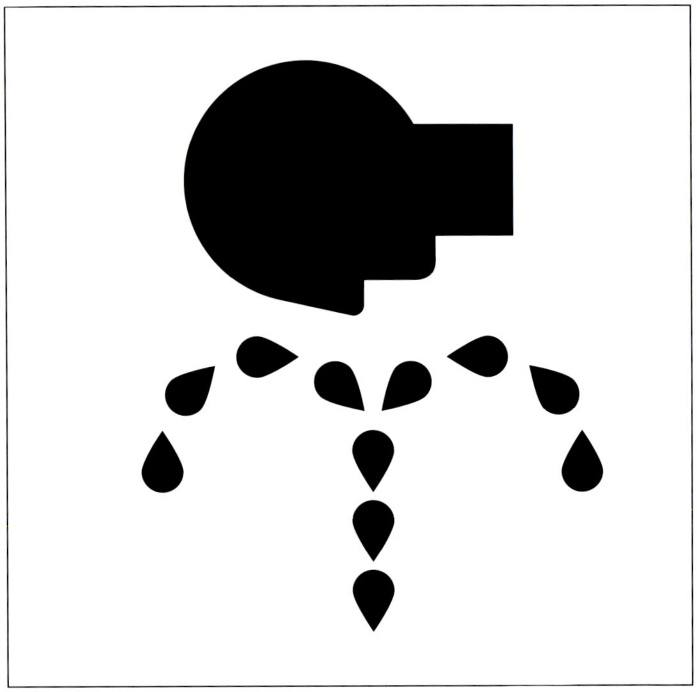

1.1

1.2

2.1

2.2

3.1

3.2

6026

SAFETY GLOVE

1.2 Hand protection must be worn

3.2 Safety gloves

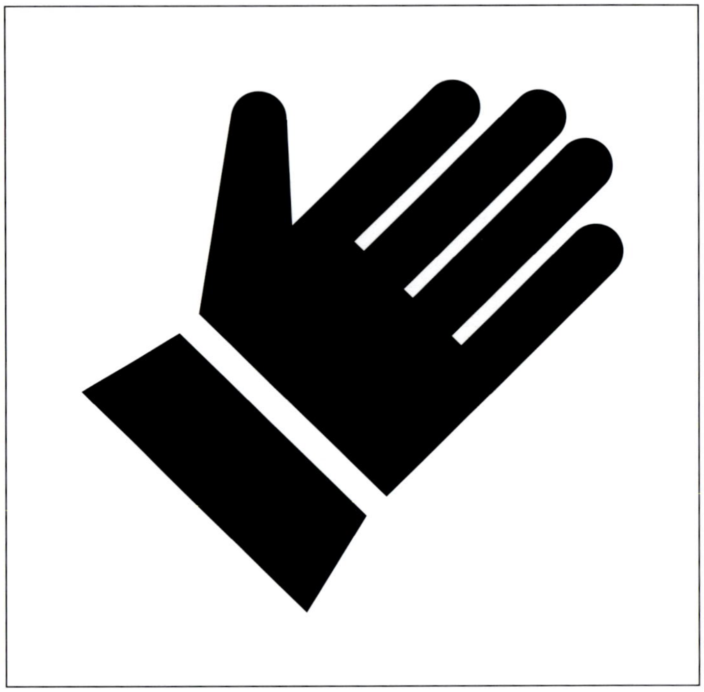

1.1

1.2

2.1

2.2

3.1

3.2

6027

LATEX GLOVE

1.2 Latex gloves must be worn

3.2 Latex gloves

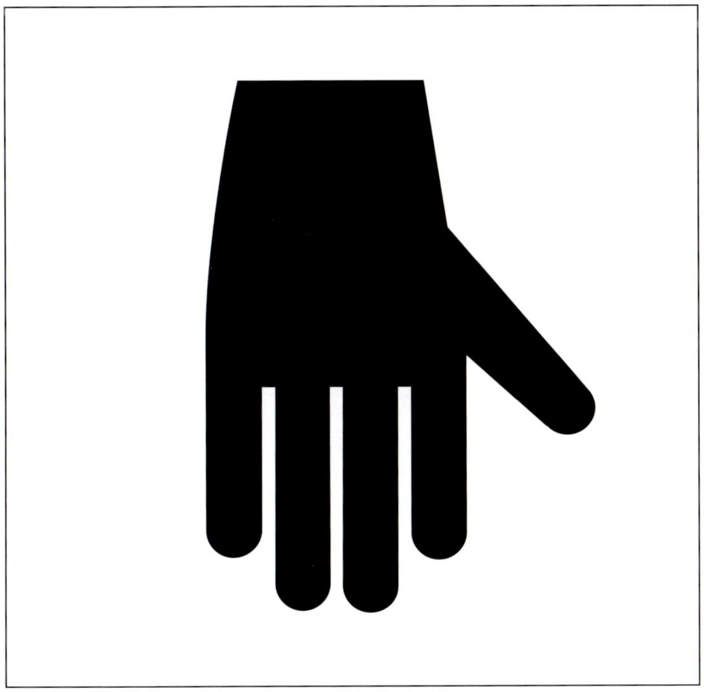

1.1

1.2

2.1

2.2

3.1

3.2

6028

SAFETY BOOT

1.2 Foot protection must be worn

3.2 Safety boots

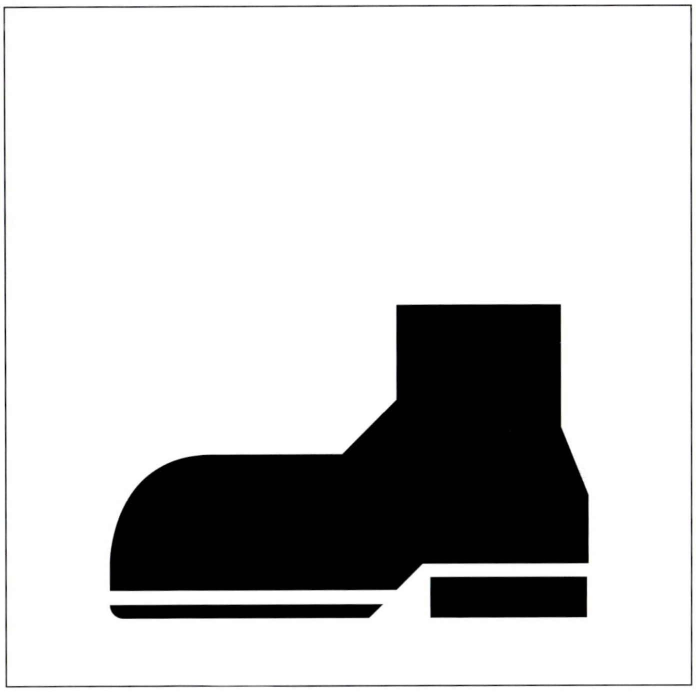

1.1

1.2

2.1

2.2

3.1

3.2

6029

SHIRT, WITH LONG SLEEVES, BUTTONED UP TO THE NECK

1.2 Long sleeves must be worn

3.2 Protective suits

1.1

1.2

2.1

2.2

3.1

3.2

6030

HUMAN FIGURE, IN ENVIROSUIT

1.2 Envirosuit must be worn

3.2 Envirosuit(s)

1.1

1.2

2.1

2.2

3.1

3.2

6031

HUMAN FIGURE, WITH SHOVEL IN HANDS, DIGGING

1.1 No digging

2.1 Caution! Men at work, work in progress

1.1

1.2

2.1

2.2

3.1

3.2

6032

HUMAN FIGURE, WITH CHAINSAW IN HAND

1.1 No logging

2.1 Caution! Logging

1.1

1.2

2.1

2.2

3.1

3.2

0
1
2
3
4
5
6
7
8
Index

6033

LIQUOR AND WINE BOTTLES

1.1 No drinking and driving, no alcohol allowed

1.1

1.2

2.1

2.2

3.1

3.2

6034

HUMAN FIGURE, FALLING, WITH HARNESS AND SAFETY ROPE

1.2 Fall protection must be worn

1.1

1.2

2.1

2.2

3.1

3.2

6035

HUMAN FIGURE, OFF BALANCE, OVER HORIZONTAL BAR

2.1 Caution! Slippery floor

1.1 1.2

2.1

2.2

3.1 3.2

6036

HUMAN FIGURES, MAN, WOMAN, CHILD

1.1 No families allowed

3.2 Family (families)

1.1

1.2

2.1 2.2

3.1

3.2

6037

HUMAN HEAD, WITH EARMUFFS

1.2 Hearing protection must be worn

3.2 Earmuffs

1.1

1.2

2.1

2.2

3.1

3.2

6038

HUMAN HEAD, WITH HAIR NET

1.2 Hair net must be worn

3.2 Hair net(s)

1.1

1.2

2.1

2.2

3.1

3.2

6039

HUMAN HEAD, WITH HARD HAT

1.2 Head protection must be worn

3.2 Hard hat(s)

1.1

1.2 

2.1 

2.2 

3.1 

3.2 

6040

HUMAN HEAD, WITH RESPIRATOR

1.2 Respirator must be worn

3.2 Respirator(s)

1.1

1.2 

2.1 

2.2 

3.1 

3.2 

6041

HUMAN HEAD, WITH RESPIRATOR

1.2 Respirator must be worn

3.2 Respirator(s)

1.1

1.2

2.1

2.2

3.1

3.2

6042

HUMAN HEAD, WITH MASK

1.2 Mask must be worn

3.2 Mask(s)

1.1

1.2

2.1

2.2

3.1

3.2

6043

HUMAN HEAD, WITH SAFETY GLASSES

1.2 Eye protection must be worn

3.2 Eye protection, glasses

1.1

1.2

2.1

2.2

3.1

3.2

6044

EYE, DROPS, SPRAYING UPWARD

3.1 Eye-washing station

1.1

1.2

2.1

2.2

3.1

3.2

6045

WATER DROPS, OVER CLASPED HANDS

1.2 Wash your hands

3.2 Hand-washing station

6046

SHOWER STAND, WATER DROPS

3.1 Emergency shower

6047

STRETCHER, GREEK CROSS ABOVE

3.1 Stretcher, first aid

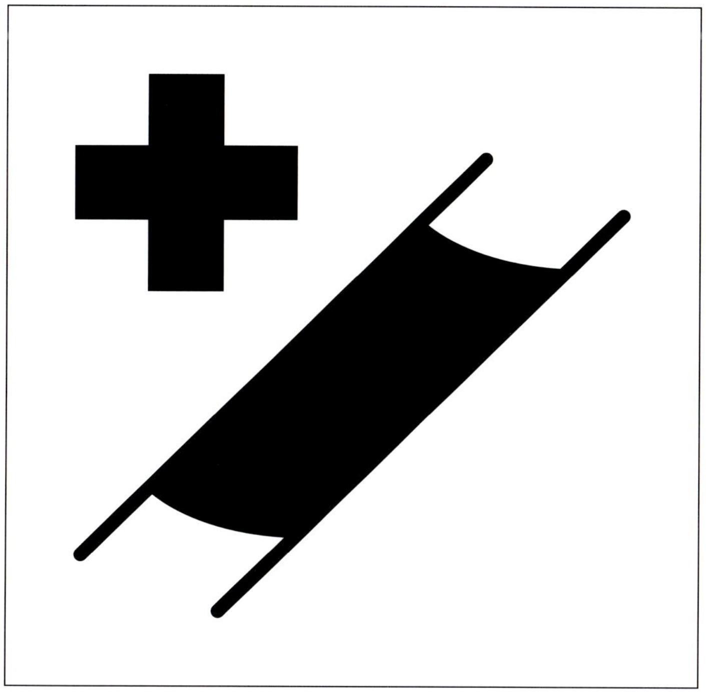

1.1

1.2

2.1

2.2

3.1

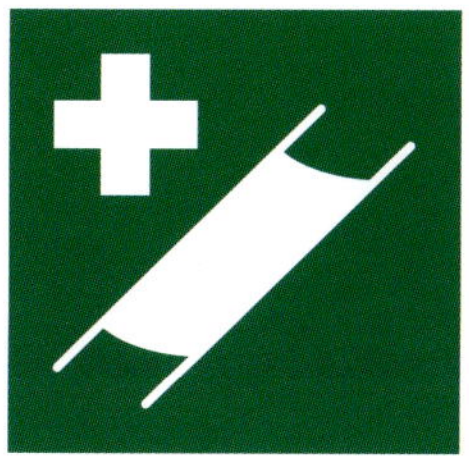

3.2

6048

GREEK CROSS, OVER BANDAGED HAND

3.1 First aid station

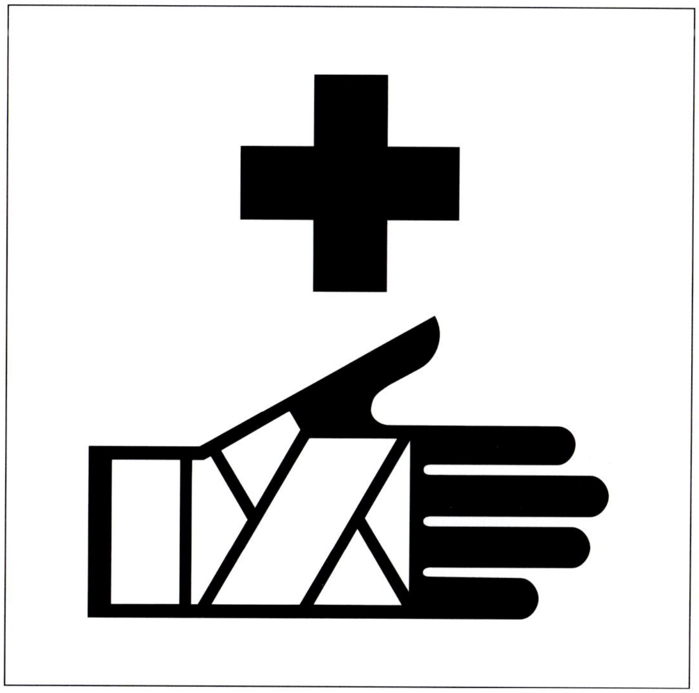

1.1

1.2

2.1

2.2

3.1

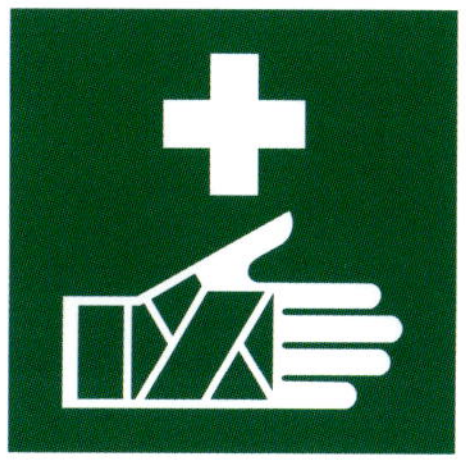

3.2

0
1
2
3
4
5
6
7
8
Index

6049

FORKLIFT

1.1 No forklifts allowed
2.1 Caution! Forklift
3.2 Forklift(s)

1.1

1.2

2.1

2.2

3.1

3.2

6050

FORKLIFT, WITH PACKING CRATE ON FORK

1.1 No forklifts allowed
2.1 Caution! Forklift
3.2 Forklift(s)

1.1

1.2

2.1

2.2

3.1

3.2

6051

CONCRETE MIXER TRUCK

1.1 No concrete mixer truck(s) allowed
2.1 Caution! Concrete mixer trucks
3.2 Concrete mixer truck(s)

1.1

1.2

2.1

2.2

3.1

3.2

6052

LOADER

1.1 No loaders allowed
2.1 Caution! Loader(s)
3.2 Loader(s)

1.1

1.2

2.1

2.2

3.1

3.2

6053

TRACTOR, BULLDOZER

1.1 No escavating

2.1 Caution! Bulldozer

3.2 Bulldozer(s)

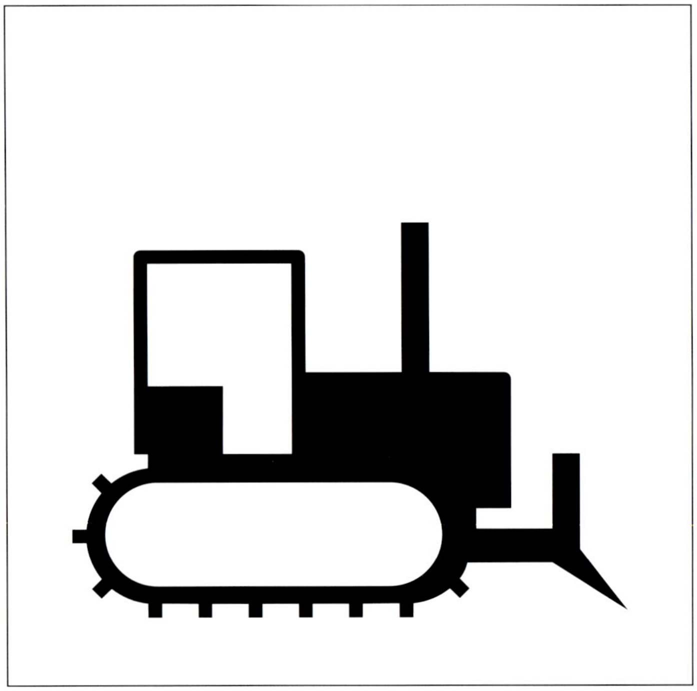

1.1

1.2

2.1

2.2

3.1

3.2

6054

HEAVY TRUCK

1.1 No heavy trucks allowed

2.1 Caution! Heavy trucks

3.2 Heavy truck(s)

1.1

1.2

2.1

2.2

3.1

3.2

6055

TRUCK, WITH LOGGING TRAILER

1.1 No trucks allowed
2.1 Caution! Logging trucks
3.2 Logging truck(s)

6056.

DOTTED STEM ARROW, OVER CYLINDER

2.1 Caution! Roll conveyor

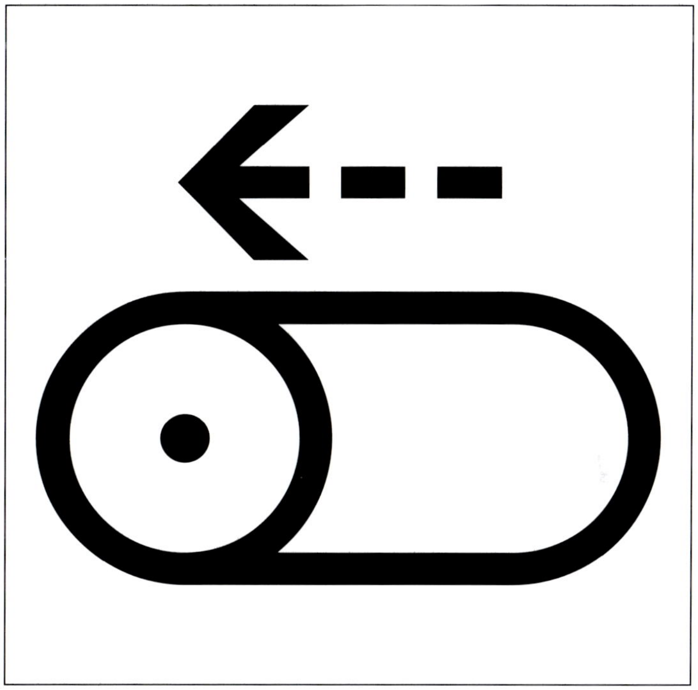

1.1

1.2

2.1

2.2

3.1

3.2

1.1

1.2

2.1

2.2

3.1

3.2

6057

HUMAN FIGURE, FALLING, OVER SHAFT, CIRCULAR BLADES INSIDE

2.1 Caution! Tirturator (tree bark peeler)

6058

ROOF EDGE, SNOW COVERED, WEDGE-SHAPED ICICLES

2.1 Caution! Falling ice

6059

WALKIE-TALKIE

1.1 No wireless devices allowed

3.2 Walkie-talkie(s)

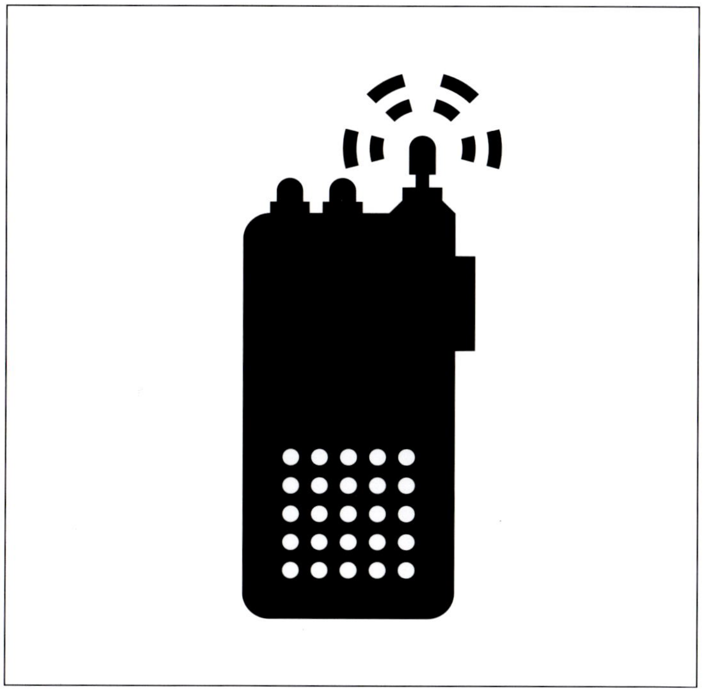

1.1

1.2

2.1

2.2

3.1

3.2

6060

CAMERA

1.1 No cameras allowed, do not take photos

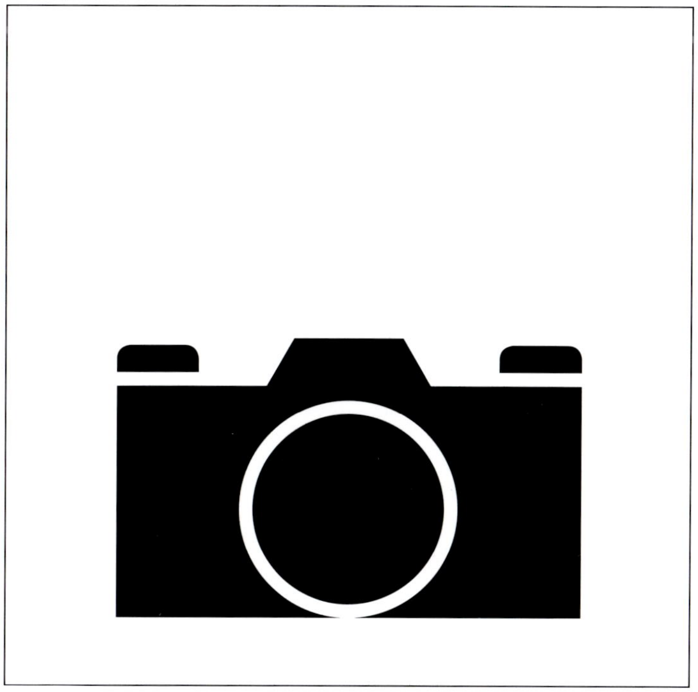

1.1

1.2

2.1

2.2

3.1

3.2

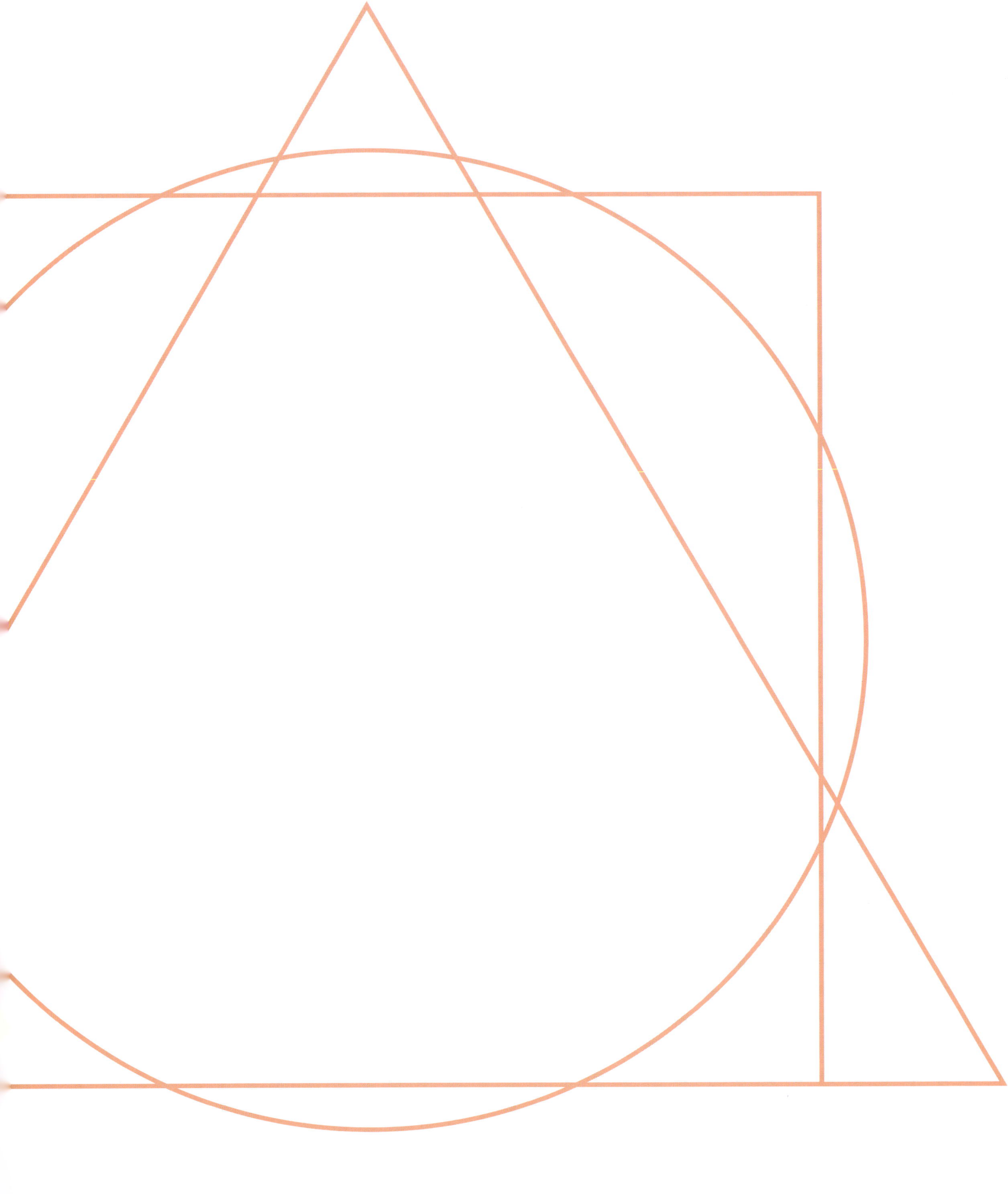

7001* (See page 309.)

DANGEROUS CURRENTS

HUMAN FIGURE, IN WATER, FIGHTING CURRENTS, CIRCULAR ARROWS

2.1 Caution! Dangerous currents

1.1

1.2

2.1

2.2

3.1

3.2

7002* (with 7001)

HUMAN FIGURE, RUNNING AWAY, ARROW ABOVE, WATER

1.2 Stay back from water

1.1

1.2

2.1

2.2

3.1

3.2

7003

RAPIDS, FALLS

CANOE, ANGLED AT 45°, OVER WATERFALL, HUMAN FIGURE, FALLING, OVER WATER

2.1 Caution! Falls or rapids ahead

1.1

1.2

2.1

2.2

3.1

3.2

7004

SWEEPERS

FALLEN TREE, PARTIALLY IN WATER, HUMAN FIGURE, IN CANOE, PADDLE, FLYING AWAY

2.1 Caution! Fallen trees in river

1.1

1.2

2.1

2.2

3.1

3.2

7005

COLD WATER

THERMOMETER, OVER WATER

2.1 Caution! Frigid water

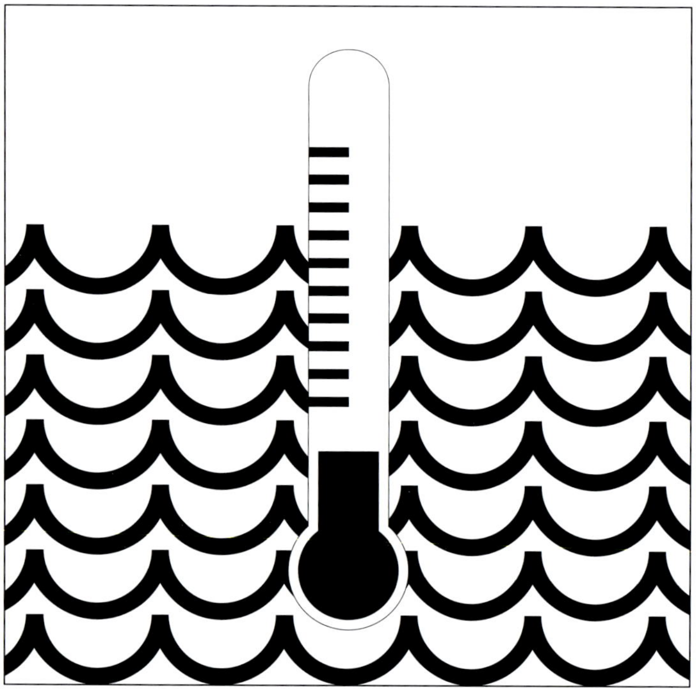

1.1

1.2

2.1

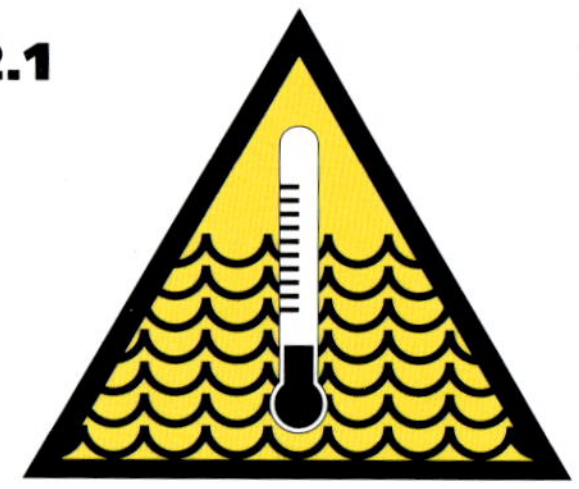

2.2

3.1

3.2

7006

DEADHEADS, ROCKS

HUMAN FIGURE, IN CANOE, PADDLE, FLYING AWAY, ROCK, LOG, IN WATER

2.1 Caution! Rocks and logs under water

1.1

1.2

2.1

2.2

3.1

3.2

7007*

STRONG CURRENTS

HUMAN FIGURE, IN WATER, FIGHTING CURRENTS, CIRCULAR ARROWS

2.1 Caution! Strong currents

1.1

1.2

2.1

2.2

3.1

3.2

7008* (with 7007)

HUMAN FIGURE, RUNNING AWAY, ARROW ABOVE, WATER, ARROWS

1.2 Stay out of water

1.1

1.2

2.1

2.2

3.1

3.2

7009*

ROGUE WAVES

LARGE WAVE, BUBBLES, HUMAN FIGURE, SWEPT AWAY, OVER WATER

2.1 Caution! Large waves

1.1

1.2

2.1

2.2

3.1

3.2

7010* (with 7009)

LARGE WAVE, BUBBLES, HUMAN FIGURE, STANDING ON SHORE, OVER WATER

1.2 Stay away from beach

1.1

1.2

2.1

2.2

3.1

3.2

7011*

SURGE CHANNELS

HUMAN FIGURE, JUMPING, OVER WATER

2.1 Caution! Water may rise suddenly

1.1

1.2

2.1

2.2

3.1

3.2

7012* (with 7011)

HUMAN FIGURE, RUNNING AWAY, ARROW ABOVE, CIRCULAR ARROWS, OVER WATER

1.2 Stay well back

1.1

1.2

2.1

2.2

3.1

3.2

7013

SLIPPERY ROCKS

HUMAN FIGURE, FALLING, OVER ROCKS, WATER

2.1 Caution! Slippery rocks

1.1

1.2

2.1

2.2

3.1

3.2

7014

STEEP DROP-OFF

HUMAN FIGURE, LOOSING GROUND, OVER WATER

2.1 Caution! Bottom drops off suddenly

1.1

1.2

2.1

2.2

3.1

3.2

7015*

BEACH LOGS

CLOUD, BLOWING, ARROWS, HUMAN FIGURE, DROWNING, LOGS, IN WATER

2.1 Caution! Logs may move in stormy weather

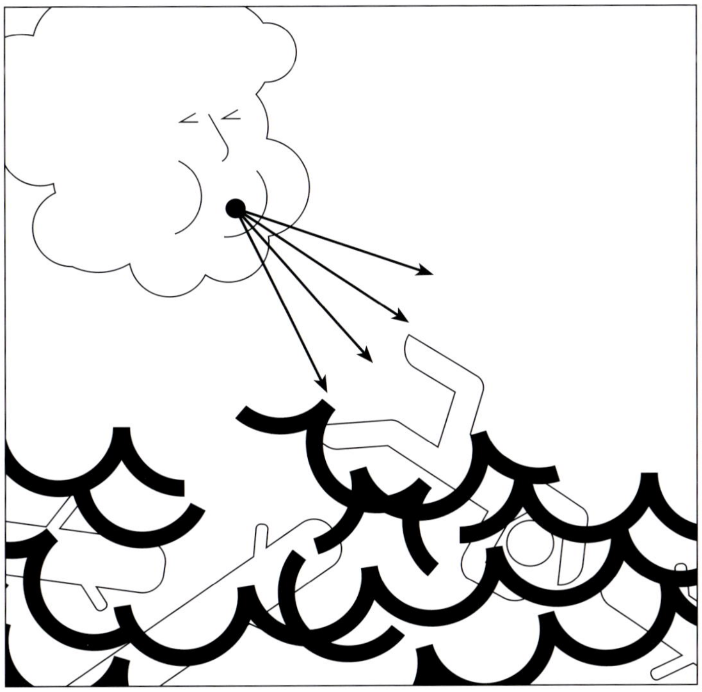

1.1 1.2

2.1

2.2

3.1 3.2

7016* (with 7015)

HUMAN FIGURE, RUNNING AWAY, ARROW ABOVE, LOGS, WATER

1.2 Stay away from beach when stormy

1.1

1.2

2.1 2.2

3.1 3.2

7017*

SHELLFISH

SKULL AND CROSSBONES

2.1 Caution! Poisonous shellfish

1.1

1.2

2.1

2.2

3.1

3.2

7018* (with 7017)

SHELLFISH

1.1 Do not eat shellfish

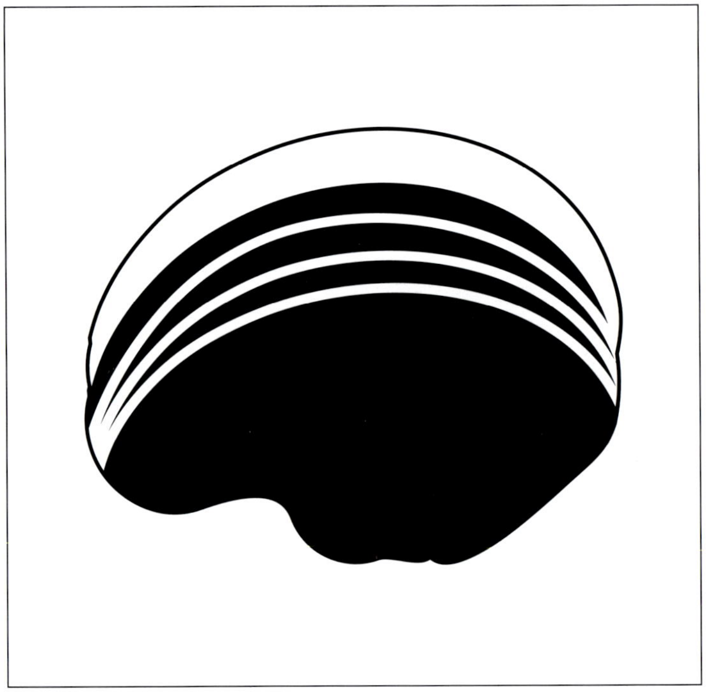

1.1

1.2

2.1

2.2

3.1

3.2

7019*

UNPROTECTED STEEP TERRAIN

STEEP CLIFF, HUMAN FIGURE, FALLING

2.1 Caution! Dangerous cliff

1.1

1.2

2.1

2.2

3.1

3.2

7020* (with 7019)

STEEP CLIFF, HUMAN FIGURE, STANDING, ARROW

1.2 Stay back from edge

1.1

1.2

2.1

2.2

3.1

3.2

7021*

STEEP DROP-OFF

HUMAN FIGURE, STUMBLING, OVER STEEP SLOPE

2.1 Caution! Dangerous slope

1.1

1.2

2.1

2.2

3.1

3.2

7022* (with 7021)

HUMAN FIGURE, STANDING, OVER STEEP SLOPE, ARROW

1.2 Stay back from edge

1.1

1.2

2.1

2.2

3.1

3.2

7023*

PROTECTED STEEP TERRAIN

FENCE, HUMAN FIGURE, FALLING

2.1 Caution! Dangerous cliff

1.1

1.2

2.1

2.2

3.1

3.2

7024* (with 7023)

HUMAN FIGURE, STANDING, BEHIND FENCE, ARROW

1.2 Stay behind fence

1.1

1.2

2.1

2.2

3.1

3.2

7025

ROCKFALL

ROCKS, FALLING, HUMAN FIGURE, FALLING, HIT BY ROCKS

2.1 Caution! Falling rocks

1.1

1.2

2.1

2.2

3.1

3.2

7026

STRONG WINDS

CLOUD, BLOWING, ARROWS, HUMAN FIGURE, BLOWN AWAY

2.1 Caution! High winds

1.1

1.2

2.1

2.2

3.1

3.2

7027

FALLING BRANCHES

TREE, FALLING BRANCHES, HUMAN FIGURE, HIT BY BRANCHES

2.1 Caution! Falling branches when windy

1.1

1.2

2.1

2.2

3.1

3.2

7028

SNOW ON TRAILS

STEEP TERRAIN, COVERED WITH SNOW, HUMAN FIGURE, FALLING

2.1 Caution! Slippery snow patches on trail

1.1

1.2

2.1

2.2

3.1

3.2

7029

UNSTABLE GROUND

ROCKS, ROLLING, HUMAN FIGURE, FALLING

2.1 Caution! Surface loose or slippery

1.1

1.2

2.1

2.2

3.1

3.2

7030

ICE ON TRAILS

HUMAN FIGURE, FALLING, OVER ICE

2.1 Caution! Ice on trail

1.1

1.2

2.1

2.2

3.1

3.2

7031*

HYPOTHERMIA

TWO THERMOMETERS, ARROW, POINTING TO LOWER LEVEL OF MERCURY

2.1 Caution! Temperature may drop quickly

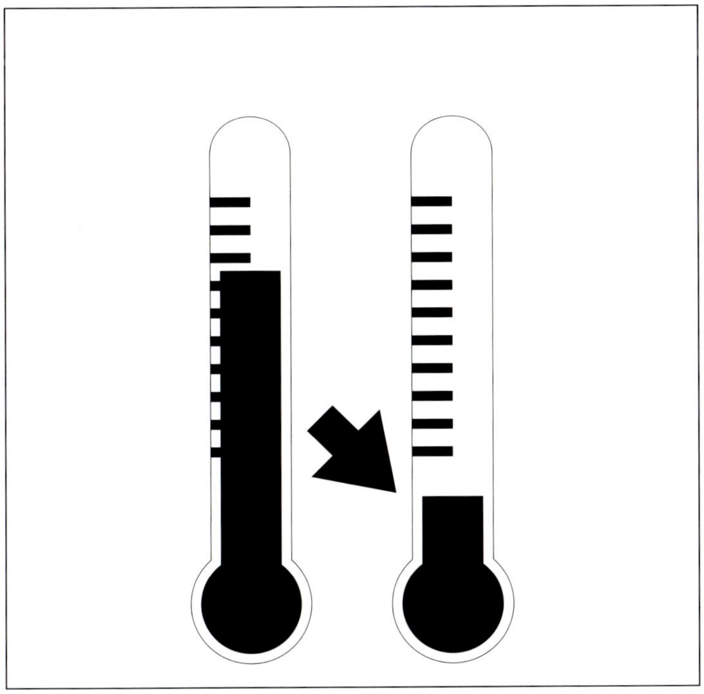

1.1

1.2

2.1

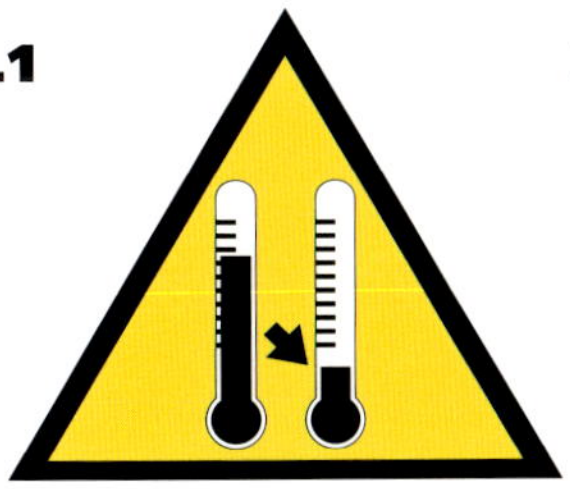

2.2

3.1

3.2

7032* (with 7031)

CAP, SWEATER, SOCKS

1.2 Carry warm clothing

1.1

1.2

2.1

2.2

3.1

3.2

7033

BEAR

2.1 Caution! Bears in area

1.1

1.2

2.1

2.2

3.1

3.2

7034

COUGAR

2.1 Caution! Cougars in area

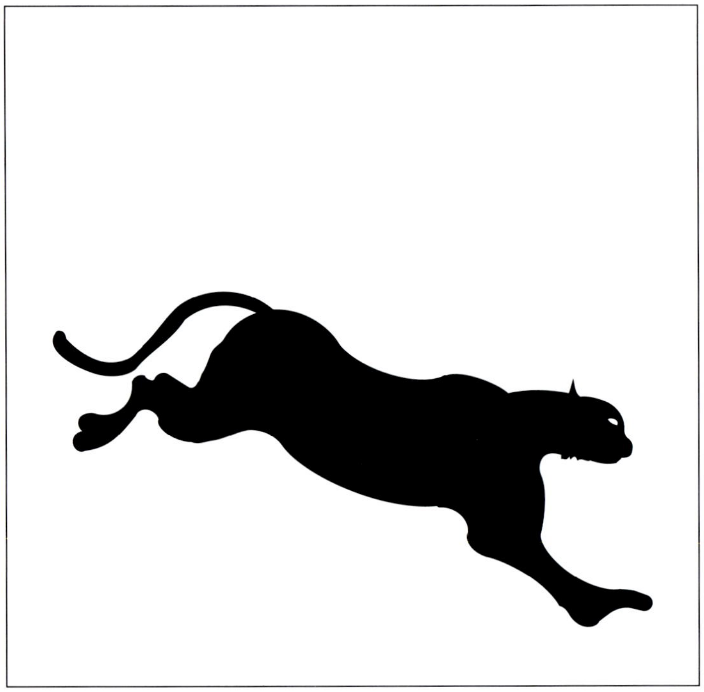

1.1

1.2

2.1

2.2

3.1

3.2

7035

COYOTE

2.1 Caution! Coyotes in area

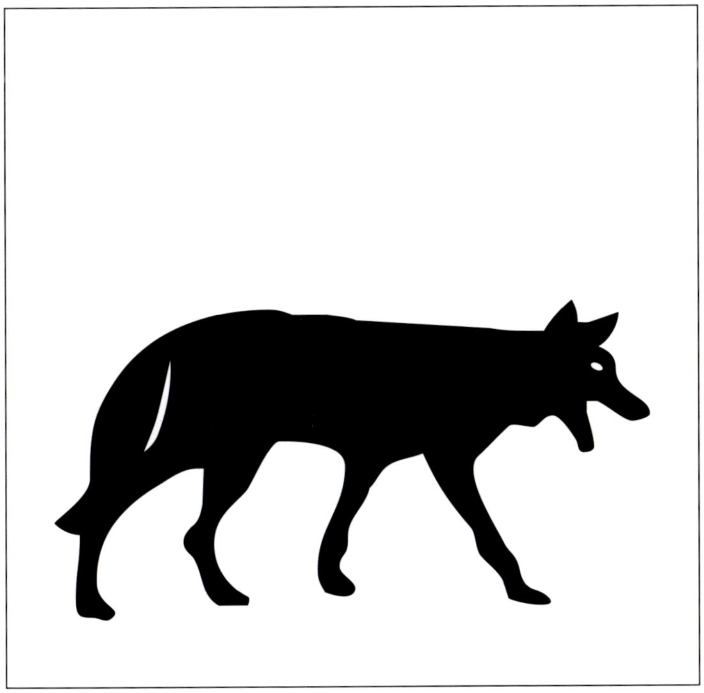

1.1
1.2 

2.1 
2.2 

3.1 
3.2 

7036

ELK

2.1 Caution! Elk may attack you

1.1
1.2 

2.1 
2.2 

3.1 
3.2 

0
1
2
3
4
5
6
7
8
Index

7037*

BISON

2.1 Caution! Bison may attack you

7038* (with 7037)

MOTOR VEHICLE, OPEN DOOR ON DRIVER'S SIDE, HUMAN FIGURE

1.1 Do not get out of your car

7039*

TICK(S)

MAGNIFYING GLASS, OVER TICK

2.1 Caution! Ticks in area

1.1

1.2

2.1

2.2

3.1

3.2

7040* (with 7039)

HUMAN FIGURES, ADULT CHECKING CHILD'S HEAD

1.2 Check yourselves for ticks after hiking

1.1

1.2

2.1

2.2

3.1

3.2

7041

RATTLESNAKE

COILED

2.1 Caution! Rattlesnakes in area

1.1

1.2

2.1

2.2

3.1

3.2

7042

WASPS

FLYING AROUND HIVE

2.1 Caution! Wasps in area

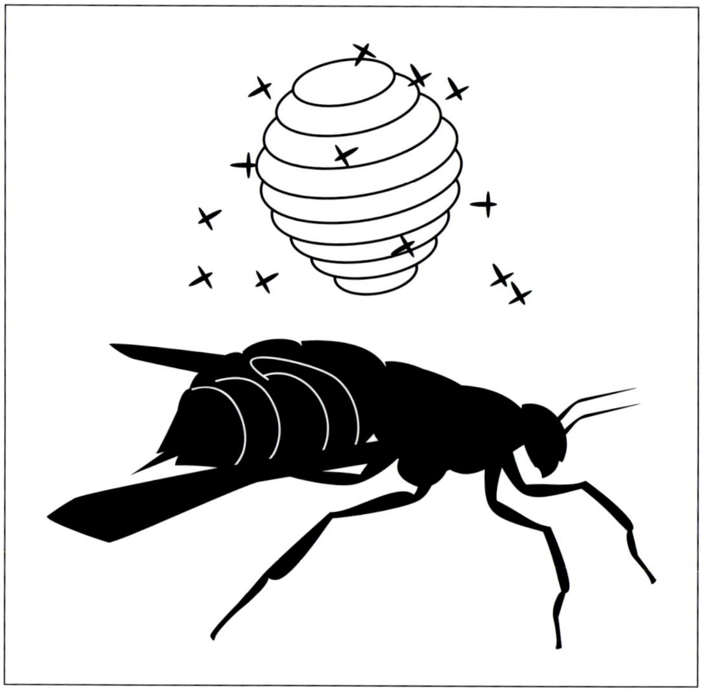

1.1

1.2

2.1

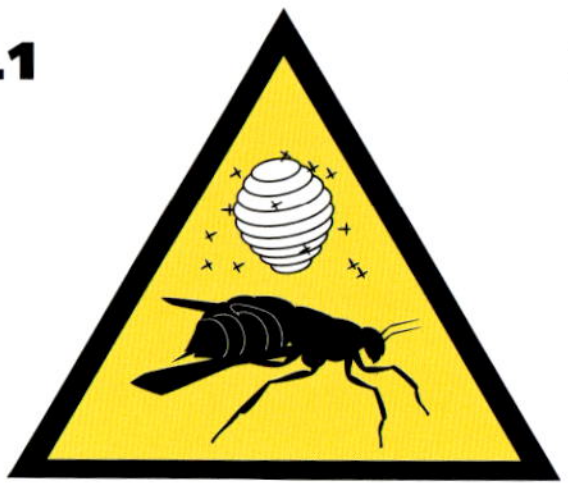

2.2

3.1

3.2

7043*

THIN ICE

HUMAN FIGURE, FALLING, THROUGH ICE, OVER WATER

2.1 Caution! Thin ice

1.1

1.2

2.1

2.2

3.1

3.2

7044* (with 7043)

HUMAN FIGURE, WALKING, ON ICE, OVER WATER

1.1 Stay off the ice

1.1

1.2

2.1

2.2

3.1

3.2

7045

AVALANCHE

SKI, HAND, SKI POLE, STICKING UP FROM SNOW, ICE

2.1 Caution! Avalanche danger ahead

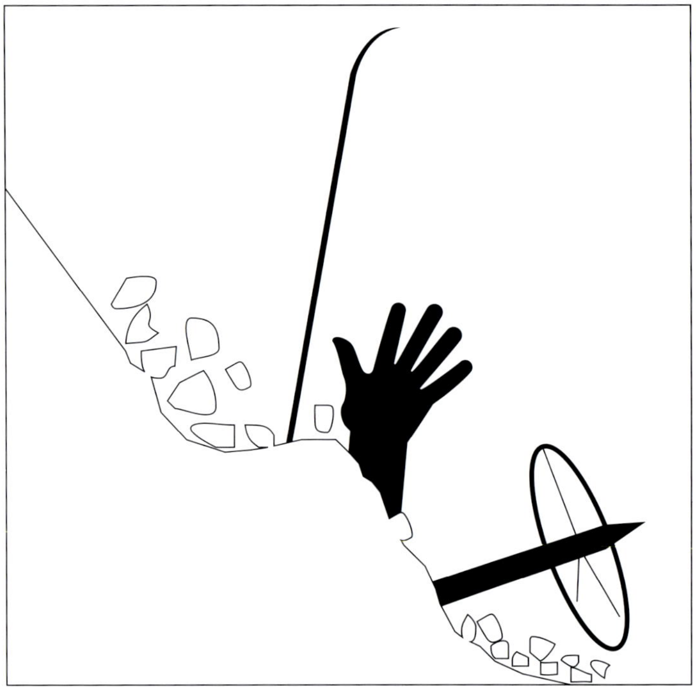

1.1

1.2

2.1

2.2

3.1

3.2

7046

UNPROTECTED CREVASSES

HUMAN FIGURE, FALLING, INTO HOLE, PATCHES OF SNOW

2.1 Caution! Hidden crevasses

1.1

1.2

2.1

2.2

3.1

3.2

7047*

PROTECTED CREVASSES

FENCE, HUMAN FIGURE, FALLING, INTO HOLE, PATCHES OF SNOW

2.1 Caution! Hidden crevasses

1.1

1.2

2.1

2.2

3.1

3.2

7048* (with 7047)

HUMAN FIGURE, STANDING, BEHIND FENCE, ARROW

1.2 Stay behind fence

1.1

1.2

2.1

2.2

3.1

3.2

7049*

ICE BRIDGES

HUMAN FIGURE, FALLING, INTO HOLE, PIECES OF ICE, OVER WATER

2.1 Caution! Thin ice

1.1

1.2

2.1

2.2

3.1

3.2

7050* (with 7049)

HUMAN FIGURE, WALKING, ON ICE, OVER WATER

1.1 Stay off the ice

1.1

1.2

2.1

2.2

3.1

3.2

SNOW BRIDGES

HUMAN FIGURE, FALLING, INTO HOLE, PATCHES OF SNOW

2.1 Caution! Snow bridges may cave in

1.1

1.2

2.1

2.2

3.1

3.2

The pictographs in Series 7 – Hazards in Parks & Recreational Areas – were originally developed as warning signs for Parks Canada. In *PictografIcSystems: Nonverbal. Universal.*, we made them consistent with the rest of the pictographs in the **PictograficSystems**©, using mostly image content descriptors published in this book.

The pictographs in Series 7 should be used as text signs along with their messages.

* Pictograph pairs with asterisks after their serial numbers should always be used together in signs, as indicated.

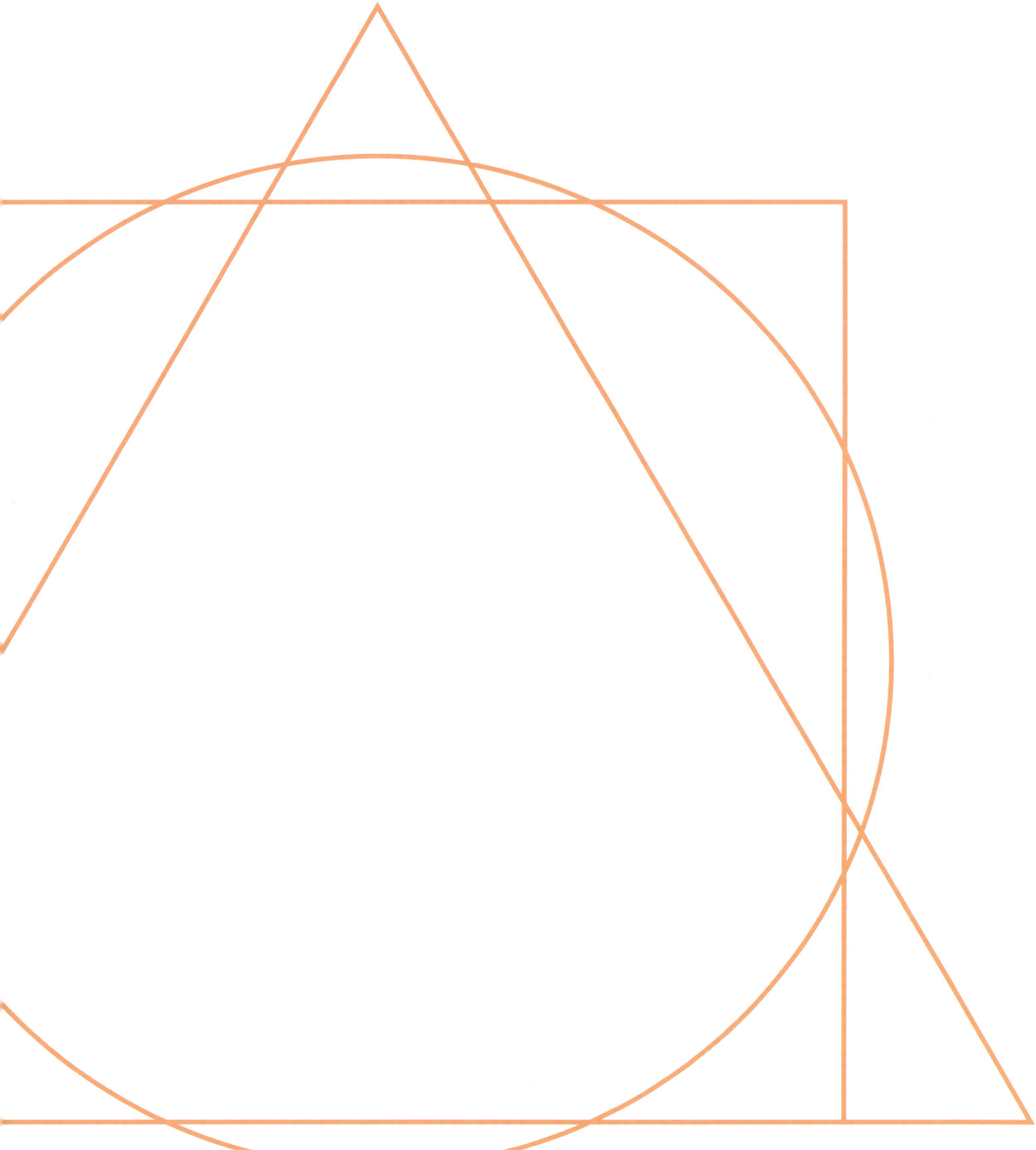

STRAIGHT ARROW

1.25 width stem

3.2 This way

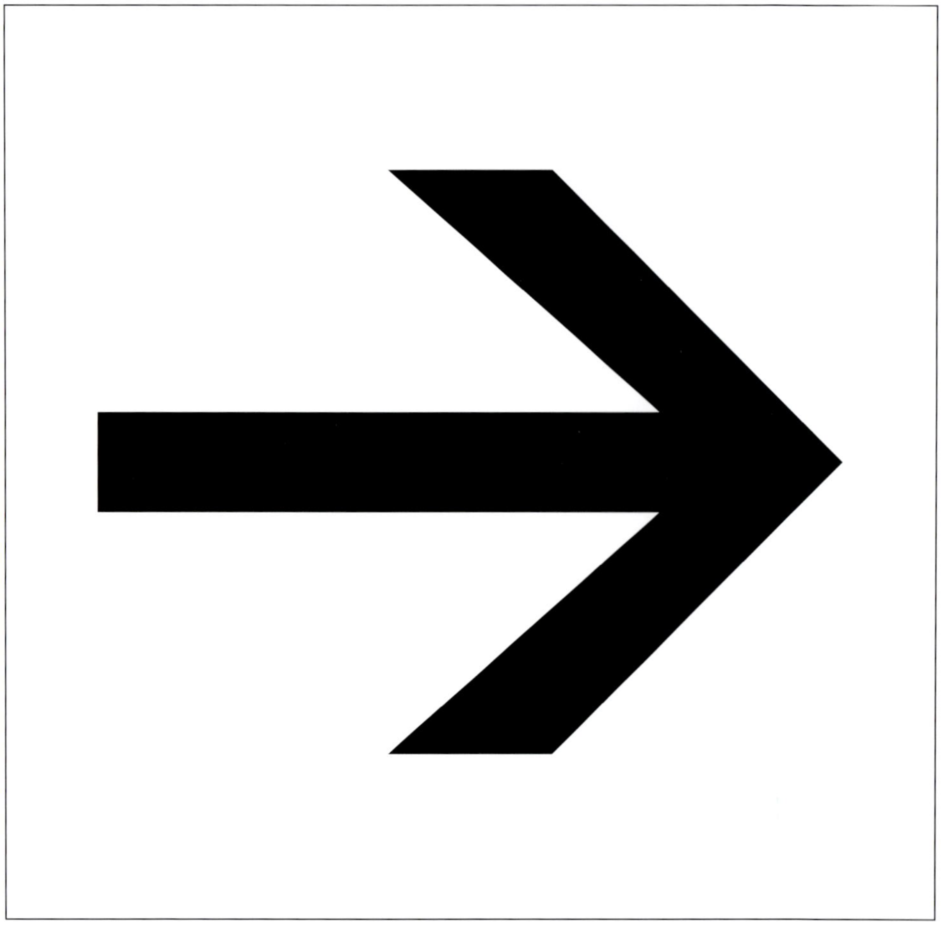

3.2

BENT ARROW

1.25 width stem

3.2 This way

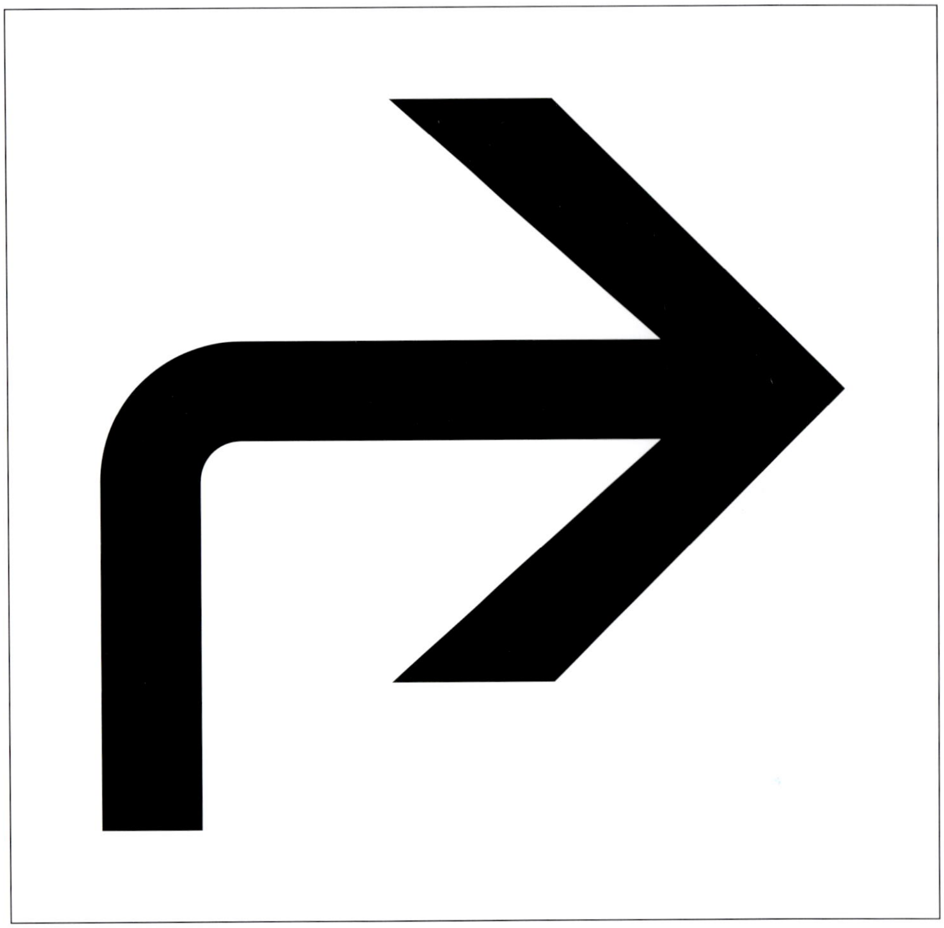

3.2

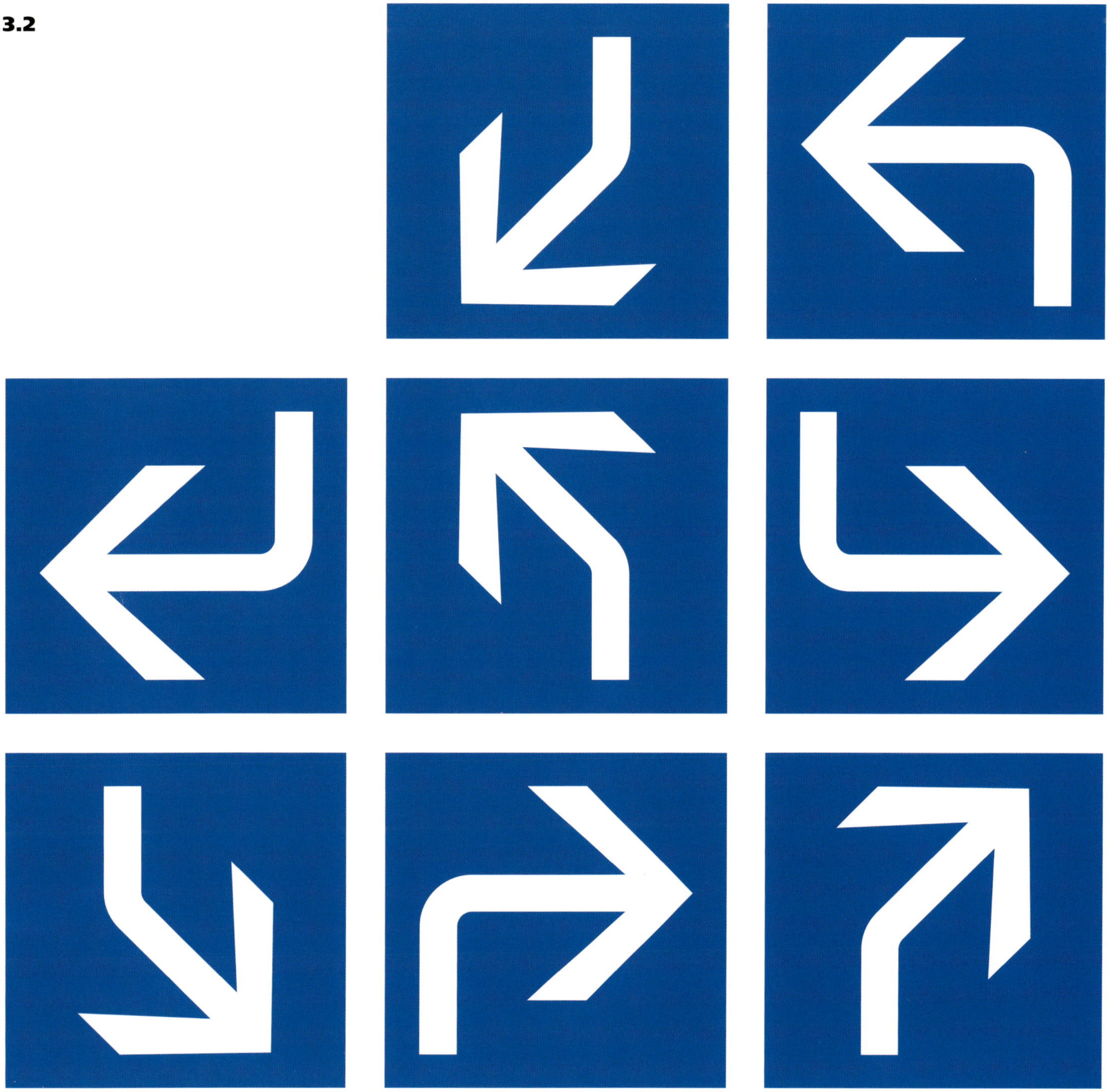

0
1
2
3
4
5
6
7
8
Index

8017–8024

STRAIGHT ARROW

1.5 width stem

3.2 This way

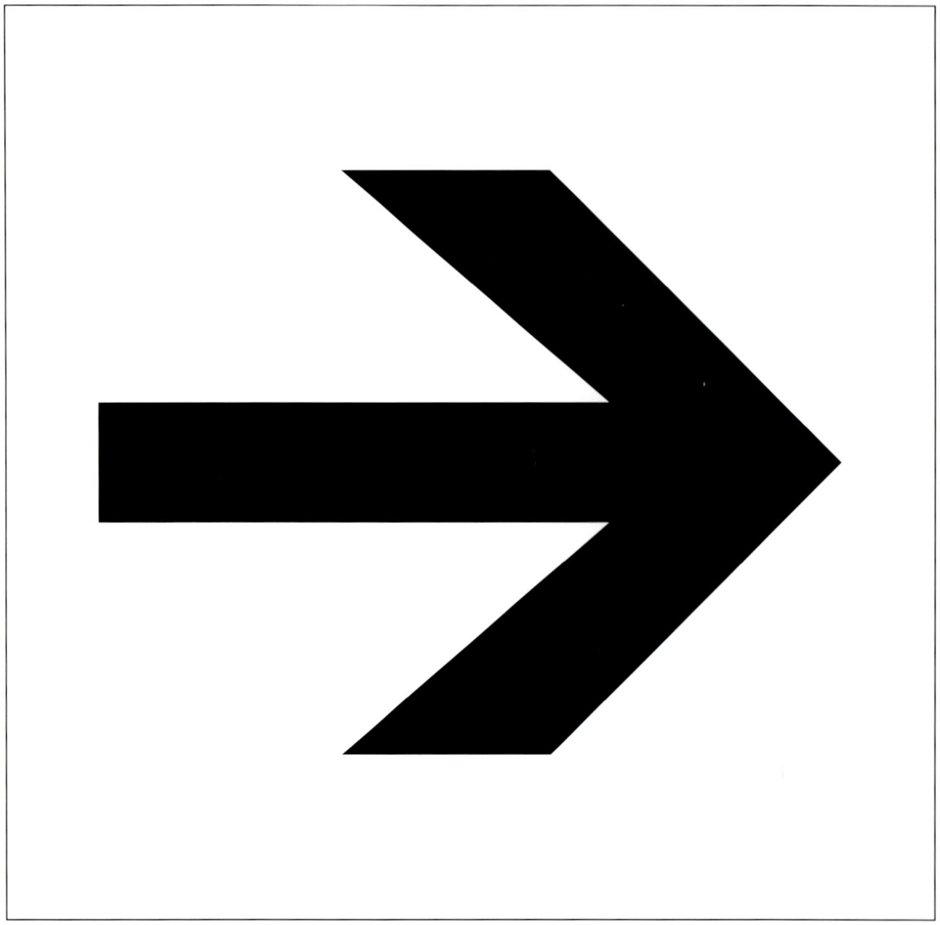

3.2

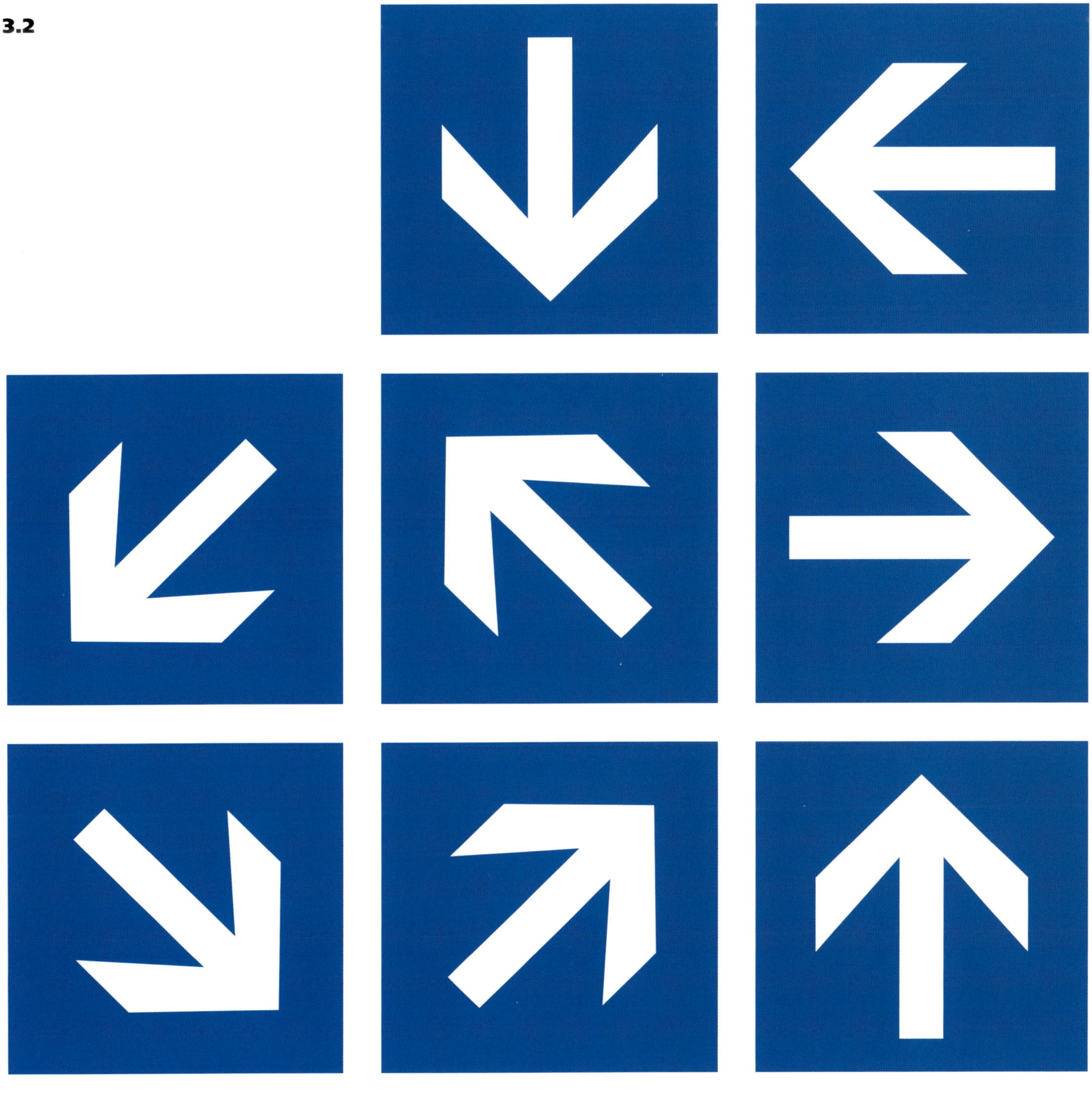

BENT ARROW

1.5 width stem

3.2 This way

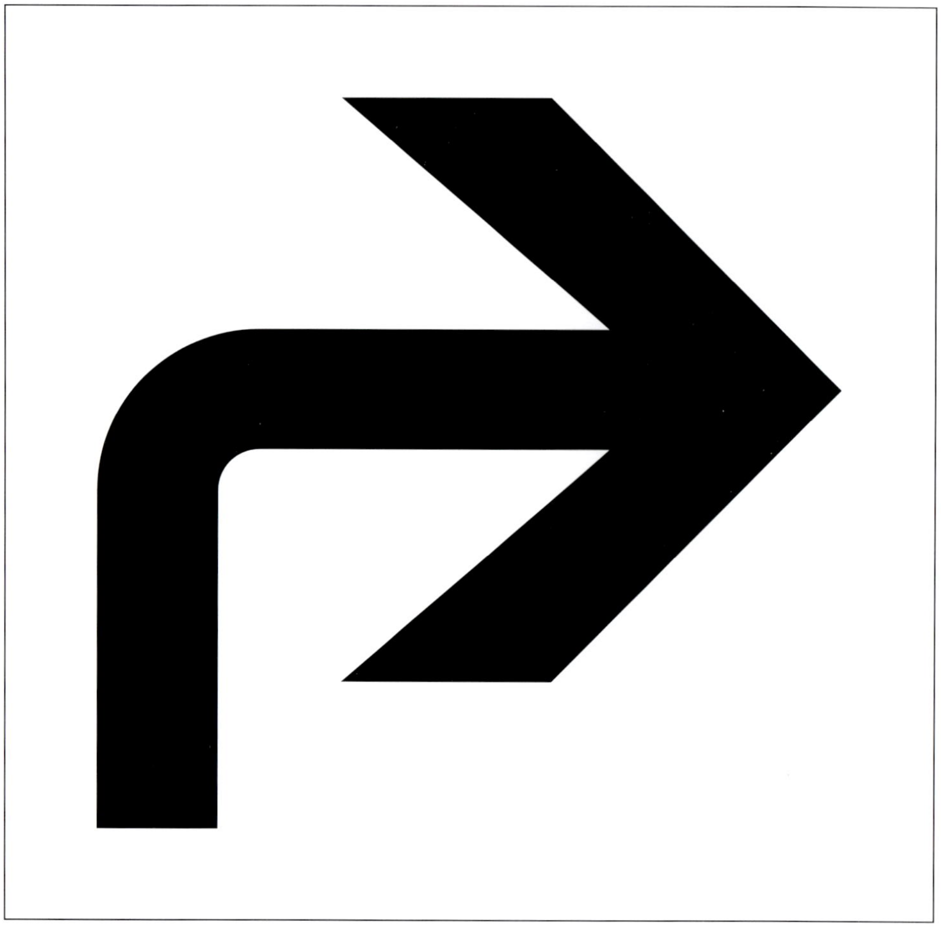

3.2

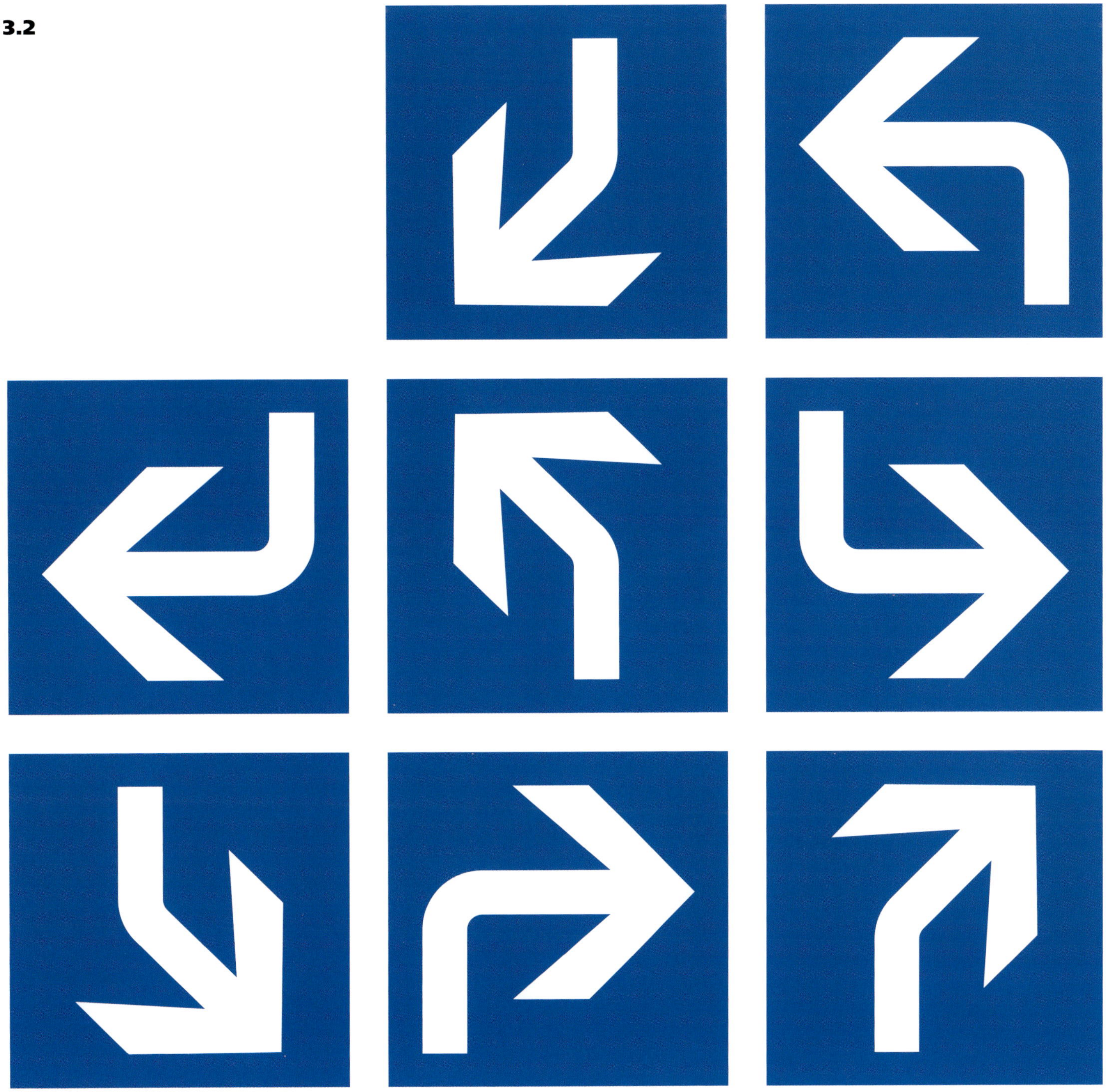

0
1
2
3
4
5
6
7
8
Index

WEDGE-SHAPED ARROW

3.2 This way

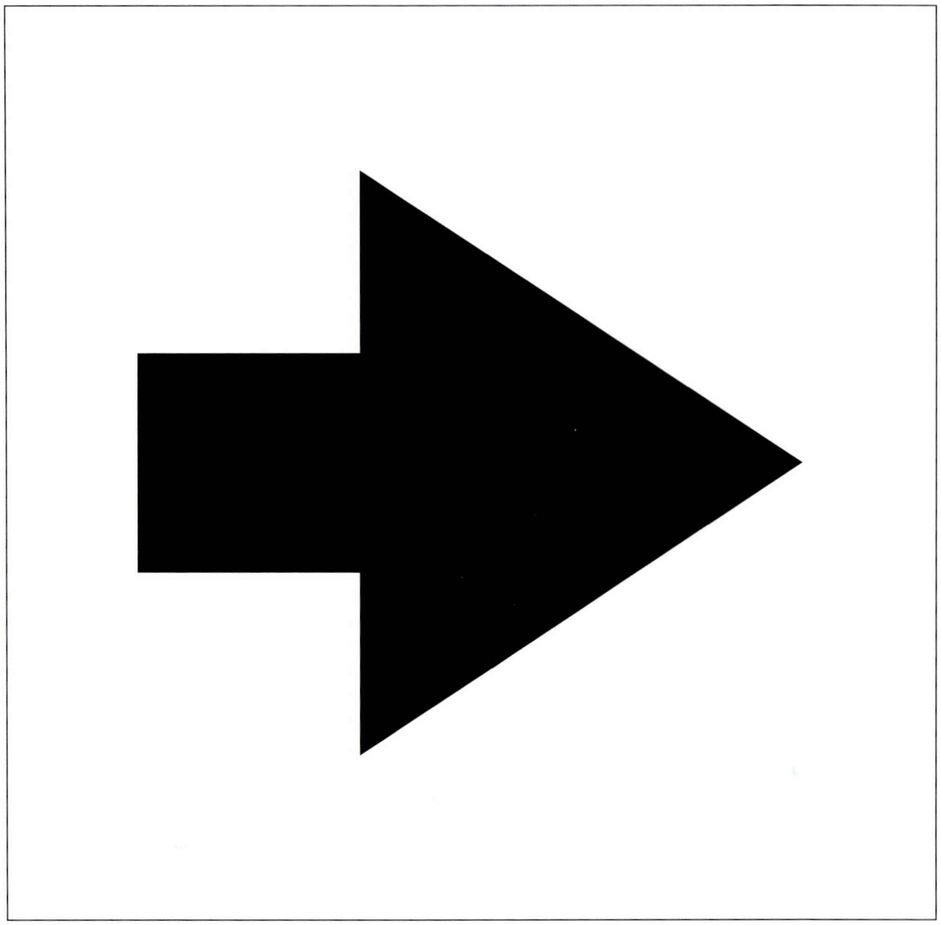

3.2

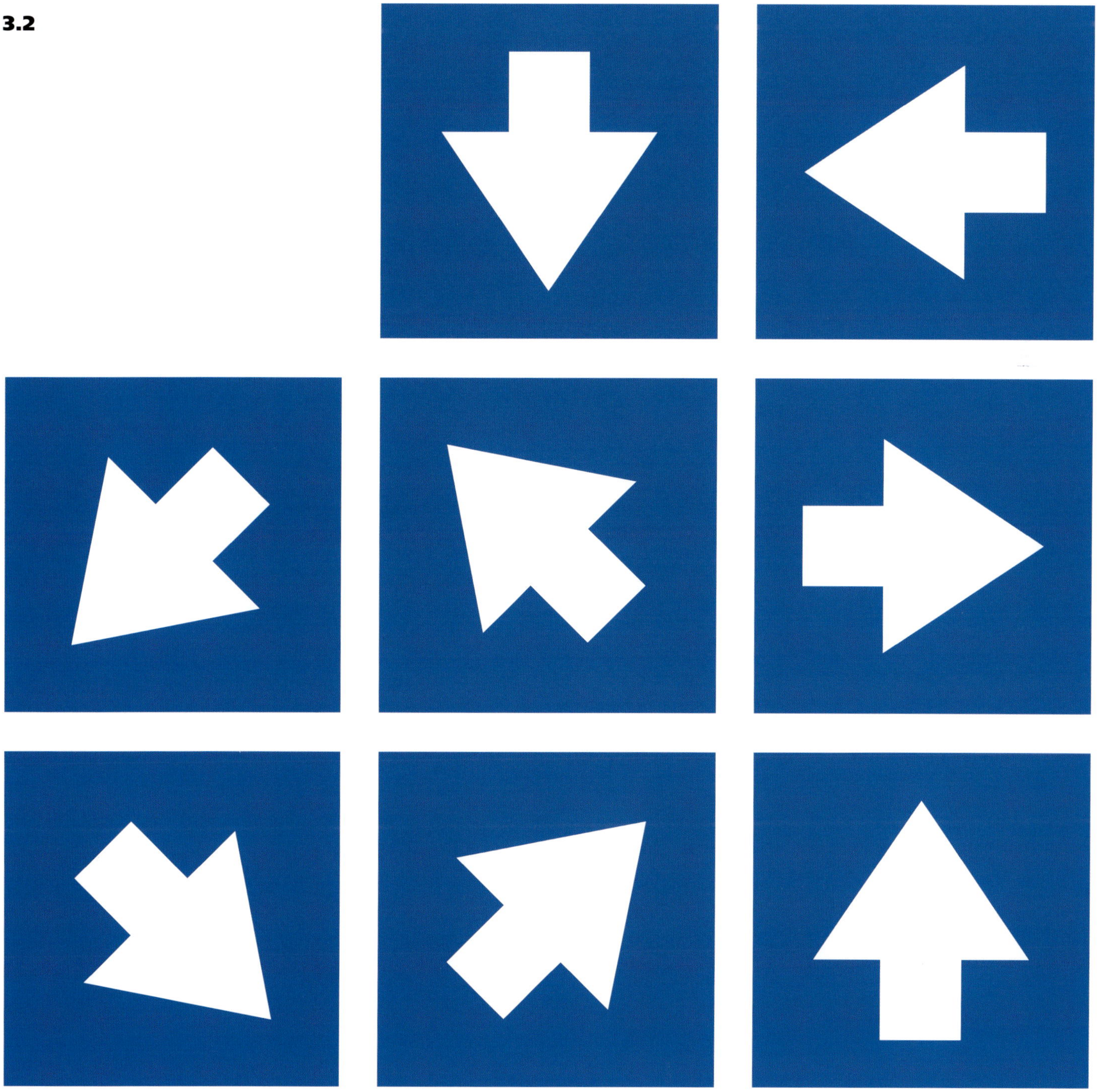

0
1
2
3
4
5
6
7
8
Index

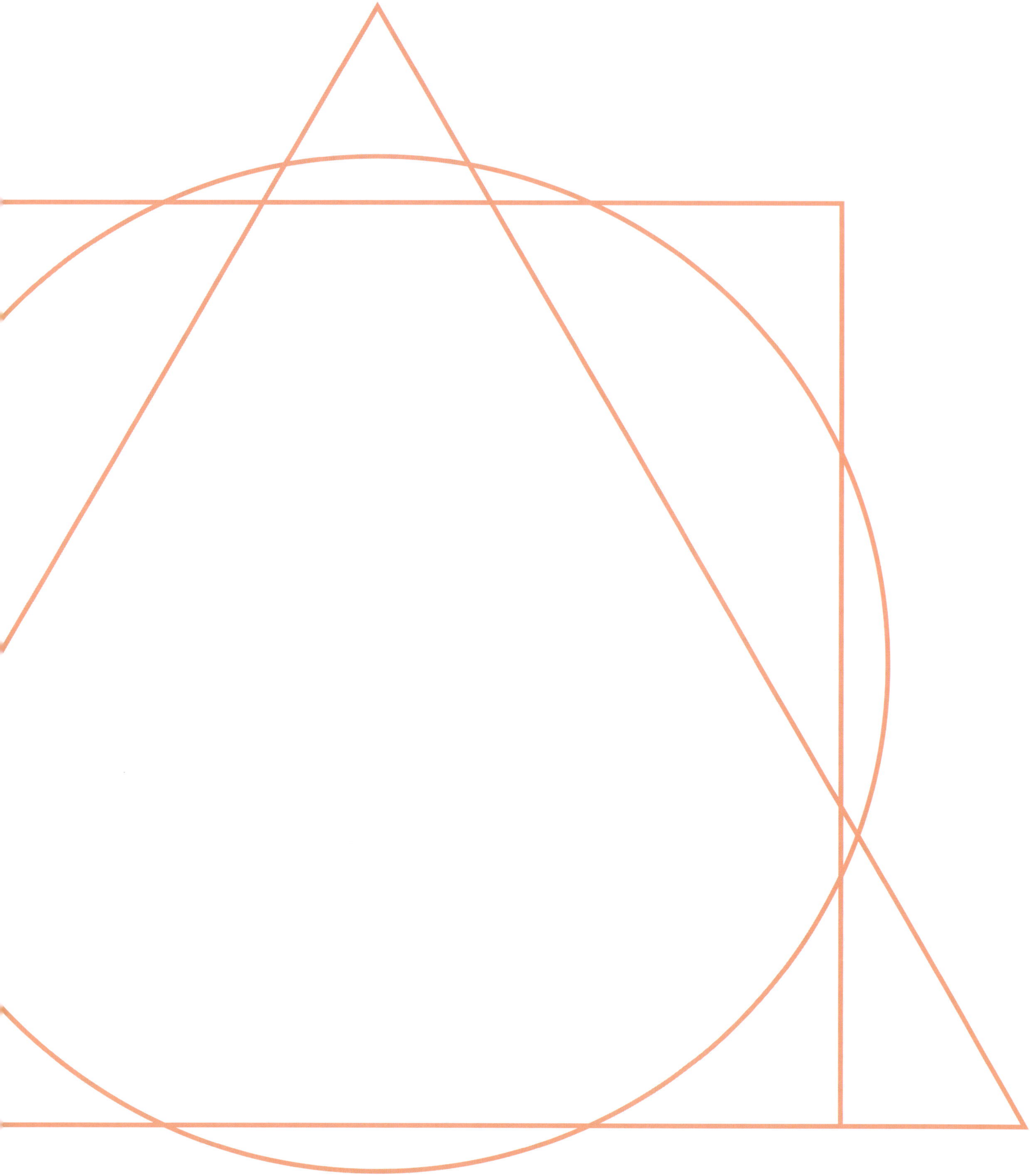

Index